OF GOD AND GODS

GEORGE L. MOSSE SERIES
IN MODERN EUROPEAN CULTURAL AND
INTELLECTUAL HISTORY

Advisory Board

Of God and Gods

Egypt, Israel, and the Rise of
Monotheism

Jan Assmann

THE UNIVERSITY OF WISCONSIN PRESS

This book was published with support from
the George L. Mosse Program at
the University of Wisconsin–Madison.

The University of Wisconsin Press
1930 Monroe Street, 3rd Floor
Madison, Wisconsin 53711-2059

www.wisc.edu/wisconsinpress/
3 Henrietta Street
London WC2E 8LU, England

I   3   5   4   2

Printed in the United States of America

Library of Congress Cataloging-in-Publication Data
Assmann, Jan.
Of God and gods : Egypt, Israel, and
the rise of monotheism / Jan Assmann.
p.   cm.—(George L. Mosse series in modern European
cultural and intellectual history)
Includes bibliographical references and index.
ISBN 0-299-22550-X (cloth: alk. paper)
ISBN 0-299-22554-2 (pbk.: alk. paper)
1. Henotheism—Egypt—History.   2. Henotheism—Israel—History.
3. Monotheism—Egypt—History.   4. Monotheism—Israel—History.
I. Title.   II. Series.
BL221.A88   2008
211′.309—dc22   2007040021

For

OTHMAR KEEL

In friendship and gratitude

CONTENTS

ACKNOWLEDGMENTS

I am grateful to the Mosse Foundation—in particular Steven Aschheim, its scientific advisor, and John Tortorice, its director—for having been given the chance to rethink various issues in the right place and in the right format: in Jerusalem and in a series of lectures. I could not have wished for a better context to present and discuss my thoughts on monotheism, in a place where over the course of fifteen years so many discussions and related activities have helped them to take shape.

Chapters 1, 3, and 6 were originally delivered as lectures in early December 2004 at the Van Leer Institute in Jerusalem. Chapters 2, 4, 5, and 7 were substantially rewritten for this study in order to place the revolutionary character of biblical monotheism within a broader context. Chapters 2 and 4 derive from lectures given in Solymite contexts. Chapter 2 deals with the question of religious violence in the context of Egyptian polytheism and is based on an unpublished lecture presented in June 2000 in Jerusalem in the context of the conference entitled "Good and Evil" organized by Moshe Idel. Chapter 4—which situates the monotheistic revolution within the broader context of the "Axial Age" and looks for antecedents of this Great Transformation in ancient Egypt—is based on a lecture originally entitled "The Axial Age in World History," presented at a 2001 conference organized by Shmuel N. Eisenstadt and Johann Arnason (published as "Axial 'Breakthroughs' and Semantic 'Relocations' in Ancient Egypt and Israel"); I am grateful to these colleagues and friends for their critical and stimulating input. Chapter 5, which traces the various steps that eventually led to the formation of the Hebrew canon, is based on a paper I contributed to a conference entitled "Forms of Transmission," organized by Ulrich Raulff and Gary Smith at the Einstein Forum in Potsdam (published as "Fünf Wege zum Kanon").

Maria S. Rost polished my English and spared the reader more than mere linguistic slips. I dedicate this book to my friend Othmar Keel, a true cultural scholar among theologians, who has devoted his life to the rediscovery of those cultural dimensions that tend to be excluded and suppressed by an all too narrow and schematic application of the Mosaic Distinction.

OF GOD AND GODS

Introduction

This study examines the relationship between God and gods. Perhaps the most important word in the title is "and," in which the various forms of this relationship are implied, ranging from total absorption ("All gods are one") to denial and destruction ("[Thou shalt have] no other gods"). What this study is *not* about—at least not primarily—is the history of biblical religion. There is an abundance of recent books about the "Early History of God";[1] the "Origins of Biblical Monotheism";[2] the "Rise of Yahwism";[3] the "History of Israelite Religion"[4] in its various evolutionary stages, from polytheism or syncretism[5] to monolatry and eventually to monotheism; and the political background of this development[6] and its reflection in the growth of biblical literature in its various redactions. The histories of God,[7] of Israelite religion, and of biblical literature are fields that have been richly cultivated. My concern is not with the history of monotheism but rather of a concept that I call "the Mosaic distinction," the idea of an exclusive and emphatic Truth that sets God apart from everything that is not God and therefore must not be worshiped, and that sets religion apart from what comes to be shunned as superstition, paganism, or heresy. This idea finds its clearest expression not in the phrase "God is one!" but "no other gods!"

This idea presupposes the existence of other gods. Paradoxically, the implied existence of other gods is of fundamental importance to the basic idea of biblical monotheism. The opposition of "God" and "gods" reflects the opposition of Israel and the nations (*goyim*, or gentiles), and the difference of uniqueness that sets "God" apart from the "gods" reflects the difference of being among the chosen or choseness and of belonging within the *b'rît* ("covenant") that sets Israel apart from the nations. In the same sense that the idea of the chosen people presupposes the existence of other peoples, the idea of the "one God" (*YHWH æchad*) presupposes the existence of other gods. Decisive is not

3

the oneness of God, which is a philosophical idea, but the *difference* of God, which is a "narrative truth" and the foundation of Israel's identity. Although there are many gods, there is only one God who delivered his people out of the hands of Pharaoh and who therefore has a legitimate claim on this people as his own. It is the exclusivity of belonging that is decisive, not the exclusivity of existence. For this reason, the term "monotheism" is a misnomer. The biblical concept of God is not about absolute but about relational oneness. However, its replacement by a term such as "monolatry" merely creates new misunderstandings. "Monolatry" suggests an evolutionary process in which the biblical idea of exclusive worship appears only as an intermediary stage between "polytheism" and "true monotheism." The implications of distinction, commitment, and difference remain crucial at every stage of the Jewish, Christian, and Muslim religions. The idea of exclusivity—of God among the gods, of Israel among the nations, and of the unswerving truthfulness, loyalty, and incessant memory required of anyone wishing to remain within this exclusive relationship—implies the idea of difference, and the idea of difference implies plurality. Universalism and absolute divine uniqueness and unity are other important concepts in the history of religions—especially monotheism. However, in the present study I will focus on the idea of difference as expressed in the Mosaic distinction.

Another point that should be stressed is that I am approaching this theme, to use Nietzsche's terms, not only in the "antiquarian" but also in the "critical" mode. In his second "untimely meditation" in *The Use and Abuse of History* Nietzsche draws several distinctions. He first distinguishes between "life-serving" and "life-harming" history, in other words, between a legitimate "history for the present's sake" and an illegitimate, obnoxious "history for the past's sake," or "objective" history. Within legitimate history he next distinguishes between "monumental," "antiquarian," and "critical" history. Monumental history uses the past for models of action, antiquarian history reveres the past as the root of identity, and critical history breaks away from the past by subjecting it to the verdict of "life." Even if we do not follow Nietzsche in drawing such a sharp distinction between memory and history, nor in his elevation of "life" to the rank of a supreme authority, his distinction between a monumental, antiquarian, and critical approach to the past nevertheless seems valid. In light of this distinction, I cannot deny that in my own treatment of the past of monotheism I may be indulging too much in antiquarianism—I am, after all, primarily an Egyptologist—while the critical approach is important and perhaps even predominant. However, this has nothing to do with "breaking away" from the past, nor do I wish to promote such a break in my own writing. Rather, I am reacting against a break that has occurred in the outside world and that in my opinion prompts us to reflect on the past in the critical mode.

The atrocities of the twentieth century—including the horrors of September 11, 2001—have lent a tremendous resonance to the sacred texts of our monotheistic tradition. It is impossible to speak of religion, especially with a focus on violence, without thinking of and referring to the Holocaust and/or to the events of 9/11. It is therefore of prime importance to make clear at the outset, before broaching the subject of monotheism, that the atrocities of the twentieth century did not stem from but rather were directed against monotheism. They were part of a modernity that had not only lost contact with but was violently reacting against its religious traditions. However, they must also not be associated with any "essence" of monotheism that would of necessity provoke such murderous reactions.[8] Yet it would be equally wrong to make the Enlightenment responsible for Auschwitz, as Eric Voegelin does.[9] For Voegelin the Enlightenment is a modern form of "Gnosticism," which he defines as the program of human self-perfection independent of any religious ties.[10] Instead of opposing monotheism to the Enlightenment, I would prefer to see the two movements in closer proximity to one another, subscribing—*pace* Schäfer[11]—to Sigmund Freud's phrase "Fortschritt in der Geistigkeit" (progress in intellectuality/spirituality). It is precisely this intellectual/spiritual "Geistigkeit" against which German fascism mobilized the masses and used the most unspeakable forms of violence. The events of September 11, conversely, were directed against modernity not in its aspect of Enlightenment but in its secularism, materialism, capitalism, and globalism, against which Islamist fundamentalism mobilized—and is further mobilizing—the semantic resources of monotheism, such as murder and martyrdom, killing and dying for god. The times are over when religion could be viewed as the "opium of the people." Nowadays, in the hands and minds of certain movements, religion appears as the "dynamite of the people."

It is as a result of these powerful resonances that during the past fifteen years monotheism has become one of the most hotly debated topics in theological and intellectual circles, at least in the Western world.[12] The change in climate may perhaps best be illustrated by the strange fate of Sigmund Freud's last book, *Moses and Monotheism*, in which he turned Moses into an Egyptian and took monotheism to be an Egyptian import. This book is a classic example of "critical history" with regard to monotheism. It reconstructs the early history of monotheism with a therapeutic intention. Monotheism is treated as a collective compulsory neurosis and the reconstruction of its genesis constitutes a kind of *Erinnerungsarbeit* (memory work), the most decisive part of psychoanalytic treatment. Despite these revolutionary theses, the book initially made only a slight impression on the intellectual world. During the first fifty years following its publication (in German) in 1939, it was hardly read even by psychoanalysts, who felt rather perplexed and embarrassed by these bold excursions into such foreign fields as Egyptology, ancient history, and biblical criticism, and it was not even read by people who were active in those fields. However, given the renewed interest in monotheism in intellectual debates in the West, Freud's study has become one of the most famous books of the twentieth century and, more narrowly, among the most important contributions to the recent debate on monotheism. Since Yosef Hayim Yerushalmi published his groundbreaking study,[13] every year witnesses the publication of several important monographs on Freud's *Moses*.

Before entering this debate, one should reflect on why and in what context one should approach the question of monotheism and what, precisely, stokes the debate and keeps it alive. My impression is that it is its revolutionary character, reflecting a break, a major turn in history, a kind of collective conversion, that may also account for such problematic implications as intolerance, violence, exclusivity, und aggressive universalism. A similar debate had already occupied intellectuals during the eighteenth century in the context of the Enlightenment and its struggle for emancipation from clerical and political control. More than 250 years ago Voltaire and others had already pointed to the striking scenes of violence in the Hebrew Bible, and David Hume had postulated a connection between monotheism and intolerance. The eighteenth century was also the time when the terms "monotheism," "polytheism," "pantheism," and "atheism"—which are still in use today—were coined. In many respects, therefore, we are taking up the debate of the eighteenth century. Then it was the advent of the Enlightenment that raised these discussions, whereas today it is, inversely, the unexpected return of religion in its aggressive, revolutionary, intolerant, and even violent aspects that has once again brought these questions to the fore. For these reasons the rise of monotheism is not just a harmless, historical topic but rather the subject of heated debate. Whoever stresses its revolutionary character and defines it as a major turn in human history is, in our post-traumatic days, running the risk of being understood as interpreting it as a turn for the worse, pleading for a return to polytheism, and even of being suspected of anti-Semitism since monotheism is a Jewish achievement. This is how my book *Moses the Egyptian* was interpreted by many—especially German—readers.[14] There I maintained that monotheism is a religion based on the distinction between true and false, that this distinction was alien to traditional religions, which, in the light of this novel distinction, were excluded as "false" by being branded with such labels as paganism, *avodah zarah,* idolatry, *djahiliya,* and *shirk,* and that for this reason monotheism can be described as a counterreligion, opposing and rejecting what went before and what goes on outside of itself.[15] I intended this diagnosis not as a critique of monotheism but rather as a framework permitting a better understanding of the role of Egypt in biblical and subsequent Western intellectual history, Egypt being the symbol or paradigm of paganism as the excluded other and of the world out of which Israel had to move, which it had to leave behind in order to enter the new world of monotheism. Viewed against this background, the boldness of those—from John Spencer to Sigmund Freud—who insist on blurring the distinction and bridging the gap by making Moses an Egyptian stands out in stark relief. This was the story I wanted to tell in that book, though it has been read by some as a severe attack against monotheism. When I wrote *Moses the Egyptian,* I was not aware of the risk of unleashing heated debate in stressing the revolutionary and polemical character of monotheism. Having learned my lesson,[16] I shall make every effort to approach the topic with due caution and circumspection.

It is for this reason that chapter 6, which addresses the problem of violence and intolerance, is preceded by five chapters dealing mostly with Egyptian but also occasionally with Mesopotamian polytheism (chapters 1 and 3), including the question of religious violence (chapter 2) and the various roads and transformations leading to biblical monotheism (chapters 4 and 5), as well as the decisive differences between the worlds of "paganism" and monotheism. The fact that I place so much emphasis on Egypt rather than on Mesopotamia is explicable for two reasons. One is the fact that I am an Egyptologist with relatively little competence concerning Mesopotamia. The other is the predominance the Bible itself gives to Egypt over Mesopotamia in recounting the introduction of monotheism to the children of Israel as the story of their exodus from Egypt. In biblical memory it is Egypt that assumes the role of the "other," which has to be abandoned in order to enter the new religion. However, this does not mean that historically Mesopotamia did not have an impact of equal if not superior importance in the formation of Israelite religion and the biblical texts. I am approaching the theme of monotheism from a double angle, namely, that of history and of "mnemohistory." I am interested not only in tracing the historical lines along which monotheism evolved or originated in reaction against polytheism but also in understanding the ways in which this historical turn was remembered in the biblical texts. As far as "mnemohistory" is concerned, I confess that I am not a biblical scholar and that my knowledge of the biblical and postbiblical forms of "remembering" the institution of monotheism is rather restricted. Concerning "history," however, I feel that Egyptology can contribute directly to the study of monotheism. Ancient Egypt provides an ideal vantage point from which to regard monotheism—not retrospectively, which is the usual approach in biblical studies, but prospectively from a period that preceded the rise of monotheism. I am convinced that the radical newness of the idea of monotheism as represented by the prophetic and the Deuteronomic movements is to be fully grasped only from this vantage point.

The structure of this study—dealing partly with ancient Egyptian matters, partly with biblical matters, and partly with ancient history generally—may initially appear somewhat arbitrary. Some additional remarks concerning my line of argumentation may therefore be in order. Chapters 1 through 3 deal with the prebiblical, pre-monotheistic world for which ancient Egypt serves as a paradigm. Chapters 4 and 5 deal with various aspects of what Karen Armstrong has termed "The Great Transformation."[17] Chapter 4 stresses the role of history, experience, and trauma in the slow development of the "Axial Age," which, for lack of more intimate knowledge of the pertinent sources, Karl Jaspers, Eric Voegelin, and others have condensed into a much too brief period of history. Chapter 5 emphasizes the role of writing in this same process, a subject that has been totally overlooked by previous scholars. Chapter 6 and the conclusion are the only parts of this study that dwell on aspects of biblical theology, which, coming after the foregoing discussion of prebiblical or "pagan" traditions, will appear in a new light.

1

Understanding Polytheism

The Three-Dimensional Structure
of the Divine World

Any reflection on the nature of those new religious movements that since the eighteenth century have been subsumed under the term "monotheism" should be preceded by an attempt at a better understanding of the term "polytheism." Up to now there has been no valid theory of polytheism.[1] There are, of course, many descriptions and histories of such polytheistic religions as the Indian, Greek, Babylonian, and Egyptian, but nowhere can one find a coherent theory, a systematic "theology" of polytheism—at least of one particular polytheistic religion. The only exception is that of ancient Greece, but Greece, with its elaborate aestheticized mythology, seems to be a rather special case that does not lend itself to generalizations. In studying ancient Egyptian religious texts (mostly hymns), my ambition has always been to detect the system behind this vast amount of material. These studies first led me to a more systematic understanding of what Egyptian polytheism—and, to a certain degree, polytheism in general—is all about, and from there to a new appraisal of its counterpart and opposite, namely, monotheism.

By way of explanation, let me offer up some biographical reminiscences. Over thirty years ago I was asked by the editors of the *Lexikon der Aegyptologie* to contribute an article on the entry "God."[2] In looking for categories to use in describing an Egyptian deity, I analyzed hundreds of Egyptian hymns and came across a number of texts that distinguished three major forms of divine presence or manifestation: "shapes" (*iru*), "transformations" (*kheperu*), and "names" (*renu*). "Shape" refers to the various cult images and representations of a deity in the temple cult. "Transformation" refers to such cosmic manifestations as sun, moon, stars, wind, light, fire, water, the Nile and its inundation, fertility, and vegetation. "Name" refers not only to proper names such as Osiris and Amun but denotes everything that may be said and told about a deity in epithets, titles, pedigrees, genealogies, myths—in short, its entire linguistic representation. I subsequently realized that these three terms referred to three dimensions of divine presence that I called the cultic, the cosmic, and the linguistic. It thus became possible to define a major Egyptian deity as a being equally present or represented in all three dimensions by having its temple and cult image, its characteristic cosmic manifestation, and a proper genealogy and mythology.

Several years later I started writing a book on Egyptian religion.[3] I consciously avoided the term "religion" because I felt very strongly that there was a major difference between the term "religion" as it was understood in the Western tradition, with all its biblical implications, and what I was about to describe with regard to the ancient Egyptian world. These differences seemed to me too decisive to be covered by one and the same term. If we call the biblical tradition and its derivatives—Judaism, Christianity, and Islam—"religions," we should substitute another term with respect to ancient Egypt and Mesopotamia. In fact, what we commonly understand by the term "religion" is as much an innovation brought into the world by biblical monotheism as the idea of the oneness of god itself. To speak of Egyptian, Mesopotamian, Greek, and Roman "religions" means to reconfigure—or even distort—the historical phenomena according to a perception of reality proper to monotheism but alien to "paganism." There were no "religions" in pagan societies, only "cults" and "cultures." "Religion," like "paganism," is an invention of monotheism.[4]

In Egypt, for example, it is virtually impossible to draw a clear-cut distinction between culture in general and religion in particular. There is a demarcation line, but it runs not between what we would call the secular and religious worlds, but between the outside world and the secluded places of cult and ritual. This demarcation line is very obvious. Sacred architecture, for example, is constructed of stone, whereas secular architecture, including the royal palace, is constructed of mudbrick. If we ask for an equivalent to our notion of "religion" in the Egyptian world, we get two very different answers, one too broad and the other too restricted. The broad answer includes nearly everything that we call "culture," because there is virtually nothing of social importance that is not religiously founded or connected in one way or another. The narrow answer includes only what the Egyptians themselves considered "sacred." Thus, I was left with two concepts of religion, a broad one and a narrow one, and I had to decide which concept to treat in my book on Egyptian religion.

There is an Egyptian text that draws the same distinction. It speaks of the role of kingship.

> The sun god and creator, Re, has placed the king on earth
> for ever and ever,
> in order that he may
> judge mankind and satisfy the gods,
> establish Ma'at and annihilate Isfet;
> giving offerings to the gods and funerary offerings to the dead.[5]

To "establish Ma'at and annihilate Isfet": this formula refers to the broad concept of religion, encompassing both cult and culture. Within this broad concept, the previous verse draws a further distinction, providing a narrower concept of religion (or of establishing Ma'at), namely, to "satisfy the gods" from a more secular way of establishing Ma'at, to "judge [i.e., administer justice to] mankind." This, incidentally, teaches us that in Egypt the law was not a sacred institution, as it was in Israel, nor was it a medium to "satisfy the gods." On the contrary, the law was kept outside the sphere of religion proper, which was exclusively concerned with communicating with the divine. Satisfying the gods meant engaging in active worship, sacrificing and giving up offerings, performing the prescribed rituals, and observing festivals. It did not mean abiding by the laws, administering justice, rescuing the poor, supporting widows and orphans, and so on.

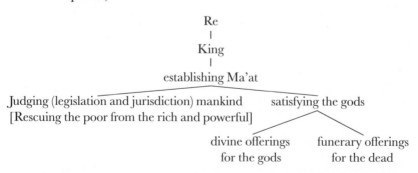

This system draws a distinction in a realm where the Bible insists on identity and it implies an indistinction where the Bible introduces a sharp distinction. The indistinction concerns the identity of state and religion. The Egyptian state resembles the Christian church in that it represents the sovereignty and the dominion of the creator over his creation on earth, among humankind. The distinction, conversely, concerns the borderline between justice and cult. To be sure, in delivering justice to mankind, the king acts on god's orders and represents divine justice among the living. But this has nothing to do with cult. Ma'at, in the cultic context, does not relate to justice and morality but rather to order and abundance. The spheres of justice/ethics and cult are carefully kept apart, whereas in the Bible—especially in the hortatory speeches of the prophets—they are constantly brought together.

One might say that this distinction between the spheres of justice, on the one hand, and of cult, on the other, has been consciously and emphatically destroyed in biblical monotheism. The famous invectives of the prophets against sacrificial cultism are well known. What they reject is the idea that God can be satisfied by priestly efforts alone. Instead, they promote the idea that in the eyes of God justice is more important than offerings. Thus, justice moves to the center of religion. This step is crucial for understanding the revolutionary innovation brought about by biblical monotheism. As soon as the latter adopted the idea of justice as its religious centerpiece, it began looking down on "pagan" religions as lacking any ethical normativeness and orientation.[6] This concept of paganism has been a commonplace of biblical scholarship and theological thought right up to the present day. However, the view of pagan religion as morally indifferent only applies to religion in its narrow sense. Here only the distinction between pure and impure matters, not the moral distinction between good and evil. Nevertheless it would be a gross distortion of historical truth to deny ancient pagan civilizations any ethical foundation and orientation. These questions are dealt with not within the context of religion proper, which is concerned to "satisfy the gods," but in the comparatively secular context to "judge [i.e., administer justice to] mankind." In the broader framework to "establish Ma'at," justice and morals play a central role and almost everything that the Bible has to say on these topics is inherited from its ancient Near Eastern and Egyptian neighbors.

It was the narrow concept of religion—namely, to "satisfy the gods" in the sense of divine communication—to which I finally decided to limit myself in the book I intended to write about Egyptian religion. It appeared in 1984 under the title *Ägypten: Theologie und Frömmigkeit einer frühen Hochkultur,* thereby avoiding the term "religion" altogether, and subsequently appeared in English under the title *The Search for God in*

Ancient Egypt. Several years later I dealt with the broader concept of religion in a book entitled *Ma'at: Justice and Immortality in Ancient Egypt.*[7] I wondered if this twofold form of description applied solely to Egyptian religion or if it could also apply to other traditional religions not based on revelation that have evolved in the course of centuries together with the other institutions of culture and civilization from which they cannot be separated.

In preferring the term "theology" to religion, I distinguished between "explicit" and "implicit" theology." By explicit theology I mean a discourse about God and the divine world that, in contrast to "mythology," is not structured according to the rules of narration but rather those of argumentation. Explicit theology is a specific phenomenon that does not necessarily exist in every religious tradition. There are doubtless many tribal and traditional religions that did not develop an explicit theology. Even in Egypt explicit theology did not exist right from the start but instead developed slowly in the Middle and Early New Kingdoms, and exploded in the Ramesside Age, following the monotheistic revolution of Amarna. Judging from hundreds of preserved texts, ancient Egypt seems to have turned into a country of theologians, with explicit theology becoming the major concern of the time. Implicit theology, by contrast, is a necessary prerequisite of every cult or religion "in the narrow sense" in the same way that grammar is a necessary prerequisite of every language irrespective of whether an "explicit" grammar of that language exists.

The implicit theology of Egyptian religion in its narrow sense of satisfying the gods, the "deep structure," as it were, of worship and sacrifice, consists precisely of those three dimensions that I found to be characteristic of the Egyptian notion of deity: the cultic or politic, the cosmic, and the linguistic. I was now able to realize that the Egyptian pantheon was anything but a random accumulation of deities. The common view of Egyptian polytheism interpreted the pantheon as the result of political unification. According to common opinion, these deities were originally worshiped more or less in isolation by tribes and villagers living in Egypt in similar isolation. Through the process of increasing alliances and of final unification these originally unrelated deities were brought into contact with one another. Their familial and other relations reflected the emerging state and society of Pharaonic Egypt. This explanation may hold for Mesopotamia and other early states and societies, but not for ancient Egypt. Here most of the deities are not autochthonic to their places of worship. Rather, the relationship between place and pantheon is the reverse: it is not the interrelation and unification of places that structures a previously unstructured set of deities but the structured pantheon, or "Divine World," that lends structure to human reality, including the various tribes and towns that comprised the Egyptian state and society.

Dimensions of Divine Presence

jrw: *The Cultic/Political Dimension*

With this observation we are already moving in the first dimension of divine presence, which in Egyptian thought is related to the concept of *jrw* (shape), the cult-image of a deity and its place of worship. This is the local and cultic dimension. Here the main topic is the specific relationship that exists between a deity and a place. All of the major Egyptian deities are lords of towns, and each of the major towns or cities is the realm of a specific deity. The Egyptian concept of "city" has distinct religious connotations. A major city is a sacred city inasmuch as a major deity is the ruler of a city: *Stadtgötter und Gottesstädte* (city gods and god-cities). This principle proved most useful when the Greeks conquered Egypt and had to rename the towns and cities in order to make them pronounceable for Greek tongues. They just took the names of the Egyptian deities in their already conventional Greek translation and added the suffix "polis." Thus, Thebes became Diospolis (the city of Amun = Zeus), Dendera became Aphroditopolis (Hathor = Aphrodite), Shmun became Hermopolis (Thot = Hermes), and On (the city of the sun god Re) became Heliopolis (Re = Helios). The institution of divine sovereignty served as a representation of social and political identity. An Egyptian thought of himself primarily as a citizen of a specific town or city and not as an Egyptian, that is, a member of a nation or country. The foci of social and political identification were the temple and its lord, a specific deity. To enter another town meant to enter a foreign country. To be at home meant to stay in one's native town or village. Belonging to a town, being a citizen of a town, meant to be a member of a festive community, to participate in the feasts that were celebrated in the form of processions. The concept of civic allocation was thus invested with religious meaning. Being a citizen of a town meant to be a follower of its ruling deity. Residence determined religious belonging. It was a kind of covenant, where the religious tasks of the citizen corresponded to the political role of the deity.

The principle of political identity and representation, however, was not limited to the level of villages, towns, and cities. The gods Horus and Seth represented Lower and Upper Egypt, respectively, and, later, Egypt and the foreign countries. The sun god Re (later Amun-Re) represented the unified empire. Consequently the cultic dimension of divine presence can also be called the political dimension. Cult and political identity are aspects of one and the same concept of divine presence and communication. The relationship between the divine world and the terrestrial sphere of Egypt—her towns and temples—may be described as one of mutual structuring and modeling. In a sense, the structure of the pantheon and the properties of its constituent deities mirror the structure of Egypt and her political organization. This structural relationship, however, also works in reverse: the divine world gives structure, identity, and meaning to the country in its different units of state, nome, district, town, and neighborhood.

The structure of an Egyptian temple reveals much about the nature of an Egyptian deity. It normally houses three or more sanctuaries. A deity never occupies his/her temple alone but is always in the company of *theoi synnaoi* (deities inhabiting a common temple), typically in the form of a family with father, mother, and child. The rooms of a temple are arranged along a central axis, stressing and mediating the distance between inner and outer, darkness and light, narrowness and breadth, closure and openness. The Egyptian temple is both the residence of a deity and the start and end point of a processional route. The cult is subdivided into everyday and festive cults. The difference between these two forms is extreme. The rites of the everyday cult are performed backstage in extreme seclusion—*in camera*, so to speak—whereas the feasts are celebrated in the form of a procession involving the entire population of a town or district. The procession is the form in which the gods exert their sovereignty over their territory and in which lay humans participate in their religion, since the temples are closed to the public. The feasts celebrate divine sovereignty, civic belonging, and religious participation. The cultic dimension of the divine is a matter of structuring not only sacred space but also sacred time.

The religious feast in ancient Egypt was the only occasion when the gods left their temple and appeared to the people at large, whereas they normally dwelt in complete darkness and seclusion inside the sanctuaries of their temples, inaccessible to all save the officiating priest. The Egyptian temple was definitely not a place where a person could enter and pray; for the common people it was more a symbol of absence and inaccessibility than of presence and contact. The Egyptian concept of the holy is connected with the secret, the hidden, the inaccessible. Contact and communication did, of course, take place in the temple, but this contact was of a very symbolic, indirect, and complex nature. It was nothing in which the ordinary person could participate. Secular people knew they were somehow distantly represented and involved in this sacred communication—which went on constantly inside the impenetrable temple walls, inside the endless sequence of courtyards, pylons, halls, and chapels—but there was no possibility for them to play an active part in this sacred game. The cult, by its very complexity, makes the gulf between the spheres of the holy and of everyday life, which it is meant to bridge, all the more palpable. On the occasion of a feast, however, these boundaries between secrecy and publicity, sacred and profane, inner and outer, were suspended. The gods then appeared to the public outside the temple walls. Every major Egyptian religious feast was celebrated in the form of a procession.[8]

The Egyptian concept of the feast finds its verbal expression in the songs chanted on this occasion and revolves around two basic ideas: a union of heaven and earth and the "coming" or "advent" of God.[9] The image of a union between heaven and earth is a precise translation of what I have described as the suspension of the boundaries between inner and outer, secrecy and publicity, sacred and profane. It is these boundaries that demarcate the normal state of reality. According to Egyptian belief, the gods are real, living powers, but they do not reside on earth among men. They are not to be encountered and experienced in everyday life. Certainly there was a time when they did live on earth, but on account of some tragic events they withdrew to heaven and the underworld, leaving the earth to mankind and thus creating that relatively secular sphere of human order and activity that is indispensable for daily life.[10] However, on the occasion of the feast this state of affairs is reversed and the original paradisiacal state of divine presence is restored to the world—or at least to the city where the feast takes place. Heaven and earth unite and God returns to mankind.

The idea of the "coming" god is the other aspect of the Egyptian concept of the feast. It is this "coming" that is expressed in the symbolic form of processional motion. The oldest processional song runs: "The god comes; beware, earth!"[11] The earth must be warned and prepared since it must give up its usual profanity and adapt to the heavenly conditions the divine presence requires. During the feast God—who is usually absent, residing far above in heaven and only symbolically present on earth within the inaccessible secrecy of his sanctuary—comes to his city. It is he who takes the initiative. While in the temple, he is passive and attended by the priest. However, during the feast he is active, the motion of the procession symbolizing his living activity and real presence. This turn from passive to active marks the event celebrated by the feast. The whole city participates in this happening ("is in feast" runs the Egyptian phrase). What the temple normally is for the god the city now becomes, namely, a vessel for his earthly presence.

The Egyptian idea of the city is centered on and shaped by this festive situation.[12] The city is the place on earth where, during the main processional feast, the divine presence can be sensed by everyone. The more important the feast, the more important the city. People from all parts of the country assemble there during the festival period to participate in the event and to "see the god." The latter phrase, in Egyptian language, has the precise meaning of participating in a feast. Being an inhabitant of a city means being granted the chance to see the god of the city on the occasion of his "coming." The inhabitants of a city form a festive community (*Festgemeinschaft*) and conceive of themselves as "followers" of their particular city-god. It is the feast that establishes and secures their identity as "Thebans" or "Memphites." Festive participation is for the concept of the Egyptian city what political and commercial participation are for the Greek city and the city of the Italian Renaissance. It is the focus of civic identity.

However, the nature or essence of the gods is not completely defined by their cultic/political role. This is just one aspect of their much more comprehensive nature. It is just a form of their "turning toward the world" (*Weltzuwendung*) or immanence.

Kheperu: *The Cosmic Dimension*

Another aspect or form of divine presence and immanence is the cosmic dimension. This aspect presents us with the Egyptian idea of the cosmos as a sphere of divine manifestation. According to the Egyptians, the world or cosmos is a process rather than a space, and the idea of order is more a matter of successfully overcoming disorder and destruction than of spatial structure and harmonious arrangement. Virtually all of the gods cooperate in the project of maintaining the world, of keeping the cosmic process going. The core of this process is what the ancient Egyptians conceived of as the "solar circuit," the daily course of the sun across the heaven and the netherworld. In the eyes of the Egyptians, the success of this project was never assumed. Like the Mesopotamians, Chinese, and Romans, ancient Egyptians were constantly preoccupied with watching the sky and observing all kinds of natural phenomena. However, unlike these other peoples, the Egyptians had as their goal not divination—that is, discovering the will of the gods and foretelling the future—but rather assisting the gods in maintaining the world. Thus, the Egyptians observed the regular and recurrent, whereas the divination cultures observed the exceptional and deviant. In the course of this intellectual pursuit, the Egyptians accumulated an incredible amount of knowledge, a kind of sacred cosmology.

All the major Egyptian deities had given roles in this project of world maintenance, as well as specific cosmic manifestations, in the same way they had a place on earth to exert their terrestrial sovereignty. The term used in explicit theological discourse involving "cosmic manifestation" is *kheperu* (transformation), a term with strong temporal connotations. A transformation is something you take on for a while, a form of being or, rather, *becoming* within time. Time is absolutely primary in the cosmic dimension of divine presence, which relates to time as the cultic dimension relates to space. The Basic structure of cosmic time is provided by the apparent circular movement of the sun around the earth. There is no clearer expression of this time-based cosmology than the Egyptian term for creation, *sep tepi* ("the first time"), corresponding to the Hebrew *Be-reshit* ("in the beginning"), referring to the first sunrise as the first time of a never-ending cyclical process. There is also no clearer expression of the huge difference between Egyptian and biblical cosmology than the demotion of the sun from its Egyptian position as the origin of the universe to the biblical position of a clock and a lamp that God suspended in the sky—and not until the fourth day of creation.

The movement of the sun, according to Egyptian religious belief, generates time and light, which are interpreted in terms of sovereignty and life. In crossing the sky, the sun god exerts his sovereignty over the cosmos in the same way that divine sovereignty on earth is performed by means of processions. Yet the solar circuit also has the meaning of a life cycle. The sun god is born every morning and dies every evening, enters the netherworld, and is reborn the next morning. Again we encounter the principle of mutual modeling. I shall return to this issue in the next section, where the establishment of this relation of mutual transparency and modeling is primarily the achievement of language.

rnw: *The Linguistic Dimension*

The third dimension of divine presence consists of what the Egyptians meant by the term "name." A name in the ancient Egyptian sense is not just a name or title as we understand it today but everything that can be said about a person. A name is not just an identifier but also a description, a linguistic representation of a person's essence. Enumerating the names of a deity means reciting hymns and eulogies in his or her honor. According to the ancient Egyptians, the linguistic dimension refers to sacred language and texts whose recitation in the appropriate context has magical power and contributes to the maintenance of the world. The whole complex of mythology also belongs to this dimension.

The concept of language as a means of summoning divine presence involves questions of how to approach the gods, address them, and describe their power and actions. Through the medium of their linguistic representation—recited by the right person at the right time and place, who names the names and tells the stories—the gods take shape and become present and immanent in the same way as they are present and immanent in their cult-images (*jrw*) and cosmic manifestations. This idea of divine presence may perhaps be compared to the Jewish concept of *Shekhina* (literally, indwelling): the gods come to "dwell" in their temples, in their cosmic manifestations, and in their sacred recitations or "names."

Language, however, also serves as the "cement" that binds the three dimensions and integrates the human, the social, the political, and the cosmic spheres into a single coherent system of cultural semantics. The linguistic representation of the cosmic process makes it transparent for the concerns of the state as well as the individual human being. The structure of mutual modeling is primarily a question of speech and language, of the kind of linguistic representation that we call myth. Myth is not merely a story about the gods but a form of thought, a way of world-making, a deep-structural generator of stories. The underlying principle of Egyptian mythmaking is the establishment of a connection between the three spheres of cosmos, state, and individual life and death in the form of mutual modeling. The solar myth represents the sun god's encircling of the earth in terms of sovereignty, which obviously mirrors Pharaoh's terrestrial sovereignty, as well as in terms of performing a life cycle by being born, dying, and being reborn, which mirrors human fate and hope. Pharaoh's rule and man's life cycle clearly serve as models for investing the solar circuit with meaning, but the sun god's ride across the sky and through the netherworld also serves as a model for Pharaoh, the state, and the life and hopes of the individual human being. The one serves as an allegory of the other. Similarly, the myth of Osiris mirrors, models, and structures the human hope of overcoming death, the political idea of Pharaonic legitimacy and succession, and the cosmic concept of the netherworld.

The stories told about the gods present them in a very human—almost all too human—form. Only in this dimension do the deities assume personal traits. However, they reveal these personal characteristics not in relation to the human world but in relation to each other. The gods are interconnected within constellational networks. They display their personalities in the frame of divine "constellations," in which they play such roles as fathers, mothers, sons, daughters, brothers, sisters, lovers, warriors, murderers, avengers, kings, viziers, judges, priests, and scribes. There is no myth about a god that does not mention other gods. Myths are the stories in which the gods relate to one another. We may call this kind of mythology *historia divina,* a history taking place in the divine world, where the human world is involved only in terms of mirroring but not as an object of divine action. The gods are acting upon each other but not—or only very rarely—on the human sphere. They relate to the human world in the first dimension by animating their cult-images, inhabiting their temples, and ruling their cities, but not in the third dimension of linguistic representation. The mythology or "narrative theology" of the Egyptians is anthropomorphic, not anthropocentric. This changes drastically as soon as one leaves the level of implicit theology and enters the universe of explicit theological discourse. It also changes in the course of history. I shall return to these questions in the next chapter. Here I am concerned not with historical changes but with the Basic structures.

The three-dimensional Basic structure of Egyptian religion is certainly not to be generalized. However, it finds a striking parallel in the stoic theory of tripartite theology, *theologia tripertita,* for which the Roman antiquarian Varro, as quoted by Saint Augustine, is the most explicit authority.[13] Continuing Stoic traditions and translating Greek terms, Varro distinguishes three forms of theology: *theologia physike* or *naturalis; politike* or *civilis;* and *mythike* or *fabularis.* In this concept one can easily recognize the three dimensions of implicit theology. According to Varro, *theologia naturalis* is the concern of philosophers; *theologia mythike* or *fabularis* is the concern of poets; and *theologia politike* or *civilis* is the concern of priests. Thus, according to this theory the political and cultic aspects were considered identical, just as they were in Egypt. The only difference between the Egyptian and Varro's distinctions seems to be the attribution of different truth values to the different theologies. For Varro only the *theologia naturalis* of the philosophers has any claim to truth, whereas the two other theologies, namely, the political theology of the priests and the mythical theology of the poets, are based on fiction and imagination. In Egypt all three dimensions of divine presence were equally valid, and no approach was given precedence over the two others; all were equally close to or distant from the truth. In Egypt the division of labor was not as advanced as it was in Rome, with the Egyptian priests acting both as philosophers and poets. The three dimensions complement each other. It is obvious that such a conception is ruled out in the contexts both of scientific thought, as in Greece, and of revelation, as in Israel, where there is a single knowledge about the divine that is privileged.

History, the Missing Dimension

When one compares the three-dimensional structure of Egyptian polytheism to biblical religion, it immediately becomes evident that the dimension of divine presence or impact that is most prominent in the Bible is completely lacking in Egyptian religion. This is history or, more precisely, sacred history, history understood as a dimension of encounter and communication between god and man. In the Bible sacred history (*historia sacra*) takes the place of myth (*historia divina*).[14] The biblical God develops and reveals his personal characteristics not in relation to other gods within a framework of mythical constellations—there are no other gods around him—but rather toward mankind. Many of his most characteristic traits, such as his loving kindness and mercy or furious anger and inexorable judgment, belong to his role as overlord and legislator within the covenant. They are not yet present in Genesis and appear only after the delivery of the Torah on Mount Sinai. Whereas in Egypt narrative theology deals with actions and events among gods, in the biblical form of historiography it deals with the actions and events between God and his people. History becomes the privileged dimension of God's closeness or remoteness to man, at the expense of both the local and cosmic dimensions. Many of the biblical books are pure historiography. Flavius Josephus noted that in Israel the writing of history was assigned to the prophets,[15] a reflection of the theological importance attributed to history in biblical religion.

I suspect that the sanctification of history, that is, the process of elevating history to a dimension of divine presence, has much to do with the strong connection the Bible establishes between history and justice, or doing and faring. History is seen as the manifestation of the will of God, of a god who reacts to the deeds of mankind by punishing, rewarding, guiding, and, eventually, redeeming. History, or God's interaction with humanity (or with his chosen people), is based upon justice. The latter, in other words, appears to function as a generator of history.

History seen as a dimension of religious experience and divine immanence marks a distinctive difference between biblical religion, on the one hand, and the Egyptian, Greek, and Roman religions, on the other. This might seem trivial since the difference between biblical and "pagan" religions is obvious enough. However, it becomes less trivial as soon as one recognizes that the same difference that sets biblical religion apart from the Egyptian, Greek, and Roman religions links it to Mesopotamia and the Hittite world. One can even observe the slow rise of history in Egypt as a fourth dimension of divine immanence and religious experience and how this changes the entire structure of Egyptian religion. The origins of this conception point to Mesopotamia. Here one encounters the idea of divine intervention into human affairs in Sumerian texts dating back as early as the third millennium BCE. In Egypt this idea of divine intervention does not appear until the thirteenth century BCE.

Historiography in the form of longer narratives reaching back into greater periods of the past did not exist in ancient Egypt. To be sure, an articulation of history in the form of a great number of "historical inscriptions" and even annals did exist. Although all kinds of documents exist, no comprehensive retrospective historiography and no narrative accounts of any longer sequences of reigns or dynasties have surfaced. It seems as if the Egyptians had no real use for the past.[16] They lacked mastery over any semantic connectives that would have transformed a number of singular events into a coherent history.

The absence of history, that is, of historical narrative, in ancient Egypt seems to depend on the Egyptian construction of time and identity.[17] The Egyptians experienced time not as a natural phenomenon past their control but as something to be ritually maintained. To be sure, we are dealing here with cyclical time, but not in the rather banal sense in which Egyptians imagined time as a cyclical phenomenon. Rather, they were convinced that they had to "cyclicize" time through cultural efforts, to give time a circular shape in order to enable time and the world continuously to regenerate itself and to prevent it from being reduced to chaos. Cyclical time is a cultural form that has to be constructed and maintained through a meticulous observance of rites and feasts. It is only natural that a society accustomed to thinking along these lines would not make much of linear sequences and developments. Such a worldview excludes history and prevents it from entering tradition and communication.[18] The Egyptian word that comes closest to our concept of history is *kheperut* (events), which has negative connotations.[19] An event is something that had best not happen. In an important work of wisdom literature one reads that God has given man magic as a weapon to ward off the blow of events.[20] This concept of magic settles the question of history. The latter is something to be avoided, with God providing humankind with the necessary means to do so. It is certainly not a dimension of divine immanence and religious experience.

In Mesopotamia the gods intervene into history because they are explicitly invited to do so. The theologizing of history results from certain institutions of international law. Unlike Egypt, which possessed a central government right from the start, Mesopotamia went through a long period of polycentrism, with city-states linked to each other through treaties and conflicts. Given this situation, Mesopotamia formed concepts and institutions not only of national but also of international law. The political institutions of the city-state were able to maintain justice within the state, but the gods were made responsible for the maintenance of law and order among the various states. They were called upon to ensure the strict observance of treaties between states and to punish any transgressors. Treaties had to be sealed by a solemn oath sworn by both parties, thereby submitting themselves to divine supervision.[21] Just as the legal institutions of the state maintained justice inside the state, so the will and "wrath" of the gods maintained justice among the various states.

This institution also explains the strong connection between justice and history. Divine intervention occurred within the framework of the legal institutions of treaty and alliance. However, it was soon extended to other frames of human action, where the gods were believed to intervene generally in the course of history by meting out punishment and reward.[22] This leads to the redaction of royal inscriptions providing an account of a king's reign, and even of texts that stretch back over a series of different reigns into the remote past. An early text belonging to this genre, known as the "Curse on Aggade,"[23] recounts the rise and fall of the Sargonid dynasty in the twenty-third and twenty-second centuries BCE. Among other events, it relates how King Naramsin destroyed the temple of Enlil in Nippur and how Enlil responded to this crime by sending in the Guteans, who put an end to the ruling dynasty. Here it is clearly the idea of law and justice that acts as a connective principle linking distant events involving crime and punishment.

The much later neo-Babylonian "Weidner chronicle" (first century BCE) reaches even farther back in time. This chronicle describes a succession of dynasties and connects the success of a king's reign with his attitude toward the Esagila, the temple of Marduk in Babylon. In various cases the fall of dynasties is explained as being the result of guilt accumulated by one or several rulers during their reigns. The fall of the empire of Ur is traced back to certain forfeits committed by King Shulgi.[24] The judicial concept of guilt and punishment gives meaning to history and coherence to the chain of events and the sequence of dynasties. Here, as in Egypt, the concept of "event" is invested with negative connotations. However, the difference between the Egyptian and Mesopotamian versions is obvious. In Egypt the event is a manifestation of chaos and contingency, without any meaning. In Mesopotamia the event is full of meaning, viewed as the manifestation of the punitive will of a divinity whose anger has been roused by the king.[25]

In Mesopotamia the concept of the gods as the agents of historical justice also had much to do with divination, which played a central role in Babylonia. Everything depended on the correct interpretation of signs expressing the will of the gods. A sign pointed to a future event and presupposed a finality between the will of the gods and the vicissitudes of history. In Egypt the will of the gods was absorbed into the task of maintaining the world. In Mesopotamia the divine will was sufficiently free to extend its range into human affairs. As a result, Mesopotamian history created a realm of religious meaning and experience and became a matter of discursive communication and representation.[26] Later on, during the New Kingdom or Late Bronze Age, this model grew increasingly influential—even in Egypt—and led to considerable changes, especially in the historiographical genres of private autobiography and royal inscriptions.[27] The traditional theology of maintenance was complemented by a theology of will that invested the realm of historical and biographical events—or *Kheperu*—with meaning.

In the Hittite Empire the Mesopotamian tradition of international law led to the formation of three different contexts for the theologizing of history and representation of the past. The first is the context of guilt. When a catastrophe occurs, it is traced back to the intervention of an offended deity who can only be reconciled with humanity through the latter's confession and repentance. This led to important discourses of historical reconstruction. The most elaborate example is the confessional prayers of King Mursilis, who, after enduring years of pestilence, tried to appease the gods by publicly confessing a sin committed by his father more than twenty years earlier. These prayers, together with the annals of his father, Suppiluliuma, which tell the same story, represent some of the most elaborate pieces of cuneiform historiography.[28]

A second context of historical reconstruction is the Hittite custom of introducing state treaties with a long flashback into the common history of both parties forming an alliance. The alliance is built upon the foundation of a past of mutual friendship and support, giving reason to believe in the future stability of the contract and the loyalty of the partners.[29]

A third context of historical discourse is the royal apology. This genre also flourished in Hittite historiography, which has left us the most impressive and elaborate examples, especially the historical accounts of usurpers such as Telepinus or Hattusilis III. Both tried to justify their illegitimate ascent to the throne by pointing out the blessings the gods had bestowed on their reigns, in contrast to the injustices of their predecessors, with their ensuing misfortunes, which was reversed during their own rule.[30]

All three of these traditional genres of cuneiform historiography reached their fullest fruition only in the Bible, where they developed into large-scale compositions comprising one or more entire books. The first form, confessional historiography, led to the "Deuteronomic" tradition of historiographical writing in the Bible. Here every reign is judged according to the principle of the king's obedience to the law. With few exceptions, it is a long story of disobedience, disloyalty, apostasy, injustice, idolatry—in short: of accumulation of guilt, ultimately leading to the destruction of Jerusalem and the Babylonian exile. The second form, covenantal history, underlies the books of Exodus and Deuteronomy, where the law, that is, the treaty proper, is introduced by the history of how God intervened on behalf of the redemption of his chosen people. Deuteronomy contains not only the historical introduction and the body of stipulations of the treaty but even the curses that traditionally form its conclusion.[31] The third form, the royal apology, is represented in the Bible by the elaborate accounts of the reigns of Saul, David, and Solomon—especially David, whose dynastic legitimacy was certainly dubious.[32]

The theologizing of history reached its apogee with biblical—especially Deuteronomic—historiography.[33] The idea of forming an alliance with God himself instead of appointing certain deities as supervisors of political alliances draws God more intimately into human affairs than had been the case in Mesopotamia and its neighboring civilizations. There history was just a field of possible favorable or punitive interventions by the gods, whereas now it becomes a single coherent series of events stretching from the creation until the end of the world, a sequence known as *historia sacra* in the Judeo-Christian tradition.

Nothing of this sort is to be found in Egypt, at least not until the Late Period. Yet even here one encounters a certain connection between history and justice. Here, too, justice functions as a generator of history. However, it is restricted to the sphere of biography because justice appears only in the form of a judgment following death, when every individual must give an account of his or her life. In Mesopotamia the idea of a divine agency monitoring royal behavior presents history in a much more comprehensive form both socially and temporally. In Mesopotamia it is precisely the absence of ideas of immortality and of reward and punishment in the hereafter that favors the sanctification of history. The absence of the idea of immortality means that every account has to be settled on earth. Whereas in Egypt the consequences of human actions were extended into the hereafter, in Mesopotamia they were confined to the terrestrial world, only extended into the future across generations and dynasties—which we now call history. What immortality and the hereafter were to the Egyptians, history was to the Mesopotamians, namely, a horizon of fulfillment. In Mesopotamia, however, this form of historical thinking was only rudimentarily developed and only gained its full articulation in Israel. Spinoza had already remarked that in the Old Testament there is no trace of the concept of immortality or of reward and punishment in the hereafter. Instead there is the sequence of generations. Instead of the judgment of the dead, there is the verdict of history, world history as the world's court of justice ("die Weltgeschichte ist das Weltgericht," as Hegel, quoting a poem by Schiller, put it). History is a substitute for immortality or paradise.

As we have seen, this conception of history emerged in the context of legal thinking and remained closely associated with the notions of law, guilt, verdict, and punishment throughout the biblical tradition and right up to its secularized version in Hegel's philosophy of history. In Israel it is this fourth dimension of theology that prevails and eventually replaces the others. With the rise of monotheism, the cosmos ceases to appear as a "manifestation" of divine presence and is seen as the "creation," the work of God. Following the reform of King Josiah at the end of the seventh century BCE, the cultic dimension is reduced to the temple at Jerusalem and no longer reflects the pluralistic identity of various centers and regions. *Historia divina,* the stories told about the gods that reveal their personalities and vicissitudes, is turned into *historia sacra,* the story of the one God and his chosen people.[34] *Historia sacra* is the successor to the third, mythic dimension of narrative articulation of divine constellations. Its written codification no longer serves as a magical presentation of the divine the way sacred texts had been used in the context of the third dimension of divine presence, namely, the linguistic. The rise of monotheism necessitated the destruction of this multidimensional structure of divine presence or immanence in order to pave the way for a totally new conception of reality.

2

Seth the Iconoclast

Polytheism and the Language of Violence

Pagan and Monotheistic Violence

If there is one iconic image, an emblematic expression of Egyptian political self-definition, it is the image of Pharaoh smiting his enemies. This image appears in the political iconography of Egypt as early as the formation of the Egyptian state at the end of the fourth millennium BCE. It is first seen as a mural painting in the tomb of a prehistorical chieftain, then in its canonical form on the ceremonial slate palette of king Nar-mer, which depicts and commemorates the very act of uniting the empire. It served throughout Egyptian history, until as late as the third century CE, when the Roman emperor Decius had himself represented in this pictogram on the walls of the temple of Esna. In this icon the Egyptian state defines its relation to the outward world, which is also the reason why it typically adorns the pylons and outer walls of a temple. It fulfills the apotropaic and almost magical function of warding off the peoples and tribes that surround Egypt and who might be tempted to attack and invade it. A clearer and starker expression of sheer violence is hardly imaginable. It contradicts all attempts at presenting the "pagan" or "polytheistic" civilizations, such as that of ancient Egypt, as particularly peaceful, tolerant, and nonviolent. However, the kind of violence expressed in this pictogram is not that of religious intolerance. We are dealing here with political violence, without which no political order can exist. To quote Niklas Luhmann, "Politics and law are only possible if they are able for their enforcement to use physical violence and efficiently to exclude counterviolence."[1] No one denies that the states that emerged in the Ancient Near East out of the tribes and chiefdoms of prehistory based themselves on the possibility of using physical violence and proclaiming this possibility or readiness in the symbolic forms of political iconography and rhetoric.

One must distinguish between so-called pagan and monotheistic violence. Pagan violence stems from the indistinction between state and religion. If Pharaoh acts as god's deputy on earth, extending the task of world maintenance into the realm of the human world under the conditions of the separation of heaven and earth, his political actions assume a religious character because they represent the world-preserving power of the creator. Theoretically monotheism should have put an end to these conceptions of divine immanence within the political institutions of the state and the person of its ruler since it implies a strict separation between religion and state. Religion is now constituted as a sphere with its own normativity, which might even override the political normativity of the state. In political practice, however, the pagan principles of indistinction and representation frequently return even under the conditions of monotheism. Well known instances include Byzantine caesaropapism, the Muslim caliphate, the status of the French king as head of the church of France, and other forms of medieval Christian political theology, many of which survived well into early modernity. Political violence executed in the name of God, with each of the warring parties claiming that God is on its side, has to be classified as sheer pagan violence. As far as political theology is concerned, many pagan ideas survived in Islam and Christianity. Monotheistic violence, conversely, is directed against paganism—typically against the "pagan within"—and not against political enemies.

In this chapter I will deal with notions of specifically ritual violence within polytheism, in contrast to political and legal violence. Ritual violence is committed in the name of some specific god, political violence is directed against an enemy or rebel in the name of the ruler, and legal violence is directed against a criminal in the name of a law. All these forms of violence, finally, are to be distinguished from mere "raw" violence, which is committed without reference to any legitimizing authority. Against whom is ritual violence directed? The present chapter will attempt to answer this question, and to explore the conception of evil in the context of polytheism.

Intrasystemic and Extrasystemic Ritual Violence

As far as the distinction between ritual and political violence is concerned, Assyria represents a borderline case. Given the extreme indistinction there between state and religion, Assyrian violence is clearly pagan and not monotheistic. However, it nevertheless seems to have a religious character that greatly exceeds what may be observed in ancient Egypt. The objection that this violence was essentially political and had nothing to do with religion is easily countered by the observation that it was normally not only acted out in the name of the god Assur but was also directed against the gods of the conquered towns and countries, whose images were either destroyed or removed along with the captive inhabitants. Under certain conditions—for example, the breaking of a treaty sealed by an oath to Assur—political enemies were also considered enemies of Assur. Such religious foes had to be punished in the name of Assur, with the king and his army acting as Assur's willing executioners. Moreover, the Assyrians practiced a form of warfare that also involved the gods of their enemies.[2] For the Egyptians this was a traumatic experience whose memory lasted for many centuries; the same certainly holds true for many other victims of this policy who did not leave behind similar documents. In order to understand this form of ritual violence, one first has to distinguish between internal and external and then between intrasystemic and extrasystemic violence. The violence that the Assyrians inflicted upon the images of other gods in the name of Assur was external in the sense that it was always directed against foreign gods but intrasystemic in that it did not transcend the system of polytheism. The foreign gods whose images were subjected to violent treatment were taken seriously. The idea was not that there should be no other gods besides Assur but that the conquered town or country should be shorn of its tutelary deities. Thus, Esarhaddon says of Babylon, "The gods who dwelt therein flew off, like birds, and went up to heaven."[3] Even the strategically contrived sacrileges that Ashurbanipal committed against the temples and deities of Elam ("I considered its gods [and] goddesses as [mere] ghosts") should be considered intrasystemic. This is political violence directed against a people and its gods, who are believed to be their protectors, but not against a foreign religion as such.[4]

The distinction between intrasystemic and extrasystemic refers to two different constructions of otherness. The intrasystemic other is typically a member of a foreign country, civilization, language community, and/or religion with whom communication is nevertheless possible under the conditions of general translatability. By contrast, the extrasystemic other belongs to a system with which such conditions of translatability are not given and are even impossible. It is easy—or at least not impossible in principle—to translate Egyptian into Assyrian gods, but there exists no possible translatability between monotheistic and pagan religions. Translatability does not preclude conflict and violence; the Assyrians took violent action against a people on the basis of principal translatability.[5] The "enemy" is an intrasystemic other who may, however, be integrated into one's own political system without being forced to convert to a different construction of reality. The "idolater" and the heretic, conversely, are extrasystemic others who can be integrated only through conversion.

The iconoclastic actions of Akhenaten, who closed the Egyptian temples, smashed the cult-images, erased the names of the gods—especially Amun—consequently have to be classified as internal but extrasystemic because they were directed against the traditional polytheism of Egypt. The same applies to the satirical representations of image worship that one finds in the Bible and in the apocryphal Wisdom of Solomon, though one is dealing here not with violence proper but only with a derisory treatment of another religion or religious practice It is extrasystemic in that it treats the images of the gods as mere pieces of wood or stone, willfully disregarding their intrasystemic function as consecrated media of divine presence. The Assyrians act within the system, however violently, taking the gods of the enemy seriously, whereas the Hebrew prophets posit themselves outside the system. The violence with which the texts are concerned is also to be interpreted mostly as internal, directed against one's own group or people; but it is also extrasystemic, considering the people to be killed as followers of or converts to a foreign religion held in abhorrence and considered an abomination.

The classic case of intrasystemic ritual violence is human sacrifice.[6] Human sacrifice plays a central role in the case which monotheism makes up against paganism. In the Bible human sacrifice is repeatedly alluded to as an abomination, which in biblical religion is replaced by other forms of atonement. Isaac is not to be sacrificed but instead will be released and replaced at the very last moment by a sacrificial animal, a ram. One of the many interpretations of the *Akedah* (Gen. 22)—and certainly not the most profound and most interesting one—is that it teaches us about the abolition of human sacrifice and its replacement by animal sacrifice. Conversely, there is strong evidence in the Bible that human sacrifice—especially the sacrifice of the firstborn—was practiced in preexilic Israel and that the abolition of human sacrifice is part and parcel of the message of the prophets and the turn to monotheism during and after the exile.[7] Monotheism, however, is not specific in this respect. The myth of Iphigenia tells a similar story in the context of a polytheistic religion.[8] The rejection of human sacrifice seems to have been widespread in the ancient world and to have had little to do with the difference between monotheism and polytheism. Rather, it has to be seen as part of the much more general transformation that K. Jaspers once called the "Axial Age." (In the New World, of course, human sacrifice was practiced by the Aztecs to an unparalleled extent well into the fifteenth century CE, but this lies outside the biblical context.)

There is no clear evidence that human sacrifice was ever practiced in Egypt,[9] but in Palestinian and especially Phoenician contexts (above all at Carthage) hundreds of human remains have been unearthed that confirm the practice of human sacrifice beyond any reasonable doubt. Walter Burkert is certainly right in identifying *homo religiosus* as *homo necans*. For Burkert "blood and violence lurk fascinatingly at the very heart of religion."[10] Nietzsche interpreted the role of violence in religion as a method of "creating a memory":

> If something is to stay in the memory it must be burned in: "only that which never ceases *to hurt* stays in the memory"—that is a main clause from the oldest (unhappily also the most enduring) psychology on earth. . . . Man could never do without blood, torture, and sacrifices when he felt the need to create a memory for himself; the most dreadful sacrifices and pledges (sacrifices of the firstborn among them), the most repulsive mutilations (castration, for example), the cruelest rites of all religious cults (and all religions are at the deepest level systems of cruelties)—all this has its origin in the instinct that realized that pain is the most powerful aid to mnemonics.[11]

There is certainly much mythmaking and monotheistic atrocity propaganda in these representations of early religious practices, but the connection between religion and ritual violence, especially in the context of initiation rituals (creating a memory) and propitiatory sacrifice cannot be denied. Biblical monotheism must be viewed as a reaction against these forms of intrasystemic violence. In this it was certainly not alone, being part of a more general change of mentality and sensitivity in the ancient world. However, among the various movements and transformations aiming at "humanizing" religious—especially sacrificial—practices in the ancient world, biblical monotheism was the most determined and explicit. It would be absurd to contend that biblical monotheism brought violence into the world. On the contrary, it was influential in abolishing many forms of violence that had been acted out in the name of god(s) and within the framework of religion. The only new form of violence that arose with monotheism was extrasystemic violence. (This was directed against practitioners of other religions, which were subsumed under the rubric "idolatry," and against deviant beliefs and practices within one's own religion, subsumed under the term "heresy.")[12] This kind of violence originally seems to have been a matter more of theory than of practice. Moreover, this new form of violence, being extrasystemic, always tends to be acted out primarily against members of one's own group who, in one way or another, have fallen out of the system. It is extrasystemic but mostly introverted violence.

Seth as the Personification of Death and Violence

Although the Egyptians, as far as we know, did not attack the cult-images of other peoples, they used ritual or sacrificial violence against a god of their own pantheon, namely, the god Seth, who was himself considered the embodiment of violence and evil. Sacrificial violence in Egypt was based upon the distinction between good and evil, which in many ways differed from the monotheistic—especially the biblical—form of that distinction. In order to understand the intrasystemic violence that ancient Egyptian polytheism inflicted on what is seen as the personification of evil, one must take a closer look at how the Egyptians construed the distinction between good and evil, especially on the divine plane.

A passage by Jamblichos, a Neoplatonic philosopher and the author of *On the Egyptian Mysteries* (late third century CE), brings the Egyptian ideas about good and evil into focus: *"Akinēta de diatelei panta kai aeigenē, dioti oudepote histatai ho tou hēliou dromos. telea de kai holóklera diamenei panta, epeidē ta en Abydo aporrhēta oudepote apokalyptetai"* [Everything remains stable and ever new, because the course of the sun has never been halted; everything remains perfect and complete, because the mysteries in Abydos have never been uncovered].[13]

Good is that which keeps the world stable and ongoing; evil is what threatens its continuation by arresting the course of the sun and uncovering the mysteries of Osiris. This could be called a "cosmotheistic" conception of good and evil. By the time Jamblichos wrote these words, Re, the sun god, and Osiris, the god of the dead, had long since merged into one deity. The same applies to the two opposing principles that were fused into the figure of Typhon, the deity of absolute evil, who opposes the principles of order, stability, and continuity that keep the world going on both planes, the course of the sun and the mysteries of Abydos.

However, in the classical Egyptian tradition these two evil forces—the one confronting the sun in its course and the other threatening Osiris in his mysteries—were carefully kept apart. The cosmic personification of evil is called Apopis (Apep). Texts and images describe it as a huge watersnake or dragon that swallows the heavenly ocean across which the sun god is sailing in a boat, which is thus in danger of running aground on a sand bank. The evil that threatens Osiris with uncovering his mysteries, however, is called Seth, and this same Seth is depicted at the prow of the sun god's boat in the act of stabbing Apopis with a huge spear. On the cosmic plane, then, Seth acts on the side of Re, the personification of good, using violence to inflict death on the personification of evil. On the other plane, however, the plane of life and death represented by Osiris and his mysteries, Seth acts as evil and is himself the object of ritual violence. Seth thus personifies violent evil but not absolute evil. He represents an evil that is necessary to keep the world going in its "Re" aspect, but that must simultaneously be controlled and contained because it threatens the world in its "Osiris" aspect.

What is the nature of this violent evil? The balance of this chapter will focus on Seth, the foe of Osiris and the potential revealer of his mysteries; Seth the iconoclast, who uses anti-religious violence and is himself the object of ritual counterviolence.

According to the myth, which in Egyptian sources is never told in its entirety but only alluded to, Osiris was king of Egypt. Osiris's reign came to a violent end when he was slain by his brother, Seth. In accordance with René Girard's theory of sacrifice, this primordial fratricide was prompted by "mimetic desire" comparable to yet different from the murder of Abel by Cain. According to the biblical story, it was God's acceptance of Abel's gift and rejection of Cain's gift that aroused the latter's murderous envy. In Egyptian lore it is the throne of Egypt that is the object of Seth's mimetic desire. Seth not only killed his victim but also hacked his body to pieces and threw them into the Nile, which carried them to various places throughout the land. Isis, the sister-wife of Osiris, traversed the land to collect the scattered body parts. Together with her sister Nephthys, she was able through the power of her lamentations to reanimate the dead body so that she could conceive a son, the god Horus.

The next act of this drama is dominated by Horus, just as the first act was dominated by Isis. Whereas the activities of Isis and her assistants were directed toward the bodily aspects of the person—including animation, consciousness, memory, passion, and sexual desire—Horus directs his activities to the social aspects—including status, dignity, honor, and power. This is the point where ritual counterviolence sets in. Seth, the murderer of Osiris, has to be brought to justice. His humiliation will restore honor to the disgraced and his condemnation in court will restore the power of justice to the dethroned, powerless outcast. Assuming the role of his father's avenger, Horus is a Hamlet figure. However, unlike Hamlet he is not "sicklied o'er with the pale cast of thought" but knows exactly what to do, hesitates not a moment in translating his program into action, and succeeds in overcoming Seth and rehabilitating Osiris. The social rehabilitation of Osiris in terms of honor, dignity, status, and power consists not in his own ascension to the throne of Egypt but in that of his son. Osiris himself remains in the netherworld as the ruler of the dead and the lord of eternity.

What role does Seth play in this family drama? Seth is the personification of death. The whole mythology surrounding these various constellations of deities and their specific activities aims at making death treatable through ritual efforts, just as an injury or a malady may be treated through medical efforts. Death is made treatable by means of conceptual differentiation, which distinguishes between the active aspect of aggression, destruction, and annihilation of life and the passive aspect of the victim. According to this conception of death, there is no "natural death." Death is not conceived of as part of life but rather as its opposite, a murderous, destructive force. Every death is a murder. Death is not seen as something intrinsic to the process of life, within each living being, but as an external force. This force is personified by Seth. Death is thus dissociated from its victim, Osiris, and this dissociation from death and the dead underlies the concept of making death and the dead the object of ritual treatment.

Death, as personified by Seth, is not the end of life but an antagonistic force that is not satisfied with just killing. It continues its destructive attack against life by tearing the body apart, scattering the limbs all over Egypt, and trying to gain access to the restored body and to repeat its destruction. This is what the idea of uncovering the mysteries of Abydos means. These reside in the resurrected mummy of Osiris and its mysterious life in spite of the murder committed by Seth. Death is not seen as an event that must be accepted passively in an act of powerless surrender but as an act of violence that must be counteracted by opposing, containing, controlling, and keeping it out. The first blow of death can be ritually treated, and as long as death is prevented from dealing a second blow, a person may partake of the eternal life that the mysteries of Abydos bestow on their initiates and thus be rescued from death.

This mythology of life and death can also be read in terms of good and evil. In personifying death, Seth is also the personification of evil. If death is construed as murder, it is a crime, and the agent of death is a criminal who must be prosecuted and punished. The restitution of life and honor to Osiris is acted out primarily by inflicting ritualistic sacrificial violence on Seth. Seth is the prototype of the sacrificial animal. Every animal that is killed in order to be offered up as sacrifice is identified with Seth, and the killing is interpreted as punishment.

Seth and the Moralization of Death

This criminalization of death corresponds to a moralization of (after)life. The forces of death are seen as criminal and condemnable; the forces of life are seen as just and virtuous. The treatment of death consists mainly of restoring justice. Death, in the person of Seth, is brought to justice and condemned to death. Osiris is restored to life by being "justified against" (that is, triumphing over) Seth—or death. Justice and virtue appear as principles that have the power to save, to rescue a person from death and destruction. In the course of centuries, these mythic images developed into the idea of the judgment of the dead. Unlike Judaism and Christianity, the Egyptians did not conceive of this judgment as occurring collectively at the end of time but rather as being bestowed individually on each person after his or her death. It was believed that, following death, every person was summoned before a divine tribunal in order to be justified before God and rescued from death or to be condemned and surrendered to final death.

Within the framework of this idea, both Seth and the concept of evil undergo a transformation. Seth becomes the personification of evil not only in the form of violence and murder but as the epitome of all manner of vices and transgressions, such as lying, robbing, greed, adultery, fornication, blasphemy, and rebellion. Evil assumes the power of deadly sin, capable of causing one's final death and destruction if brought before the divine tribunal. The moralization of death, in other words, makes eternal life dependent on a person's moral behavior in this life. The mythical concept of condemning Seth in order to conquer death and gain eternal life gives way to the moral principle of conquering death by leading a good life and avoiding evil in all its various manifestations, especially vices and transgressions apt to give offense to the divine judges. During the trial following death, the heart of the deceased was weighed on a scale against a figure of truth. Every sin would make the side with the heart sink a little deeper. If it were found to be too heavy and irredeemably charged with guilt, the heart of the culprit would be swallowed by a monster, which would then also annihilate the guilty one.

Through this process of moralization, Seth, the personification of death, comes to be seen as the embodiment of all the sins and vices that cause death and destruction and prevent a person who commits them from passing the test of the scales and entering eternal life. In the context of Osiris, Seth turns into a devil, the personification of evil. However, Seth remains a great god and never turns into an absolute devil. Death is an evil force of destruction to be feared, hated, and avoided as much as possible. Nevertheless, it is an inevitable force of nature, a part of this world and its continuous course. Despite its inevitability—and this is the Egyptian conviction—there is still a lot that can be done about it.

In the Christian context, this conceptual connection of death and evil survives in the notion of "deadly (mortal) sin." Evil is defined as a kind of human behavior that prevents one from entering paradise and causes death, destruction, and eternal punishment, much the same way as in Egypt, where a sinful life that fails the test of the scales would be expelled from life and condemned to be swallowed up by the monster.

It may be useful to contrast the Decalogue of the Bible with those sins in the Egyptian Book of the Dead (especially the "Negative confession" in chapter 125) that correspond to the biblical prohibitions.

1. Thou shalt have no other gods before me.	——
2. Thou shalt not make unto thee any graven images.	——
3. Thou shalt not take the name of the Lord thy God in vain.	Ramses IV: I did not swear by the ram of Mendes. I did not pronounce the name of Tatenen.[14]
4. Remember the Sabbath day and keep it holy.	——
5. Honor thy father and thy mother.	Ramses IV: I did not contradict my father. I did not reject my mother.[15]
6. Thou shalt not kill.	B5: I did not kill a human

	being; A: I did not kill, nor ordered killing [A15–16]; B13: I did not kill the cattle of God (human beings).
7. Thou shalt not commit adultery.	B19: I did not make love to the wife of another man; B20: I did not fornicate; B27: I did not have homosexual intercourse.
8. Thou shalt not steal.	B2: I did not rob; B4: I did not steal.
9. Thou shalt not bear false witness.	B9: I did not lie.
10. Thou shalt not covet.	B3: I was not greedy; B18: I desired only my own possessions.

There are only three commandments—the first, second, and fourth—that have no corresponding prohibitions in the Egyptian context. The Egyptians did not worry about worshiping "other gods," their main concern being not to neglect any god worth worshiping. Worship required images; for the Egyptians there was no other way to reach the gods. There was also no regular "Sabbath" in Egypt, although there were a great many festival days. To follow the god—that is, to participate in the procession—was generally believed to be a great privilege, not an obligation. There was no need of a commandment here. The Egyptian commandments concerning god and the gods are not to blaspheme and not to break the taboos.

The three Jewish and Christian commandments that have no parallels in the Egyptian concept of sin—which can be neatly summarized as no other gods, no images, and keeping the Sabbath—represent the innovative and revolutionary core of biblical monotheism. The other commandments reflect the common wisdom of the Ancient Near East and were treated there—especially in Egypt—at a considerably higher level of moral sensitivity and elaboration. The prohibition against killing, for example, is extended to not causing pain, not provoking tears, and not torturing animals. The prohibition against lying is extended to all kinds of communicative misbehaviors such as calumny, prattling, slander, winking, being deaf to words of truth, and the mysterious prohibition of "knowing the nonexistent," whose meaning is still obscure.

The other seven commandments are social norms common to most societies and are not unique to monotheism. The commandments concerning the exclusive oneness of God, the prohibition of images, and
the injunction to keep the Sabbath are charged with the particular significance of being distinctive features, identity-markers of this new form
of religion by means of which Israel set itself apart from the other civilizations and religions of the ancient world. To worship other gods, to
fabricate and worship images, and to violate the Sabbath constitute
"sins" of a high order.

Despite the many parallels between Egyptian moral norms providing the criteria for a person's life following death and the Hebrew commandments as codified in the Torah, there is one decisive difference: in
the Bible God acts as legislator, whereas in the Egyptian Book of the
Dead the gods act only as judges. Moral norms are derived not from
divine legislation but from traditional wisdom and custom. The idea of
divine legislation is alien to ancient Egypt. The king and his counselors
formulate the laws; the teachers of wisdom codify the social norms of
acceptable behavior; and the gods merely extend the jurisdiction and social evaluation of this world into the other world, acting as judges along
the same lines and criteria as the social and judicial institutions on earth.

The Politicization of Evil

Seth, as we have seen, is an ambivalent figure. He is both the principle
of death and of evil—since death is seen as the source of evil and evil as
the cause of death—but he is also the bystander of the sun god, who
stands at the prow of the solar bark and directs his murderous aggression against Apep, the cosmic foe. Seth owes this promotion to his association with Ba'al and the general Canaanophilic inclinations of the
Ramesside dynasty.

The political aspect of Seth is perhaps as old as his aspect of death. In
the Old Kingdom the king is believed to incorporate both Horus and
Seth, justice and violence, reason and force. Moreover, the concept of
Egypt as an empire resulting from the unification of two kingdoms,
Upper and Lower, finds its usual symbolic expression in an icon showing Horus and Seth tying together lily and papyrus, the heraldic plants
of Upper and Lower Egypt. According to this symbolism, Seth represents Upper Egypt instead of death and evil. There is a myth describing
how Geb, the father of Osiris, first distributed the kingdom of Egypt

between Horus and Seth, giving Lower Egypt to Horus and Upper Egypt to Seth. However, he subsequently repented of this decision and gave the whole of Egypt to Horus, allotting to Seth only the desert and the foreign countries. The political myth of Horus and Seth is one of conflict rather than one of good and evil, of exclusion and annihilation. Seth is never excluded. On the contrary, he is integrated into a holistic concept of sovereignty combining death and life, violence and law, Upper and Lower Egypt, desert and fertile ground, magical and political force, and war and peace.

During the Ramesside period, the political aspect of Seth changes in a direction that will become of decisive importance in the Late Period. In order to better understand this semantic transformation of the figure of Seth, one has to travel back centuries in time. The Ramesside kings themselves took this step. King Seti I erected a stela commemorating the four hundredth anniversary of the installation of the cult of Seth-Ba'al in Avaris. It is perhaps the first erection of such a commemorative monument in recorded history.

The four-hundred-year stela takes us back into the first half of the seventeenth century BCE, a time when archaeologists ascertain a wave of Syro-Palestinian settlers in the eastern delta who a mere hundred years later were to dominate the rest of Egypt and to ascend to the Egyptian throne, forming the fifteenth dynasty, the so-called Hyksos kings. The Greek word *hyksos* transcribes their title as "ruler of foreign countries," which they bore in addition to the Egyptian royal titles. These invaders founded the town of Avaris, which became their capital, and installed the cult of Ba'al, whom they equated with Seth. This is the event that was commemorated by Seti I of the nineteenth dynasty.

This dynasty felt close to Seth. Two of their kings, Seti I and Seti II, bore names formed from that of Seth, and they descended from a family of officers living at the northeastern frontier, close to Avaris, the ancient capital of the Hyksos, the center of the cult of Seth, who was equated with the Canaanite god Ba'al. Perhaps they were partly Semitic themselves, descendants of the Hyksos tribes. In Piramesse, the newly founded capital of the Ramesside kings, a temple was erected for Seth, who became the lord of one of the four quarters into which the city was divided, like the old town of Jerusalem. No doubt Seth passed for everything but a devil during this period. He assumed unmistakable Asiatic traits, like the ruling dynasty itself, which abounded in Semitic names, and like the literature of the time, which delighted in Semitic loanwords and themes. This was a time when Egypt ruled the East and when

"Asianism" in manners, customs, and literary style corresponded to political colonialism and imperialism. Making Seth appear more Semitic and equating him with Ba'al reflected attempts to make him appear more positive. In becoming a foreigner, Seth's traditional roles or aspects of death, evil, and destructive violence did not disappear but were somehow integrated into a fuller and more positive—or, at the very least, ambivalent—personality.

However, during succeeding centuries—when Egypt not only ceased to rule the East but fell victim to a series of invasions, conquests, and domination by foreign powers, first from the east (the Assyrians and Persians), and then from the north (the Macedonians and Romans)—the character of Seth the foreigner, the Asiatic, changed yet again. The foreigner turned into a foe, and the foe turned into a devil. The two aspects of Seth—Seth-Ba'al, the Asiatic, and Seth-Death, the murderer of Osiris—merged. He now came to be regarded as the personification of absolute evil. He merged with Apep, the cosmic foe, and even lost his position in the solar bark, which he had to cede to Horus. Seth, in other words, became the personification of what could perhaps be called political or national trauma, in much the same way and in consequence of what he had always been, namely, the personification of the trauma of death.

Seth became the embodiment of the foreign invaders. The Egyptians did not differentiate much between Asians, such as Persians and Assyrians, on the one hand, and Europeans, such as Greeks and Romans, on the other. These countries were all identified with the Typhonian sphere, much as the Jews extended the concept of Edom from the mountains of Se'ir to the Roman Empire, and the concept of Amalek to Nazi Germany. Seth and Edom, moreover, share much in common, especially "redness" and "wildness." Red was the Typhonian color, and red-haired human beings were believed to belong to Seth. There are even traditions about the sacrifice of red-haired human victims. These may not be very reliable, but in any case it was certainly not very comfortable for anyone to be red-haired in Late period Egypt, and since the Egyptian language does not distinguish between red and yellow, the concept of Typhonian red-hairedness certainly included every shade of color fairer than brown.

The equation of Seth with political oppression coming from the east and north led quite naturally to the equation of Osiris with the land of Egypt. The rituals of overcoming the traumatizing effects of death, of restoring and conserving life by fashioning, burying, and redressing Osiris, were now to function as a ritualizing of "national" resistance against the traumatizing effects of foreign domination. These rituals are indicated by what Jamblichos calls the mysteries in Abydos. They keep the world going by keeping Egyptian culture, the cultural memory of Egypt, alive.

According to these mysteries, the rites of fashioning or re-membering Osiris came to be interpreted as remembering Egypt. Egypt was the body of Osiris, dismembered and scattered across the land. The fourteen, sixteen, or forty-two limbs of the dismembered body—the various traditions differ in this respect—were equated with the forty-two nomes of Egypt. The central rite of the mysteries consisted of a procession of forty-two priests. Each represented a nome of Egypt, carrying a canopic jar containing the limb specific to that nome (because it was believed to be buried there) and contributing it to the reintegration of the body. This was done by mixing sand, barley, several aromatic substances, and the water from the canopic jars in a golden or wooden mold in the form of a mummy. After a period of eight days, the barley would sprout and the mummiform body would be covered with green. The whole procedure was accompanied by the recitation of liturgies containing lamentations sung by priestesses representing Isis and Nephthys, by transfiguration spells, by rituals of execration directed against Seth and his cohorts, and by long litanies mentioning the forty-two nomes of Egypt and their specific sacred traditions. One of these rituals of fashioning Osiris is explicitly called "the ritual of conserving life in Egypt," and it is to be carried out in the "house of life." The latter was the name of an institution whose function was the conservation of the cultural memory of Egypt—a combination of library, scriptorium, and school. Every great temple had its house of life and celebrated the mysteries of Abydos, the rituals of re-membering Osiris. The cultural tradition of ancient Egypt stored in the scrolls in the library was periodically activated by ritual recitation in order to reanimate the re-collected and reassembled limbs of Osiris, the land of Egypt with its forty-two nomes.

Seth, conversely, was what he had always been: the murderer who killed Osiris, who tore his body apart, and who scattered the limbs across the country. He continued to threaten the combined efforts of Isis, Horus, Anubis, Nephthys, Thot, and their assistants, which form the mysteries of Abydos, by uncovering the mysteries, dealing the second blow, and bringing about final destruction. Now, however, this mythology was interpreted in terms of political theology. Seth dealt the first blow by invading the country, by usurping the throne, and by installing a foreign occupier. First the Assyrians and then the Persians appeared in the light of this mythology as manifestations of both death and evil, the vicious murderer who kills the country—Osiris—by neglecting or even destroying the temples, cults, and festivals; by impoverishing the country with exaggerated taxation and tribute; by deportation of its intellectual elite; by disempowering its administrative elite; by questioning its cultural, religious, and political identity—in short, through all forms of political trauma that now come to be interpreted in terms of death. By transposing onto the political level the rituals of treating and even "curing" the trauma of death, the Egyptians were able culturally to survive, in a most astonishing way, the cultural onslaught of Hellenism and the political oppression of Persian, Greek, and Roman occupation and exploitation. Egyptian culture stayed alive and even thrived well into the second and third centuries CE. It was able to impress the Greeks to such an extent as to give rise to a veritable Egyptomania among the intellectual circles all over the Mediterranean world. It even reached a large enough population—in the form of the mysteries of Isis and Osiris—to compete with Christianity.

This singular achievement was due to the Egyptian conception of death, which viewed it on both the political and the cultural plane. Egyptians knew how to transform experiences of suffering into imaginative triumphs. In the imagination of its native inhabitants, the land of Egypt presented itself as the victim of a murderous attack that was overcome annually through ritual performance. The mysteries at Abydos (which were performed not only there but in every religious center in Egypt) represented merely one such ritual of overcoming cultural death. Another important festival was the "triumph of Horus," whose annual celebration at Edfu was the most important feast in Egypt. The dramatic performance shows Seth conquering Egypt from the north and being driven back and expelled from the south by Horus. A number of other myths and legends reflecting the Assyrian trauma locate threat in the north and salvation in the south. I am almost certain that the Assyrian conquest under Esarhaddon and its three subsequent repetitions—each more cruel and destructive than the next—were experienced by the Egyptians in no less traumatic form than the fall of the northern kingdom of Israel in 722 and the Babylonian exile in the sixth century by the Israelites. This experience changed the whole system of cultural semantics and was decisive in making Seth an absolute devil and the personification of death, evil, and destruction. Seth turns into the proto-typical vilifier and desecrator, committing the very crimes that Ashur-banipal himself boasts of having committed against the gods of Elam: "The temples of Elam I destroyed so that they ceased to exist. . . . Into their secret groves into which no stranger goes, whose bounds he does not enter, my battle troops penetrated, saw their secret, and burnt it with fire. The burial places of their kings . . . I devastated, I destroyed, I let them see the sun."[16] Thus, the idea of death came to be associated specifically with Assyria and more generally with foreign—especially northern—countries, while the idea of evil came to be associated with foreign customs. This resulted in a climate of xenophobia and led to the formation of taboos and cultural abominations.

This new cultural semantics, beset with strictures and taboos of all kinds, seemed to be centered on the cult of the sacred animals, which was only now elevated to the position of *the* defining element of Egyp-tianism, in much the same way as the Jewish law—especially *kashrut*—came to be regarded as the defining element of Judaism. The compari-son with India is even more obvious, where the sacred cow came to be regarded as the most elevated symbol of Hinduism under British domi-nation and colonialism. Making identity sacred is a regular reaction for-mation in times of political and cultural oppression. The cult of the sa-cred animals served as the symbolic expression of sanctified identity in Egypt. Herodotus tells that the Egyptians would not kiss a Greek on the mouth (because this mouth might have eaten beef), nor would they use the knife, or kettle of a Greek (because they could have been used for preparing beef). Like the biblical story of Joseph (Gen. 43:23), Herodo-tus states that the Egyptians would not share their meal with foreigners.

Seth the Iconoclast and the Origins of Egyptian Anti-Judaism

In his treatise on Isis and Osiris Plutarch mentions that Seth-Typhon, the murderer of Osiris, was driven out of Egypt and spent a week jour-neying to Palestine, where he became the ancestor of the Jews by father-ing two sons, Hierosolyma and Juda.[17] He instituted the Sabbath in com-memoration of his weeklong flight and erected a statue of his sacred animal, the ass, in the temple at Jerusalem.[18] Seth is usually associated with the donkey in Egyptian mythology. In Greco-Egyptian texts, the God Iao—the Greek rendering of the Hebrew Tetragrammaton[19]—is equated with Seth and the ass because the name sounded like the—obviously onomatopoetic—Egyptian word for "ass."

Within these traditions, the xenophobic climate surrounding Seth, the Asiatic foe, assumes an unmistakably anti-Semitic ring. True, the Egyptian attitude toward Jews was no less hostile in the Greco-Roman era than was their attitude toward Greeks. In the case of the Greeks, this hostility can be explained by their occupation, domination, and colonial exploitation. The Jewish case is less easily explained. One cannot exclude the possibility that there was more to Egyptian anti-Judaism than just their notorious xenophobia.

In this respect, the story that Manetho tells about Moses seems of prime importance. We owe the preservation of this fragment from Manetho's otherwise lost work on Egyptian history to Flavius Josephus, who quotes it in his pamphlet *Contra Apionem* as a particularly flagrant case of injustice against the Jewish nation. *Contra Apionem* is a collection of, and response to, renderings of Jewish history—especially the Exodus from Egypt—by mostly Egyptian Hellenistic historians. The work is both an apologia of Jewish history, culture, and religion and an anthology of ancient "anti-Semitic" writing. It is important to realize this context before studying the Manetho fragment itself, which is quoted by Josephus for a reason. His polemical and apologetic perspective has led to an interesting case of misreading.

Manetho was an Egyptian priest who wrote his *History of Egypt* under Ptolemy II in the first half of the third century BCE.[20] King Amenophis, he tells us, wanted to see the gods. The sage Amenophis Paapis—a well-known historical personage whose presence dates the events under Amenophis III to the first half of the fourteenth century BCE—tells Amenophis that he may see the gods if he cleanses the land of lepers. This hint as to the date of the events was lost on Josephus, who was ignorant of Amenophis Paapis. He therefore took this story to be a variant of the account that Manetho gives of the expulsion of the Hyksos in another section of his work, which is also quoted by Josephus. As a Jewish historian eager to reject any manifestations of anti-Judaism in Hellenistic historiographical literature wherever he could find it, Josephus read Jewish themes into texts that dealt with something else entirely. In the case of Manetho, he read the theme of exodus into both the account of the expulsion of the Hyksos and the story about King Amenophis and his counselor, which actually refer to events separated by almost two hundred years. Josephus could not have known this because he was unable to identify Amenophis Paapis.

The king sent all lepers into the eastern desert, put them into forced labor camps, and had them work in the quarries. Amenophis, the seer, predicted divine punishment because there were priests among the prisoners. He said that they would receive help from outside, conquer Egypt, and reign there for thirteen years. Fearing to tell the king this in person, he wrote everything down and committed suicide. The lepers chose Osarsiph, a Heliopolitan priest, as their leader to enter into negotiations with the intimidated king. He received permission to settle in Avaris, the ancient capital of the Hyksos, where he organized the lepers by giving them laws prescribing all that is forbidden in Egypt and ruling out all that Egypt prescribes. The first and foremost commandment is not to worship the gods; the second, not to spare any of their sacred animals, nor to abstain from other forbidden food; and the third, not to have intercourse with outsiders.

Osarsiph's actions illustrate the principle of normative inversion, which consists of inverting the norms of the other culture. This seems to me the most forceful way of constructing extrasystemic, "untranslatable" otherness and of marking the difference. This principle recurs repeatedly where the relationship between Jews and gentiles is being discussed, not only in "pagan" and anti-Jewish argumentation but also within a Jewish context. This is especially true of Maimonides and his *Guide for the Perplexed*, where the normative inversion of the customs of the Sabians serves as a historical explanation for most of the ritual laws.[21] After establishing his anti-Egyptian and counterreligious institutions, Osarsiph fortified the city and sent an invitation to the Hyksos in Jerusalem, who had been driven out of Egypt some two or three hundred years earlier, to join the lepers in their revolt. The Hyksos returned. Remembering the prediction, King Amenophis shrank from fighting the rebels, hid the divine images, and fled with the sacred animals to Ethiopia. The lepers and the Hyksos ruled Egypt for thirteen years in a way that, in the collective memory of the Egyptians, made the former Hyksos rule appear like a golden age. Not only were the towns and temples laid waste and the holy images destroyed during this period, but the sanctuaries were turned into kitchens and the sacred animals grilled on fires. At this stage of his narrative Manetho makes the highly significant remark that Osarsiph took the name "Moses." Although this might be a later gloss, whoever wrote this sentence made it clear that in that author's view the religion of Moses was tantamount to the persecution of the gods, the destruction of their images, and the slaughter of their sacred animals. Finally, Manetho continues, Amenophis and his grandson, Ramses, returned from Nubia and drove out the lepers and their allies.

Josephus read this story as an account of the Hebrew Exodus, this despite the fact that Manetho explicitly states that the Hyksos (the

Hebrews, in Josephus's understanding of Egyptian history) had already been settled in Jerusalem for two hundred years or more. Josephus mistakenly thinks that Manetho presented two versions of the event, one taken from the "sacred scriptures" and the other from oral tradition (*mytheuomena kai legomena*). However, to what else could Manetho have been referring in his story of the lepers if not to the Exodus of the Jews?

In my book *Moses the Egyptian* I subscribed to the by now prevalent interpretation, dating back to the days of Eduard Meyer, who as early as 1904 proposed to see in this story a reflection of the Amarna experience. During the Amarna period Akhenaten (the son of Manetho's King Amenophis) shut the temples, halted the rituals and feasts, and installed a strict and exclusive monotheism for about fifteen or seventeen years (thirteen is also a possibility).[22] This experience must have had an equally traumatizing effect on the Egyptian psyche as the Assyrian conquests of Egypt six hundred years later. For the first time in recorded history someone stood up to reject and abolish a whole religious tradition in the name of truth. This experience might have given the Asiatic foe its distinctively religious or antireligious traits and enriched the nature of evil by adding the concept of iconoclasm or, rather, "theoclasm."

Theoclasm is represented in Manetho's narrative and in many similar stories as the most extreme form of impurity, namely, leprosy, in much the same way as idolatry is represented in the biblical texts as madness. On the basis of the monotheistic distinction between truth and error, idolatry appears as the worst kind of error, whereas on the basis of the traditional distinction between purity and impurity, iconoclasm appears in the shape of leprosy. However, there is an association of leprosy and idolatry in the Bible as well. In her fascinating analysis of Numbers, Mary Douglas discovered a cyclical structure that connects the laws concerning the expulsion of the lepers (Num. 5:1–4) with the laws concerning the expulsion of the idolaters (Num. 33:50–56). Leprosy and idolatry are the worst forms of pollution because they prevent God from "dwelling in the midst of his people."[23]

In the eyes of the Egyptians monotheism, or, rather, "monolatry" is evil, sinful, and criminal because the world is full of gods, and the gods must be worshiped. The gods are social beings, living and acting in "constellations"; a lonely god would be devoid of any power or personality and would have no impact on the great project of maintaining the world. However, this precisely describes Seth, who is asocial, an outcast, and condemned to solitude. He is one, who

rejoices in separation, who hates fraternity,
who relies only on his own heart among the gods.[24]

In a Ramesside tale we read that Apophis, the Hyksos king, worshiped Seth in a monolatric way:

King Apophis chose for his lord the god Seth.
He did not worship any other deity in the whole land except Seth.[25]

There is thus an obvious connection in Egyptian eyes between the asocial nature of Seth and the monolatrous exclusivity of his worship. Both are abhorred as manifestations of extrasystemic otherness and of deadly sin and evil.

Rituals of Hatred

Besides passing for an iconoclast, Seth appears as a revealer of mysteries. This brings us back to the remark by Jamblichos:

Everything remains perfect and complete,
because the mysteries in Abydos have never been uncovered.

Seth threatens all the mysteries of Egypt with his insatiable curiosity and reckless greed. He destroys every secret, breaks every taboo, defiles all that is pure, and desecrates all that is sacred. The rites are performed to ward him off

lest the movements of the sun become known,
rich in trajectories in crossing the sky,
lest the chest in Heliopolis be opened
and it be seen what it contains,
lest the garment in Memphis be loosened
and the arm of "so-and-so" become visible,
lest the lamp be extinguished in the night of evil,
in that time which must never happen,
lest the four spells in Heliopolis become known
and the heaven falls down in hearing them,
lest the seal of Anubis be broken
and the clay of Ptah be removed,
lest the hiding shrubbery be cut down
in order to expel the one whom it conceals.[26]

Seth is the god of blasphemous and scandalous curiosity. This is also the theme of a myth told by Ovid[27] and several other ancient authors that provides an explanation of animal worship in ancient Egypt.[28] The gods, it is revealed, so feared the reckless curiosity of Seth-Typhon that they decided to disguise themselves in the shapes of animals. Later they declared these animals sacred out of gratitude to them. Diodorus of Sicily, who calls the cult of the animals an *aporrhēton dogma* (unspeakable secret),[29] replaces "Seth" with "humankind" in his rendering of the story, which is how he claims to have heard it in Egypt. It seems possible that this very strong and conspicuous condemnation of curiosity reflects an Egyptian reaction to the scientific and investigative mind of the Greeks, who subjected the Egyptians to a veritable program of "Egyptological" research. It strangely foreshadows Saint Augustine's verdict on curiosity, which dominated the occidental attitude toward the world and nature until the end of the sixteenth century.[30] Another work in which the theme of curiosity plays a central role is *The Golden Ass*, by Apuleius of Madauros. Lucius, the hero, dabbles in magic out of an insatiable curiosity and is punished by being transformed into an ass, the animal of Seth, whose principal vice he practiced.[31]

In the Late Period the god Seth became the target of rituals of hatred and execration. Here one encounters the language of violence in the context of polytheism. One of these rituals of hatred is entitled "the ritual of overthrowing Seth and his cohorts." It opens with the following prescription:

> Let a figure of Seth be brought made of red wax,
> his name inscribed on its breast, saying "Seth, the miserable."
> Moreover, let his figure be drawn on an empty sheet
>   of fresh papyrus with fresh ink.
> Alternatively, bring a figure made of acacia or hema-wood.
> To bind it with the sinew of a red bull; to recite over it.
> To stamp on it with the left foot; to recite over it.
> To hit it with a spear; to recite over it.
> To cut it with a knife; to recite over it.
> To put it into the fire; to recite over it.
> To spit on it many times in the fire; to recite over it.[32]

The following pages contain the endless spells that were to be recited during the execution of these symbolic actions against the figure of Seth. Execration rituals were a familiar phenomenon in ancient Egypt. They were always directed against political enemies of Pharaoh, both inside Egypt and abroad. Pots or figurines, inscribed with the names of the enemies, were smashed, burned, and buried with the intention of putting a curse on these individuals to prevent them from hostile actions against Pharaoh and to shorten their days. The earliest examples of this custom date back to the third millennium BCE. The application of these rituals to Seth, in a highly elaborated form, marks the climax of what I would call the "politicization of evil." In a papyrus dating from about the same time period we read:

> If the ceremonies for Osiris are neglected
> in their time at this place . . .
> the country will be deprived of its laws.
> The plebs will abandon their superiors
> and there are no orders for the masses.
> If the foe is not beheaded that is at hand
> made of wax, on papyrus, or of wood
>   according to the prescriptions of the ritual,
> then the foreign countries will rebel against Egypt
> and civil war and revolution will rise in the whole country.
> The king in his palace will not be obeyed anymore
> and the land will be deprived of its defence.[33]

In the Late Period the ceremonies for Osiris and the rites against Seth are given a decidedly political meaning. Ritual violence acted out in the name of a deity—in this case Osiris—is turned into political violence acted out against rebels and foreign enemies in the name of the state and the Pharaoh The rituals acquire a political meaning and political actions acquire a religious meaning. This corresponds closely to the Neo-Assyrian system.

In Greco-Roman times, when Egypt was confronted first with Hellenism and Judaism and then with Christianity, whose success in Egypt was quite overwhelming, the image of the Asiatic foe increasingly assumed the traits of an atheist, an enemy and persecutor of religion. The evil that the foreigners were believed to have caused Egypt was described not in terms of political oppression but religious persecution. To conclude, let me quote the famous apocalypse from the hermetic treatise in which Asclepius laments the end of Egyptian religion:

> A time will come when it will appear that the Egyptians worshipped the divinity with faithful mind and painstaking reverence—for no purpose. All their holy service will be disappointed and perish without effect, for divinity will return from earth to heaven and Egypt will be abandoned. The land that was the seat of reverence will be widowed by the powers and left destitute of their presence. When foreigners occupy the land and territory, not only

will reverence fall into neglect but, even harder, a prohibition under penalty prescribed by law will be enacted against reverence, fidelity, and divine worship. [One recognizes the echo of Osarsiph's legislation.]

Then this most holy land, seat of shrines and temples, will be filled completely with tombs and corpses.

O Egypt, Egypt! Of your reverent deeds only stories will survive and they will be incredible to your children! Only words cut in stone will survive to recount your faithful works, and the Scythian or Indian or some such neighboring barbarian will dwell in Egypt. For divinity goes back to heaven and all the people will die, deserted, as Egypt will be widowed and deserted by god and human.

I call on you, most holy river, and I tell your future: a torrent of blood will fill the Nile to the banks and pollute the divine waters. . . . Whoever survives will be recognized as an Egyptian only by his language; in his actions he will seem a foreigner. . . .

A land once holy, most loving of divinity, by reason of her reverence the only land on earth where the gods settled, she who taught holiness and fidelity will be an example of utter unbelief. In their weariness the people of that time will find the world nothing to wonder at or to worship. This universe—a good thing that never had, nor has, nor will have its better—will be endangered. People will find it oppressive and scorn it. They will not cherish this entire world . . .

No one will look up to heaven. The reverent will be thought mad, the irreverent wise. Whoever dedicates himself to reverence of mind will find himself facing a capital penalty. They will establish new laws, new justice. Nothing holy, nothing reverent nor worthy of heaven or heavenly beings will be heard of or believed in the mind.

How mournful when the gods withdraw from mankind! Then neither will the earth stand firm nor the sea be navigable; stars will not cross heaven, nor will the course of the stars stand firm in heaven. Every divine voice will grow mute in enforced silence. The fruits of the earth will rot; the soil will no more be fertile; and the very air will droop in gloomy lethargy.

Such will be the old age of the world: irreverence, disorder, and disregard for everything good.[34]

This text, which was written in view of the rise of Christianity and related movements—especially Gnosticism—best expresses the Egyptian or polytheist's view of exclusive monotheism.

What one may learn from this example is how much violence there is in polytheism. Violence is expressed as existing between gods, resulting in combat, bloodshed, murder, destruction, desecration, humiliation, and other forms of conflict within the divine world. These conflicts reflect and give expression to conflicts, antagonisms, and oppositions experienced in the visible world and are, in turn, reflected and expressed by human violence in the frame of ritual performance. Violence is contained *in* but also contained—that is, held in containment—*by* polytheism. This is why polytheistic violence is intrasystemic. As Michael Fishbane has pointed out,[35] although pre-monotheistic combat myths, left many traces in the Hebrew Bible, this mythical expression of violence is excluded in monotheism. Monotheism put an end to "polytheistic," intrasystemic violence but not, unfortunately, to violence as such.

3

All Gods Are One

Evolutionary and Inclusive Monotheism

The writer and medievalist C. S. Lewis once stated that

> monotheism should not be regarded as the rival of polytheism, but
> rather as its maturity. Where you find polytheism, combined with
> any speculative power and any leisure for speculation, monotheism
> will sooner or later arise as a natural development. The principle, I
> understand, is well illustrated in the history of Indian religion. Be-
> hind the gods arises the One, and the gods as well as the men are
> only his dreams. That is one way of disposing of the many. . . . The
> gods are to be aspects, manifestations, temporary or partial em-
> bodiments of the single power.[1]

As early as the seventeenth century, when the terms "monotheism"
and "polytheism" were being coined, Ralph Cudworth stated that all
religions were basically monotheistic in that they acknowledged only
one supreme deity as origin or creator of the universe.[2] There are, in
fact, several roads that seem to lead from polytheism to monotheism, to
reduce the number of gods and to transform diversity into unity. One,
which I will call "Translating Gods," is typical of Mesopotamia but
spread all across the ancient world of classical antiquity.[3] The other is
typical of all polytheistic religions and consists of a well-defined hierar-
chal structuring of the pantheon, with a single god at the top who tends
not only to surpass the other gods but also eventually to absorb them.
This is what Eric Voegelin has called "Summodeism," the belief in a supreme god far above the other members of the pantheon.[4] In the first
model unity is a matter of common elements, of what two or three—
and eventually even all—gods have in common; in the second model
unity is a question of power.

Two Paths to Unity

Translating Gods

From the viewpoint of monotheism, polytheism seems prehistoric: original, primitive, immature, a mere precursor of monotheism. However, as soon as one changes this perspective and tries to view polytheism from within, say, from the viewpoint of ancient Egypt, polytheism appears as a great cultural achievement. In polytheistic religions the deities are clearly differentiated and personalized by name, shape, and function. The great achievement of polytheism is the articulation of a common semantic universe. It is this semantic dimension that makes the names translatable, that is, makes it possible for gods from different cultures— or different regions and traditions within a culture—to be equated with one another. Tribal religions are ethnocentric. The powers and ancestral spirits that are worshiped by one tribe are irreducibly and untranslatably different from those worshiped by another. By contrast, the highly differentiated members of polytheistic pantheons easily lend themselves to cross-cultural translation or "interpretation." Translation works because the gods have a well-defined function in the maintenance of cosmic, political, and social order. The sun god of one group, culture, or religion is the same as the sun god of another. Most of the deities have a cosmic competence and reference or are related to a well-defined cultural domain, such as writing, craftsmanship, love, war, or magic. This specific responsibility and competence renders a deity comparable to other deities with similar traits and makes their names mutually translatable.

The tradition of translating or interpreting foreign divine names goes back to the innumerable glossaries equating Sumerian and Akkadian words, among which appear lists of divine names in two or even three languages, such as Emesal (women's language; used as a literary dialect), Sumerian, and Akkadian. The most interesting of these sources is the explanatory list *Anu ša ameli,* which contains three columns, the first two giving the Sumerian and Akkadian names, respectively, and the third listing the functional definition of each deity.[5] This explanatory list gives what may be called the "meaning" of divine names, making explicit the principle that underlies the equation or translation of gods. In the Kassite period of the Late Bronze Age the lists are extended to include such languages as Amorite, Hurritic, Elamite, and Kassite in addition to Sumerian and Akkadian. In these cases the practice of translating divine names was applied to very different cultures and religions.

The origin of this practice may be found in the field of international law. Treaties had to be sealed by solemn oaths, and the gods who were invoked in these oaths had to be recognized by both parties. The list of the gods involved conventionally closed the treaty. They necessarily had to be equivalent in terms of their function and, in particular, their rank. Intercultural theology became a concern of international law.

The growing political and commercial interconnectedness of the ancient world and the practice of cross-cultural translation of everything, including divine names, gradually led to the concept of a common religion. The names, iconographies, and rites—in short, the cultures—might differ, but the gods remained the same everywhere. This concept of religion as the common background of cultural diversity and the principle of cultural translatability eventually led to the late Hellenistic outlook, where the names of the gods mattered little in view of the overwhelming natural evidence for their existence and presence in the world.

The idea that the various nations basically worshiped the same deities albeit under different names and in different forms eventually led to the belief in a "Supreme Being" (Gk. *Hypsistos*, "the Highest One").[6] It essentially comprised not only the myriad known and unknown deities but also those three or four gods who, in the contexts of different religions, play the role of the highest god (usually Zeus, Sarapis, Helios, and Iao = YHWH). This super-deity is addressed by appellations such as *Hypsistos* (supreme), and by the widespread "One-God" predication *Heis Theos*. Oracles typically proclaim particular gods to be a unity comprised of a number of other gods:

> One Zeus, one Hades, one Helios, one Dionysos,
> One god in all gods.[7]

In one of these oracles, Iao (YHWH), the God of the Jews, is proclaimed to be the god of time (Olam-Aion), appearing as Hades in winter, Zeus in springtime, Helios in summer, and "Habros Iao" in autumn.[8] These oracles and predications manifest a quest for the sole and supreme divine principle behind the innumerable multitude of specific deities. This is typical of the "ecumenical age" (Voegelin) and seems to correspond to efforts toward political unification.[9] The belief in the "Supreme Being" (Hypsistos) has a distinctly universalist character.

> The sons of Ogyges call me Bacchus,
> Egyptians think me Osiris,
> Mysians name me Phanaces,
> Indians regard me as Dionysus,
> Roman rites make me Liber,

The Arab race thinks me Adoneus,
Lucaniacus the Universal God.[10]

This tradition of invoking the highest god according to the names
given him by the various nations expresses a general conviction in Late
Antiquity regarding the universality of religious truth, the relativity of
religious institutions and denominations, and the conventionality of divine names. According to Servius, the Stoics taught that there is only one
god with various names that differ according to actions and offices. Varro
(116–27 BCE), who knew about the Jews from Poseidonios, was unwilling
to differentiate between Jove and Yahweh because he felt that it mattered
little by which name the god was called as long as the same thing was
meant (*nihil interesse censens quo nomine nuncupetur, dum eadem res intelligatur*).[11]
Porphyry felt that the names of the gods were purely conventional.[12]
Symmachus, a pagan prefect, wondered what difference it made "by
which wisdom each of us arrives at truth? It is not possible that only one
road leads to so sublime a mystery."[13] Celsus argued that "it makes no difference whether one calls god 'Supreme' (*Hypsistos*) or Zeus or Adonai or
Sabaoth or Ammon as the Egyptians do, or Papaios as do the Scythians.
The name does not matter when it is evident what or who is meant."[14] In
his treatise on Isis and Osiris Plutarch makes this point, stating that no
one would "regard the gods as different among different nations nor as
Barbarian and Greek and as southern and northern. But just as the sun,
moon, heaven, earth and sea are common to all, although they are given
different names by the various nations, so it is with the one reason (logos)
which orders these things and the one providence which has charge of
them."[15] Seneca stressed that this conviction was based on natural evidence: "This All, which you see, which encompasses divine and human,
is One, and we are but members of a great body."[16] According to Mark
Smith, "Pliny the Elder (*Natural History*, bk. 2, v. 15) put the general point
in a pithy formulation for deities in the world, that they are a matter of
'different names to different peoples' (*nomina alia aliis gentibus*)."[17]

In his book *On the Psychotheology of Everyday Life* Eric Santner proposes
the following distinction between globalism and universalism, assigning
to globalism the idea of intercultural translatability and to universalism
the idea of monotheism based on the "Mosaic Distinction" between
true and false: "For global consciousness conflicts are generated through
external differences between cultures and societies, whereas universality,
as I am using the term here, signifies the possibility of a shared opening
to the agitation and turbulence immanent to any construction of identity, the *Unheimlichkeit* or uncanniness internal to any and every space we

call home."[18] Globalism is concerned with the stranger without and may be characterized as a culture of recognition. Universalism is concerned with the stranger within and strives for a culture of tolerance. This original and intriguing understanding of universalism is based on the writings of Franz Rosenzweig and Sigmund Freud. However, even if we replace it by the commonly accepted meaning of the term "universalism," the distinction remains valid and very revealing. Universalism, as commonly understood, means the general validity of something recognized as an absolute truth. The eighteenth century, the Age of Reason, was also an age of universalism. Reason, nature, and the dignity and rights of the human being were proclaimed to be universal truths. The universalism of enlightenment conflicted with the universalism of religion. Each believed itself to be based on general truth. It was the same clash that we experience today between, on the one hand, the universalism of Western secularism, with values such as human rights, democracy, and a market economy, and, on the other, Islam, with its equally universalist perspective. I call this "exclusive universalism" because the Truth (with a capital *T*) whose universal validity it is promoting does not allow for—excludes—compromise. Globalism, conversely, is based on the idea that although the Truth is hidden, the search for Truth is common to all human societies and cultures, and that although the external differences are irreducible, they are translatable. Globalism is concerned with cultural techniques of translation and a practically and politically oriented attitude. Universalism is concerned with Truth and thus a more religiously and philosophically oriented form of thought. Given this distinction, it becomes clear that the Mesopotamian way of translating gods, which eventually led to a form of inclusive monotheism—the idea that "All Gods are One"—is connected to globalism and a kind of intellectual and spiritual by-product of processes that belong to the practical and political sphere. This is seen in the rise of the "Ancient World" in the Late Bronze Age and particularly in the emergence of the Greek and Roman empires in antiquity and late antiquity. It also becomes clear that concern over such questions as monotheism, violence, and intolerance has much to do with the process of globalization and the conflicting universalisms of our time.

In his study Mark Smith quotes a prayer of the Hittite queen Puduhepa (consort of Hattusilis)[19] that she addresses to the sun goddess of Arinna: "O Sun-goddess of Arinna, queen of all countries! In the Hatti country you bear the name of the Sun-goddess of Arinna; but in the land which you made the cedar land you bear the name Hebat."[20] Smith adds that at first glance this utterance might seem to operate with the assumption of god-lists found at Ugarit. However, a closer look would suggest that in addressing the goddess as the Sun-goddess of Arinna, this particular figure is the underlying reality for both the Sun-goddess of Arinna in Hatti and Hebat in the Levant. The theology of translation here is more profoundly an expression of theological imperialism: the goddess thought in the Levant to be Hebat is in fact actually the Sun-goddess of Arinna. This very sort of expression is one that will return in modern theological discourse attempting to come to grips with divinity across religious divides.[21]

Hyphenating Gods

Scholars conventionally refer to an Egyptian phenomenon that might be compared to the Mesopotamian technique of translating gods as "syncretism."[22] It involves the collocation of two or three different gods, leading to such hyphenated names as Amun-Re, Amun-Re-Harakhty, Ptah-Sokar-Osiris, Hathor-Tefnut, Min-Horus, Atum-Khepre, Sobek-Re, and many others. As a rule the first name refers to the cultic/local dimension, the actual temple owner and lord of the town, whereas the second name refers to a translocal—preferably cosmic—deity. Thus, Amun is the lord of Thebes in whom the Sun god Re becomes manifest. Ptah is the lord of Memphis, and Sokar is the god of its necropolis. Osiris is the god of the underworld and the dead, whose Memphite representation is thus to be seen in Ptah-Sokar. This relationship between deities does not imply equation or fusion since the gods retain their individuality. Re does not "merge" into Amun or vice-versa. The gods enter into a relationship of mutual determination[23] and complementation: Re becomes the cosmic aspect of Amun, Amun the cultic and local aspect of Re. Atum refers to the nocturnal and Khepre to the diurnal aspect of the sun god. Hyphenation implies neither identification nor subordination. Amun has no precedence over Re nor Re over Amun. In the course of time, however, this practice of "hyphenating" gods fosters the idea of a kind of deep-structural identity.

Hierarchy

Let me now turn to the most common road to unity, the way of power, leading to the primacy of one god as chief of the pantheon over the other gods. This structure is so typical of polytheistic religions that one need not go into any detail here. I am interested only in those cases where this basic structure of primacy and dominion verges on forms where dependence either turns into ontological subordination—such as in God versus angels, or demons or spirits or lesser gods of any kind—or fusion, such as in the equation of gods with aspects or bodily parts of the one supreme God. At the beginning of the eighth book of the *Iliad* Homer depicts a scene where the power structure of primacy is about to change into ontological subordination—at least in the form of a thought experiment:

> Now when Morning, clad in her robe of saffron, had begun to suffuse light over the earth, Jove called the gods in council on the topmost crest of serrated Olympus. Then he spoke and all the other gods gave ear. "Hear me," said he, "gods and goddesses, that I may speak even as I am minded. Let none of you neither goddess nor god try to cross me, but obey me every one of you that I may bring this matter to an end. If I see anyone acting apart and helping either Trojans or Danaans, he shall be beaten inordinately ere he come back again to Olympus; or I will hurl him down into dark Tartarus far into the deepest pit under the earth, where the gates are iron and the floor bronze, as far beneath Hades as heaven is high above the earth, that you may learn how much the mightiest I am among you. Try me and find out for yourselves. Hang me a golden chain from heaven, and lay hold of it all of you, gods and goddesses together—tug as you will, you will not drag Jove the supreme counsellor from heaven to earth; but were I to pull at it myself I should draw you up with earth and sea into the bargain, then would I bind the chain about some pinnacle of Olympus and leave you all dangling in the mid firmament. So far am I above all others either of gods or men."[24]

Fortunately for polytheism, Zeus renounces this manifestation of supremacy, which remains only a potentiality. However, the famous passage has always been understood as referring to the latent monotheism within polytheism.

Obviously, the power structure of a pantheon reflects the power structure of a society. In this way the strikingly loose power structure of the Greek pantheon, where Zeus reigns as first among equals (*primus inter pares*) and relies on such extreme threats in order to get his way, reflects the loose power structure of the Greek aristocracy, where the values of competition prevail over the values of cooperation. The social and political situation in the oriental states and empires was totally different.

These societies were firmly centered in a monarchy and a bureaucracy where the king reigned not as first among equals but as a god or a god-like being on earth.

In Mesopotamia, where there was originally a plurality of city-states, the situation was not very different from that of Greece. With the growing tendency toward unification, however, the pantheon increasingly became structured based on strong hierarchical relations of subordination, which over time fostered ideas of deep-structural identity.[25] The Mesopotamian creation epic entitled the *Enuma Elish* ends with a hymn to Marduk, the chief god, calling him by fifty names. The gods who are subordinated to Marduk become his names, aspects of his all-encompassing essence. Another text assembles a group of major deities, identifying them with Marduk's various roles:

> Ninurta is Marduk of the hoe,
> Nergal is Marduk of the attack,
> Zababa is Marduk of the hand-to-hand fight,
> Enlil is Marduk of lordship and counsel,
> Nabium is Marduk of accounting,
> Sin is Marduk, the illuminator of the night,
> Shamash is Marduk of justice,
> Adad is Marduk of rains.[26]

A hymn of Ashurbanipal addresses Marduk as assuming the identities of the three highest gods in the form of personal characteristics:

> You hold the Anuship, the Enlilship, the Eaship.[27]

And in another prayer one reads:

> Sin is your divinity, Anu your sovereignty,
> Dagan your lordship, Enlil your kingship,
> Adad your superior strength, wise Ea your understanding,
> Nabû who handles the griffel your efficiency,
> Ninurta is your being the first, Nergal your magnifcent power,
> The council of your heart is Nusku, the sublime minister.[28]

In Egypt, beginning at the end of the fourth millennium BCE, one sees the Pharaonic state as a very strong, centralized form of political organization where the king reigns as god, first as the incarnation of the god Horus and then also as the son of the sun and creator god Re. This state of affairs is reflected in the similarly centralized power structure of the pantheon, where Re reigns as king of the gods in the same way that

Pharaoh reigns on earth. It is similarly reflected in the Egyptian concept of cosmogony, which may also be interpreted as a power-oriented "cratogony." The emergence of the world is simultaneous with the emergence of power and sovereignty. Creation and dominion are merely two aspects of the same process. As soon as Atum, the personification of preexistence, turns into existence and rises as the sun, he starts to rule over all that is emanating from him. At first, when heaven and earth were not yet separated, the sun god ruled over both gods and humans, but then, in reaction to a rebellion of mankind against the aging sun god, he separated heaven and earth, withdrawing to heaven together with the gods. The kingship was taken over by his son, Shu, the god of the air; then by Shu's son Geb, the god of the earth; and finally by Geb's oldest son, Osiris, who was killed by his brother, Seth. In consequence of this second catastrophe, the underworld was created for Osiris, who, having been killed, became the ruler of the dead, whereas his throne on earth, which Seth had usurped, was given to his son, Horus. With Horus myth turns into history because this god is the personification of kingship, which is incarnate in each reigning king. Following four successive divine generations (Re, Shu, Geb, and Osiris)—in which the kingship reflected a downward movement from heaven, through the air and earth, to the underworld, and a voyage through the elements of fire, air, earth, and water—the office is now held by earthly kings acting as representatives or deputies of the sun god on earth. According to this mythology, the concepts of creation and sovereignty are very strongly interconnected. Creatorship is the legitimizing basis of sovereignty, and ruling means only the continuation of creation under the conditions of an existing world. This sheds light on the Egyptian concept of power. Power is the dependence of everything created on its creator. Creation generates dependence, which is power. The primacy of one god over all the other gods is grounded in creatorship, and the subordination of all the other gods under this one god is grounded in the dependency of the created on the creator. In other words, the primacy of the highest god lies in the fact that he himself was not created. We are here dealing with a form of ontological subordination. These gods were never asked whether or not they consented to the rule of the sun god because they are subjected to his rule by the natural power of creation and not the political power of subjection.

This highest god, who alone is uncreated, is called *Kheper-djesef* (literally, "who originated by himself"), corresponding to the Greek term *autogenes* and maybe even to Spinoza's concept of *causa sui*. In the early part of the second millennium a discourse began to develop around this concept of god. At first it developed slowly, then rapidly, even expanding explosively. I classify this as "explicit" rather than "implicit" theology, which is the underlying theory of Egyptian religious—cultic—practice.[29]

Explicit Theology

Non-Constellational Theology: Creation and Manifestation

Implicit theology can be called "constellational" since it deals with the deities as an interrelated plurality. Explicit theology, conversely, is non-constellational, centered on the One who is the origin and power center of all. Paradoxically, explicit theology in ancient Egypt is very different from, and almost the opposite of, implicit theology. In this sense it is different from the "explicit grammar" of any given language, which is, of course, nothing other than the codification of its implicit grammar. As may be expected, explicit theology starts with creation theology, focusing not so much on cosmogony as on sovereignty and dependence, on the caring attention of the creator toward his creatures. The first known text is *The Instruction for King Merikare*, a work of wisdom literature dating from the early second millennium BCE and thus in a comparatively "secular" context:

> Humans are well cared for,
> the livestock of god;
> he made heaven and earth for their sake.
> He pushed back the greediness of the waters
> and created the air so that their nostrils might live.
> His images are they, having come forth from his body.

> For their sake he rises to heaven.
> For them he made plants and animals,
> birds and fish,
> so that they might have food.
> If he killed his enemies and went against his children,
> this was only because they thought of rebellion.

> For their sake he causes there to be light.
> To see them he travels [the heavens].
> He established for himself a chapel at their back.
> When they weep, he hears.
> He created for them a ruler in the egg
> and commander to strengthen the backbone of the weak.

He made for them magic as a weapon
to ward off the blow of happenings.
Watching over them night and day,
he thrashed the crooked-hearted among them
as a man beats his son for the sake of his brother.
God knows every name.[30]

This is not only an extremely anthropocentric view of creation; it is also a monotheistic view of the divine. The text speaks of "God" and other gods are not mentioned. This kind of monotheism, however, is not a matter of religion but of genre and perspective. If one looks at the world in the way this text does, the principles of plurality and differentiation disappear and the ultimate unity of the divine appears. This perspective is characteristic of the genre of wisdom literature, a forerunner of moral philosophy that reflects in a very general way on the fundamentals of human existence. Egyptian wisdom literature generally speaks of "god" instead of specific gods.[31] This is not merely a generic term to be replaced by the name of a specific god in a given case ("a" god instead of "god") but rather a specific term referring to the sun god and creator, as in *The Instruction for King Merikare*. In the perspective of moral philosophy, this is the only god that really counts, the one god on whom everything else (including the other gods) depends. Such "monotheism of perspective" is conventionally termed "henotheism." On the one hand, it is distinguished from "monolatry" in the sense of a monotheism of cult, worship, and commitment, and, on the other hand, from "monotheism" in the sense of a full-fledged religion combining a monolatrous cult (that recognizes the existence of other gods but worships only one) through the henotheistic perspective in which other gods do not exist at all. The same monotheism of perspective may also be recognized in "the God" (*p3 nṯr*) in the Egyptian version and "the God" (DINGIR-*li*) in the Akkadian version of the treaty between Hattusilis III and Ramses II. This expression is certainly not to be interpreted as "'whatever god you intend,' that is, 'a template deity,"[32] but rather as "the chief god of each party."[33]

In Egypt the henotheistic perspective of wisdom literature and the polytheism of cult coexist without any apparent conflict. During the New Kingdom, however, the henotheistic perspective gradually affects certain domains of temple literature as well, especially hymns to Amun-Re, the god of the capital of Thebes, who becomes identified with the sun god of Heliopolis. An early hymn to this god, perhaps dating back to a time before the New Kingdom, adopts the anthropocentric and henotheistic perspective of Merikare:

Hail, Re, lord of justice
whose chapel is hidden, lord of the gods;
Khepry in his boat
at whose command the gods emerge;
Atum, creator of human beings
who differentiates them and makes them live,
who distinguishes people by the colour of their skin,
who hears the prayers of those in distress
and is well disposed to those who call on him,
who rescues the fearful from the overbearing,
who judges between rich and poor.
Lord of perception, on whose lips is the creative word,
it is for his sake that the inundation has come;
lord of sweetness, great of love,
it is to make people live that he has come.[34]

To be sure, the gods (plural) are mentioned in this text, which is still
a far cry from real monotheism or even henotheism. Yet these gods are
regarded no differently from other of god's creatures, including humans
and animals. Akhenaten's "monotheistic" revolution is the radical consequence of this shift from mythical anthropomorphism to "philosophical" anthropocentrism. It realizes the henotheistic perspective in terms
of cult and religious institutions, turning the sun and creator god into
the only god and denying the other gods any worship or even existence.
In the aftermath of this revolutionary step, the gods are readmitted into
cults and a general worldview. The henotheistic perspective, however,
still prevails and the gods—especially in hymns to Amun—now tend to
be demoted to "names," "manifestations," "symbols," and "limbs" of
the One.

The culmination of these tendencies is reached when the whole
pantheon comes to be seen as just aspects of one supreme god. "All gods
are three," one reads in an Egyptian text, which states that these three
gods are just aspects of one god:

All gods are three:
Amun, Re and Ptah, whom none equals.
He who hides his name as Amun,
he appears to the face as Re,
his body is Ptah.[35]

All gods are three, and these three are encompassed and transcended
by a god who is referred to only as "He," whose name is Amun, whose

cosmic manifestation is Re, and whose body, or cult image, is Ptah. Even the name of "Amun," the "Hidden One," is just an epithet masking the true and hidden name of this god, of whom another hymn states:

> People fall down immediately for fear
> if his name is uttered knowingly or unknowingly.
> There is no god able to call him by it.[36]

This text was written in the thirteenth century, when the monotheistic revolution effected by Akhenaten had already been overcome and the traditional religion, with its plethora of temples and deities, had been reestablished. Despite this external restitution, however, Akhenaten's revolution left a deep impression on Egyptian thought that led to a veritable explosion of explicit theological discourse that now increasingly concentrated on the oneness of god. The traditional paradigm of creation and sovereignty was now complemented by the new paradigm of hiddenness and manifestation.

In contrast to the "paradigm of creation," the model of manifestation does not temporize the god-world relationship. The traditional concept of primacy has both a temporal and hierarchical meaning. To be the first means to be the chief. The first contains in his essence, in a seminal way, all that comes later. Primacy means allness. The name Atum means to be complete in this very sense of primordial or preexisting primacy. By turning from creator to maintainer, however, the first and highest god has to resign from his all-encompassing, all-absorbing, omnipotent position in relation to the other gods. Creation turns into cooperation. Oneness is the quality of chaos or preexistence, whereas existence and cosmos are characterized by difference, diversity, antagonism, and cooperation. Maintenance is teamwork. The One must become a partner. The leading model for expressing the maintenance of the world in terms of cooperation and partnership is the mythology of the solar circuit, which shows the sun god sailing through the sky and the underworld in a boat, an action in which virtually all of the gods take part. This cyclical process is both one of biological regeneration—in which the sun god passes through as a newborn child, a young man, an old man, and a dead person—and of political triumph—in which the sun god is continuously defeating Apopis, the personification of chaos. In both aspects—being subject to periodical death and rebirth and being confronted by a counter-power of chaos—the sun god as maintainer of the world differs from the sun god as creator of the world in that he himself becomes dependent, integrated into a system of interdependence.

During the Eighteenth Dynasty, this traditional cooperative model of the solar circuit had already started to give way to a different model whose main tendency was to increase the distance between god and gods or god and the world. The sun god is no longer depicted as a partner in a cooperative action, embedded in varying constellations of gods, submitting to the sequence of life and death, and confronted by a counteracting foe. Rather, he circulates around the world on a solitary course and maintains the world in a way that is very similar, if not identical, to primordial creation. This already leads to a certain de-temporization of the concept of divine oneness, which is no longer restricted to chaos and preexistence but is connected to the sun in relation and opposition to the world. Thus, in a sun hymn on a pre-Amarna stela one reads:

> You have settled very remote,
> very far away;
> you have revealed yourself in heaven in your aloneness.
> Every god on earth,
> their arms are held out in praise at your rising.
> You shine, and they see,
> they raise themselves, their arms bent in respect
> before your display of power.[37]

The traditional constellations of deities have disappeared in this and several other texts dating from the time preceding the Amarna revolution. The god confronts the world in sublime solitude. The distance between god and world has become extreme. Akhenaten's revolution is a radicalization of this concept. His innovations include: (1) the complete disappearance of the many gods, who, in the stage of solar theology immediately preceding the Amarna revolution, belong to the world that the sun god creates and maintains; (2) the complete elimination of the topic of creation, resulting in a radical de-temporization of the relationship between god and world; and (3) a "pantheistic" concept of continuous creation and participation, using the term *kheperu* (transformations), as, for example, in the following passage:

> You create millions of forms [*kheperu*] from yourself, the One,
> Cities and towns
> Fields, paths and river[38]

The "millions of forms" obviously refer to the visible world in its aspect of a space made habitable by light and arranged into a cosmos.

Another hymn opposes the One and the millions as aspects of god himself:

> You made heaven remote to rise in it
> To see all that you created, you being alone.
> But there being millions of lives in you to make them live.[39]

The paradigm of manifestation was developed in reaction to Akhenaten's radical monotheism. Like Akhenaten's opposition of god and world, this new paradigm de-temporizes the relation between god and world. The difference lies in the fact that the gods are now readmitted into the world and that the relation between god and world is also interpreted in terms of a relation between god and gods, the One and the many. In the paradigm of manifestation, god is not resigning from his sublime Oneness in creating or becoming the world. In order to explain the new conception of the relationship between god and world, the theologians avail themselves of the anthropological concept of "Ba," which is conventionally translated as "soul." God remains One in relating to the world in a similar way as the Ba relates to the body, an invisible, animating principle.

Ba" is a bifocal term. It denotes both the sensible manifestation of an invisible power—in this sense the wind is called the Ba of Shu or the sun the Ba of Amun—and the one invisible power that becomes manifest in a variety of sensible phenomena. In this sense, Amun-Re comes to be called the "hidden Ba" or the "sublime Ba," whose manifestations are either the other gods or the visible cosmos itself. In a hymn dating from the thirteenth century BCE both aspects of the Ba concept are used. Verses 8–11 describe the sun as the Ba, the visible manifestation of Amun:

> His Ba, it is said, is the one who is in heaven;
> It is he, the one who is in the underworld, who rules the east.
> His Ba is in heaven, his body in the west,
> His image is in the southern Heliopolis and wears his diadem.

The concluding verse 28, however, refers to the soul-like hidden nature and namelessness of God:

> He is Ba-like, hidden of name like his secrecy.[40]

In opposition to the monotheistic view of Akhenaten, god does not animate the world from without, in distant contraposition, but rather

from within. This is the great innovation that I propose to interpret as a
response to the monotheistic revolution of Akhenaten. To be sure, restoration is also a kind of response, but it means just going back to a discontinued tradition. It is a reaction, not a real response. It does not take
into account what Akhenaten has achieved, whereas the Ba theology
does. It responds to Akhenaten by surpassing him. It preserves Akhenaten's de-temporized concept of Oneness by further elaborating his
model of manifestation, for which Akhenaten had made ample use of
the term *kheperu,* and the motif of One-and-millions:

> Hail to you, the One who transforms himself into millions,
>   Whose length and breadth are limitless![41]
> Power in readiness, who gave birth to himself,
>   Uraeus with great flame;
> Great of magic with secret form,
>   Secret Ba, to whom respect is shown.[42]

The opposing terms "One" and "millions" are linked here by the
concept of self-transformation, *jrj sw* (who made or makes himself into).
"Millions" clearly refers to the world of creation, which is interpreted as
a transformation of god himself. Creation is emanation. The world is
created not out of chaos, nor *ex nihilo,* out of nothing, but *ex Deo,* out of
God. God is limitless; so is the world; god is the world. The preceding
verses oppose two aspects of god, namely, *sekhem seped* (power in readiness) and *Ba' sheta'* (Secret Ba), the first referring to the sun and the second referring to the hidden aspect of god as a soul animating the world
from within. In Amarna, the One is the sun, the absolutely and over-
whelmingly manifest and visible god, opposite to and animating the
world, which has no divinity of its own. In Ramessid Thebes the One is
the absolutely hidden and secret Ba animating the world from within.
Thus, the Ramessid theology is able both to retain and to surpass the
Amarna idea of Oneness.

In this context, the motif of One-and-millions returns frequently
and in a number of variants. The "millions" are stated to be god's
body,[43] his limbs,[44] his transformation,[45] and even his name: "million of
millions is his name."[46] By transforming himself into a millionfold reality, God has not ceased to be a unity. He is both one and millions, unity
and plurality, simultaneously hidden and present in that mysterious way
in which this theology is trying to grasp by means of the Ba concept. A
frequently attested text even goes so far as to describe god as the Ba (and
not the creator) of gods and humans (i.e., "the millions"):[47]

The One Alone who created what is,
The illustrious Ba of gods and humans.[48]

In my *Moses the Egyptian* I suggested that this new concept of god is not only a response to Amarna but also the origin of the Hermetic idea of god—*le dieu cosmique, deus mundus*—a god who is *anima mundi* and whose body is the world. I also proposed that the Ramesside formula of One-and-millions not only echoes the corresponding Amarna formulations but also anticipates such Hermetic formulations as *Hen kai pan, una quae es omnia*, etc. There is an uninterrupted line of textual tradition from the Ramesside age down to the Greco-Roman era. The Ramesside Ba-theology reached its apex in the Late Period with the cult of the Ten Ba's.[49] This theology uses the Ba concept not with regard to the unity of the hidden power but to the plurality of its manifestations. The first two Ba's are the sun and the moon, which can also be explained as the right and left eyes of god. Then come the Ba's of Shu and Osiris, representing air and water. The fifth is that of Tefnut, the goddess of fire. The theological interpretation is given in the hymn. Sun and moon represent not light but time, which also appears here as a cosmic, life-giving energy. Light is attributed to the Ba of Tefnut, the "flaming one," the fire-spitting Cobra at the head of the sun god, the lioness personifying the heat and aggressiveness of the African sun. Her creation at the beginning of the world, together with her twin brother, Shu, refers to the primordial position of light, which is also the meaning of the biblical creation account, where the creation of light comes first. The life-giving divine manifestations in the ritual of the Ten Ba's are thus time, air, water, and light.[50]

The second group of five Ba's represents five classes of living creatures: human beings, quadrupeds, birds, aquatic creatures, and creatures living in the ground, such as snakes, scarab beetles, and the dead. Hence this theology distinguishes between cosmic and animal life. It understands the "Ba's" of God not as the visible world in itself but as ten mediating powers that animate and sustain the world. A magical text from about the same period as the ritual of the Ten Ba's of Amun counts seven Ba manifestations of Amun:

The 'Bes' with seven heads . . .
He is [embodies] the Ba's of Amun-Re, lord of Karnak, chief of Ipet-Sut,
The ram with sublime face, who dwells in Thebes.
The great lion who generated by himself,
The Great god of the beginning,

The ruler of lands and the king of gods,
The lord of heaven, earth, underworld, water, and mountains
Who conceals his name from the gods,
The giant of millions of cubits,
The strong . . . who fixed the sky on his head,
From whose nose the air comes forth,
In order to animate all noses,
Who rises as sun, in order to illuminate the earth,
From whose bodily secretions the Nile flows forth in order
    to nourish every mouth.[51]

This text illustrates what I would call the cosmotheistic turn of post-Amarna theology. God is the hidden power manifesting himself in the world. The ten Ba's of Amun are a symbolic expression of the polytheistic universe as an "interface" between god and the world. Bes, the god of the mask, embodies this interface. However, the world—with sky and earth, sun, air and water—appears as the body of the One. The visible cosmos is the body of a god, animating it from within.

Cosmotheism

The origins of this cosmotheistic theology date back to the post-Amarna period. Its mature state is reached in the time of Ramesses III, where in a hymn this king addresses to Amun one reads:

Your skin is the light, your breath is the "fire of life,"[52]
all precious stones are united on your body.
Your limbs are the breath of life to every nose,
inhaling you brings life.
Your taste is the Nile,
people anoint with the radiance of your light-eye . . .
Coming and going is possible when you appear
as earth god.[53]

In a hymn to Ptah from about the same period one encounters the same concept of the cosmic god:

For it is from your nose that the air comes
and from your mouth that the flood comes.
The "tree of life" grows upon you;
you make the earth green, so that the gods have more than enough,
as well as human beings and animals.
It is your light that makes them see.

When you set, the darkness comes.
Your eyes create light . . .
Your right eye is the sun,
your left eye is the moon.[54]

A hymn from the tomb of Imiseba (Thebes, no. 65) dating from the time of Ramesses IX reads:

Your eyes are the sun and the moon,
your head is the sky,
your feet are the underworld.[55]

The idea of the world as the embodiment of a soul-like god and of god as a soul animating the world remained central in Egyptian theology even after the New Kingdom and the flourishing of theological discourse. One is dealing here with the origin of a conception of the divine that was to become supremely important in late antiquity, namely, the "cosmic god," the supreme deity in Stoicism, Hermetism, and related movements,[56]

whose head is the sky,
whose body is the air, whose feet are the earth.
You are the ocean.[57]

With this last quotation we have entered another time and language. This text and many similar ones are in Greek and date from late antiquity. They belong to a syncretistic religion combining elements of Egyptian theology with Stoicism, Neoplatonism, and various other influences. The concept of the cosmic god also seems to be particularly well attested in Iranian and Indian texts dating from about the same period as the Greek texts:

Fire is my mouth,
Earth is my feet,
Sun and moon are my eyes,
Heaven is my head,
The firmament and the regions of heaven are my ears.[58]

Sun and moon are your eyes,
your face shines like fire,
you fill the universe with your light.[59]

His head is fire,
his eyes are moon and sun,

the celestial regions are his ears,
his voice is the revelation of the Veda,
the wind is his breath,
his heart is the world,
the earth is his feet,
he is the innermost self [*atman*] in everything existing.[60]

Despite these changes, however, the theological discourse continues, and there is a remarkable consistency of questions and answers. Their most explicit codification is to be found in the texts comprising the *Corpus Hermeticum*. The "pantheistic" motif of One-and-millions appears in the Greek texts as the One and the All, *to hen kai to pan*, or *hen to pan*, and similar expressions,[61] and in a Latin inscription to Isis as *una quae es omnia*.[62] The cosmotheistic aspect is expressed in statements about the world as the body of god, such as the oracle reported by Macrobius:

The celestial universe is my head,
my body is the ocean,
the earth is my feet,
my ears are in the ether,
my far shining eye is the light of Helios.[63]

With these texts of late antiquity one has reached the kind of monotheism C. S. Lewis defined as the maturity of polytheism, which may be summarized by the formula "All gods are One."

Hypercosmism

However, even this form of cosmotheism[64] does not seem to constitute the final stage of evolutionary monotheism. In his *Speech of Praetextatus* Macrobius distinguishes between "encosmic" and "hypercosmic" gods.[65] This points to a further evolution of cosmotheism into what could be called "hypercosmism," a religion not of immanence but of transcendence or, rather, of both. Hypercosmism has a long tradition in Greek philosophy, going back (at least) to Plato's idea of Go(o)d "beyond being" (*epékeina tês ousías*) and Aristotle's "unmoved mover."[66] Praetextatus was a typical proponent of the principle "All gods are One," holding not only that all gods are aspects of a single supreme deity but also identifying this deity with the sun. However, he applied this principle only to the "encosmic" gods. All encosmic gods are One, but beyond the One, who is the sun, there is the hypercosmic divine. There are no limits to "going beyond," even along the evolutionary lines of cosmo-monotheism. One might even wonder whether the previously cited excerpt from an Egyptian hymn dating from the thirteenth century BCE may not already express a similar thought. Here is the hymn in its entirety:

Secret of transformations and sparkling of appearances
marvelous god, rich in forms:
All gods boast of him
to make themselves greater with his beauty to the extent of his divinity.

Re himself is united with his body.
He is the Great One in Heliopolis;
He is called Tatenen/Amun,
who comes out of the primeval waters to lead the "faces."

Another of his forms is the Ogdoad,
primeval one of the primeval ones, begetter of Re.
He completed himself as Atum, being of one body with him.
He is Universal Lord, who initiated that which exists.

His Ba, it is said, is the one who is in heaven;
it is he, the one who is in the underworld, who rules the east.
His Ba is in heaven, his body in the west;
his image is in the southern Heliopolis and wears his diadem.

One is Amun, who keeps himself concealed from them,
who hides himself from the gods, no one knowing his nature.
He is more remote than heaven.
He is deeper than the underworld.

None of the gods knows his true form.
His image is not unfolded in books;
nothing certain is testified about him.

He is too secretive for his majesty to be revealed.
He is too great to be enquired after,
too powerful to be known.

People fall down immediately for fear
that his name will be uttered knowingly or unknowingly,
There is no god able to call him by it:
He is Ba-like, hidden of name like his secrecy.[67]

This text is divided into two parts. The first part (stanzas 1–4) may be described as "cosmotheistic," the second (stanzas 5–8) as "hyper-cosmotheistic." The cosmotheistic part is a piece of "positive theology" and describes how the god is personified on earth in the other gods. This personification is represented by the eight primeval gods (verses 9–10), who, according to Egyptian traditions, are embodiments of chaos or preexistence, and the three gods of the "imperial triad,"[68] namely, Re-Atum (5–6, 11–12) (Ptah-)Tatenen (7) and Amun (7, 17), who represent the divinity of the existing world. The "hyper-cosmotheistic" second part is a piece of "negative theology" and reads like a revocation of all the theological scholarship displayed and developed in the first part. The subject of the first part was the multitude of encosmic gods that reflect the nature of the One. Amun of Thebes also belongs here. The "one Amun" of the second part is not only hidden "from them"; he is hidden absolutely. No statement about him is possible. He is beyond heaven and the underworld, the holy and otherworldly regions of the world. He is even hidden from the gods, who reflect his unfathomable nature in this remote sphere. He is even more completely hidden from humans. The scriptures give no information about him. He cannot be explained by any theory. He belongs to that realm of hyper-cosmic deities that, to quote Macrobius, "not only pass the bounds of speech but that of human comprehension as well."[69] The final stanza clearly expresses the concept of the Ineffable God and associates it with two significant epithets, namely, "having the quality of Ba" and "he who keeps his name hidden." This proves that they belong together. The god is called "Ba" because there is no name for him. His hidden, all-embracing abundance of essence cannot be apprehended. "Amun" is merely a pseudonym used to refer to the god in that worldly, albeit otherworldly, sphere of personification. Every divine name is essentially a name of the hidden one, but the term "Ba" is used when the hidden one behind the many personifications is meant. It is striking to see that even the evolutionary lines of cosmotheism may lead to positions verging on negative theology.

It may now have become obvious, however, how far removed this kind of monotheism is from what the Bible tells us about the god of the Israelites. It may also have become clear that there is no evolutionary line that leads from polytheism to biblical monotheism. Concerning the main difference between biblical and evolutionary monotheism, the Bible does not say "All gods are One" but rather that God is One and "Thou shalt have no other gods. . . ." It does not establish a connection but rather draws a distinction between God and gods. Ultimately this distinction is one between God and world. Evolutionary monotheism does not draw this distinction. On the contrary, God *is* the world.

By distinguishing between God and world, revolutionary monotheism, conversely, severs the links between creation and sovereignty as well as between cosmic and political order, which were based on the centralized power structure common to both the divine and human worlds. It creates that Archimedean point from which to lift any given political system off its hinges. The king is no longer the representative of God on earth, continuing the work of creation and maintenance under the conditions of the created world. He is just a creature and servant of God, like everything else, apt to give in to the priest or to the people or to any other form of political organization and representation. To be sure, even revolutionary monotheism has been used or abused to legitimize political power. Its original meaning, however, seems to point to critique and delegitimization of the political super powers of the ancient world: Egypt, Assyria, Babylonia, the Seleucid, and above all the Roman Empire. The original impulse of revolutionary monotheism, that is, of the prophets and the Deuteronomic tradition—even of the Jesus movement—seems to me to consist in tearing apart the archaic unity of creation and dominion, or cosmic and political power, and to conceive of religion as a means of emancipation from the politico-cosmological power structure of the ancient world.

4

The Axial Age and the Separation of State and Religion

Monotheism as an Axial Movement

The emancipation from the politico-cosmological power structure of the ancient world is certainly not the exclusive achievement of biblical monotheism. Rather, it belongs within the wider context of cultural transformations commonly believed to have affected almost all of the high civilizations of the ancient world from Rome to China and to have taken place more or less simultaneously around the middle of the first millennium BCE.[1] The common denominator of these different movements may be seen in various forms of "standing back and looking beyond,"[2] that is, in adopting positions whereby the conditions and institutions of mundane life could be viewed from a distance and critiqued in the light of new "transcendental" concepts of truth and order. These "transcendental visions" enabled extraordinary individuals to look beyond the given by subjecting it to criticism, reformation, or even revolution. This is how a pastoral theologian and a psychologist have summarized the popular version of this theory: "The period between 600 and 300 BCE witnessed an explosion of human consciousness. Simultaneously in the geographically disparate cultures of China, India and the Mediterranean region, urgent questions about the meaning of human life arose. From Confucius in China to Socrates in Greece, from Buddha in India to the prophet Jeremiah in Israel, thoughtful people confronted anew the puzzle of humanity. What is the purpose of living? Are our lives governed by more than fate? For what are we responsible? How are we to make sense of suffering and death?"[3]

This theory, which Karl Jaspers popularized by coining the term *Achsenzeit* (Axial Age), was first formulated during the latter part of the eighteenth century by A. H. Anquetil-Duperron, a scholar of Zoroastrianism, who postulated a "grande révolution du genre humain" (a great revolution of humankind). This was to have taken place around 500 BCE when charismatic individuals arose in the East and West who founded new religions and philosophical systems, such as Confucius and Laotse, Buddha, Zoroaster, the Hebrew prophets, and the early Greek philosophers.[4] However, it was taken up and elaborated again only after a period of latency of more than 150 years by three thinkers: sociologist Alfred Weber, whose *Kultursoziologie* (Sociology of Culture) appeared in 1935; philosopher Karl Jaspers, whose *Vom Ursprung und Ziel der Geschichte* (On the Origin and Aim of History) followed in 1949; and political philosopher Eric Voegelin, whose monumental *Order and History* began to appear in 1956.[5] Alfred Weber stressed the synchronicity and similarity of events and processes over huge distances. Although Jaspers coined the term "Axial Age" and popularized the theory, it was Voegelin who gave a comparably clear description of the "pre-axial" world, the world that Israel and Greece left behind. A theory that in Weber's and Jaspers' reconstruction was nothing more than a pale counterimage of Europe, a mere "not yet," assumed a positive coloring in Voegelin's description as a world in its own right, a positive alternative to monotheism and philosophy. Voegelin's term for the pre-axial world was "cosmological."

Voegelin explained the decisive axial transformation as a breakthrough (or "leap in being") from the "cosmological myth," leading in Israel to history and monotheism and in Greece to philosophy and metaphysics. He described this breakthrough as a process of conceptual transformation from "compactness" to "differentiation." Israel and Greece were able to recognize differences and to draw distinctions, whereas the oriental societies used "compact" concepts that blurred these differences in a systematic way.

The Egyptian evidence confirms this approach, especially with regard to the distinction between the political and religious spheres.[6] The specific axial transformation that the Bible represents as the Exodus from Egypt by the children of Israel and their entering into a new form of religious and political order primarily involves the distinction between and separation of state and religion and must be reconstructed and interpreted in terms of political theology. However, what Voegelin was unable to see and what only Egyptology is able to bring to light is that this axial breakthrough had forerunners or foreshadowings in Egyptian history, a fact that profoundly affects the chronological implications of the Axial Age theory. These forerunners may be explained historically by breakdowns and disappointments in the political sphere, historical experiences of a rather traumatic character.

The ancient Egyptian evidence invites us to modify the Axial Age theory in two respects that are of some importance in our general search for the roots of monotheism. One is the differentiation of the all-too-compact notion of an "Axial Age" into a gamut of smaller-scale transformations or into different degrees of "axiality." Another is the possibility—and even necessity—of integrating those transformations into a larger context of historical changes and experiences. According to this theory, the separation of state and religion, or *Herrschaft und Heil* (Sovereignty and Salvation), has been forced upon some peoples—especially those who adopted the name "Israel"—by historical events of a traumatic nature. Is there a connection between breakdown and breakthrough, between trauma and innovation?

Antecedents in Ancient Egypt

The Judgment of the Dead

The first of these traumatic experiences concerns the breakdown of the Old Kingdom (2800–2150 BCE), which gave rise to the idea of a general judgment of the dead.[7] In the Old Kingdom the concept of a judgment following death was modeled upon a terrestrial court, which is only in session when there is a litigant. A dead person had to be prepared for any and every possible accusation, including not only human but also deceased and divine accusers. Without an accuser, there was no lawsuit. This form of postmortem litigation was considered just one of the many dangers of the liminal state between this world and the next. However, it was not yet considered the necessary and inevitable threshold or passage between this life and the afterlife.

The idea of an examination that each and every dead person had to pass before entering the other world developed only after the demise of the Old Kingdom at the beginning of the second millennium BCE. Here one is clearly dealing with a tribunal where all must present themselves following death. The decisive difference between the old and new conception is the fact that now the accuser is a god. However, according to the Old Kingdom conception of a judgment in the hereafter, this god is not a successor to whoever appeared as accuser and defendant before the court. Rather, he plays a role that was formerly performed by the king and the society. During the latter half of the third millennium biographical inscriptions begin to appear in the tombs of the Old Kingdom in which a tomb owner addresses posterity and renders an account of his achievements. A proverb held that "the true monument of a man is his virtue; the evil character will be forgotten."[8] The immortality of the tomb owner depended on the verdict of posterity, the collective memory of future generations and their willingness to read the inscriptions and to recall the personality of the deceased. Their judgment determined his immortality. Regarding their immortality—or at least a prolongation of their existence beyond the threshold of death—the Egyptians believed in the possibility of communicating with posterity by means of a monumental tomb that could receive visitors for hundreds or even thousands of years, who would read the inscriptions, look at the scenes, and be so impressed by the virtue of the tomb owner and the importance of his biography that they would recite a prayer in his name.

However, the dissolution of the Old Kingdom in the last quarter of the third millennium shattered this belief in the continuity of social memory and the durability of monuments. During this period of anxiety and reorientation, the Egyptians put the verdict of posterity on a more stable basis in the form of a divine judgment at the court of Osiris. This is the first instance of the transposition of an idea or institution from the earthly sphere involving the social and the political to the transcendent sphere of the divine, which is the hallmark of "axiality." The concept of such a general judgment of the dead—where the decision about immortality or annihilation rested with a divine authority— may be interpreted as a breakthrough into a kind of transcendence.[9] Compared to such earthly institutions as kingship, society, and posterity, the divine tribunal obviously has a transcendent, otherworldly character. However, I prefer to speak not of "breakthroughs" and "transcendental visions" but rather of "semantic transpositions,"[10] where ideas or semiologies are transferred from one sphere to another, that is, from the sociopolitical sphere of social memory to the divine sphere. In this case the semantic transposition was caused by a traumatic disappointment in the political sphere. In the Old Kingdom people of high rank invested their fortunes toward the erection of a monumental tomb, which they considered a secure fundament of immortality. By means of such a tomb they hoped to continue their existence in the vicinity of their lord, the Pharaoh, and in the collective memory of posterity. The breakdown of the Old Kingdom, which witnessed the spoliation and destruction of the tombs and the disappearance of kingship, underscored the illusory nature of these hopes. Longing for safer warrants of immortality, people looked beyond the social sphere. In this case the breakdown of political order led to a breakthrough in "metapolitical" foundations of order. The god Osiris and his court filled the place left empty by the vanished Pharaoh of the Old Kingdom. Osiris continued to remain in office even after the reestablishment of Pharaonic monocracy in the Middle Kingdom. Henceforth burial, tomb, and immortality were transferred from the political sphere of Pharaonic competence to the divine sphere, where they were placed into the hands of Osiris, who became the lord of death and the afterlife. However, the criteria and the norms according to which a dead person is judged by the divine tribunal are the same as those that would warrant his or her success in life and memory on earth. Until quite late—and probably only under Jewish influence—there was no thought of a discrepancy between divine and social verdicts.

The Rise of Personal Piety

My next example represents the most conspicuous case of such a transposition in Egyptian religious history. It concerns the rise and the final breakthrough of a religious trend Egyptologists call "Personal Piety."[11] An individual forms a special relationship with a certain deity, which in Egyptian is paraphrased in formulas such as "putting god N into one's heart" and "walking (or acting) on the water of god N." This new trend finds its first expression in prayers and tomb inscriptions of the fifteenth century. On the following tomb inscription one reads:

> God is father and mother to him who takes him into his heart.
> He turns away from him who neglects his city, . . .
> But he whom he leads will not lose his way.[12]

And in a prayer one reads:

> I gave you into my heart because of your strength. . . .
> You are my protector. Behold: my fear has vanished.[13]

The language of these texts has a long history.[14] Many expressions can be traced back to the First Intermediate Period (2150–2000 BCE), where they describe the relationship of patron and client. During the Middle Kingdom (2000–1750 BCE) the ruling dynasty adopted this formula, together with its rhetoric, as a model for the new relationship between king and official, based on the latter's heart, that is, his internal motivation, virtue, and sense of responsibility. Following the breakdown of the Amarna revolution, this attitude (loyalism) was transferred to the divine sphere, where it served to describe the relationship between god and man. Typical of the rhetoric of loyalism was the opposition between wrath and mercy, involving the formulae of "putting god into one's heart" and "walking or acting on God's water," and especially the stylistic device called "macarism" or "beatitude" ("Happy the man who . . . ," "Blessed is he who . . ."), which appears at the beginning of the book of Psalms.

The rhetoric of loyalism experienced an important revival during the Amarna period, around the middle of the fourteenth century BCE, where one often encountered sentences like:

> Blessed the man who puts you into his heart,
> For he will spend his old age in perfection.[15]

The Amarna period was known as an age of religious revolution in Egypt.[16] Akhenaten put an end to the countless traditional cults and substituted the cult of the one single Aten, the god of light and time. Akhenaten wished to reduce all of reality to the workings of light and time. In his eyes the other deities appeared as inert, superfluous, fictitious, and false, contributing nothing to the explanation of reality. Akhenaten was the first in the history of mankind to apply the distinction between true and false to religion, the same distinction that later led to a transformation of "axial" dimensions in the form of biblical monotheism. He was also the first to formulate the principle of exclusive monotheism, namely, that there be "no gods but god!" "O sole god beside whom is none!" was how he addressed his god. "There is no other except him," he said of god.[17]

Although Akhenaten radically changed Egyptian cosmology, he did not transcend it. His god was the sun, a form of cosmic energy, the source of light and time, without any personal and ethical traits. Above all, however, he did not alter the "compact" unity or indistinction between religion and politics. On the contrary, he did everything to cement it and to counteract the beginnings of Personal Piety, which he seems to have felt caused a rift in the politico-religious unity. Whereas Aton presented himself to humanity as a cosmic energy, it was Akhenaten who presented himself as the personal god of the individual and the object of Personal Piety:

He shows his wrath against him who ignores his teachings
And his favour to him who knows it.[18]

Whereas Personal Piety tended to create a direct relationship between a deity and an individual outside the official institutions of cult and temple, Akhenaten reinstalled the king as the sole mediator between god and man. In this respect, the Amarna religion was more of a restoration than an innovation. However, Akhenaten failed in his project, and this failure led to a complete breakthrough of what he had wanted to suppress. Following his death, the Egyptians not only returned to their traditional deities but to the beginnings of Personal Piety, which had developed into the dominant outlook and religious attitude of the time. It was for this reason that, as early as 1912, James Henry Breasted labeled this period the "Age of Personal Piety."[19] This new form of Personal Piety is best described as a semantic transposition according to which the concepts and rhetoric of loyalism were transferred from the political to the divine sphere, where they served as a model for the relationship between god and man. God acceded to the role played by Akhenaten in the Amarna period—and, earlier, by the king in the Middle Kingdom and by the patron in the First Intermediate Period—acting as protector for all: father of orphans; husband of widows; refuge for the persecuted; protector of the poor; good shepherd; judge; pilot and steering oar; merciful toward his followers; wrathful toward his enemies. The concept of transposition means that something is withdrawn from one sphere and transferred to another. Thus, protection was no longer sought on the "mundane" plane, from king or patrons, but rather on the divine plane, from a deity. In prayers one frequently encounters sentences like the following:

I have not sought for myself a protector among men,
God N is my defender.[20]

In the time of Ramses II, a man called Kiki, a follower of the goddess Mut, who donated all his property to her temple, wrote in his tomb autobiography:

He bethought himself
That he should find a patron:
And he found Mut at the head of the gods,
Fate and fortune in her hand,
Lifetime and breath of life are hers to command. . . .

I have not chosen a protector among men,
I have not sought myself a patron among the great. . . .
My heart is filled with my mistress.
I have no fear of anyone.
I spend the night in quiet sleep,
because I have a protector.[21]

The catalyst for this process of transaction seems obvious: the traumatic failure on the political level of the Amarna revolution, which must have seemed a major disappointment to the majority of Egyptians, the spectacle of kingship turning sinful and criminal toward the gods in the most radical and terrible way. The breakdown of the political system, which had stressed the religious monopoly of the state, led to the rise of personal forms of religiosity.

Trauma and Reorientation

It is precisely along these lines of historical trauma and semantic transpositions that the rise of biblical monotheism and covenant theology has to be interpreted. It involves the transference of the political institutions of alliance, treaty, and vassaldom from the mundane sphere of politics to the transcendental sphere of religion. In this respect, covenant theology may be compared to Personal Piety in Egypt, which, as we have seen, involved a transposition of the semiology of loyalism from the political to the religious sphere. In Israel one is dealing with the sanctification and theologizing of the semiology of Egyptian, Hittite, Babylonian, and especially Assyrian foreign politics (vassal treaties). What is most obvious in the case of Israel, however, is the connection with historical trauma. Covenant theology (and monotheism) developed after the fall, first of Samaria and then of Jerusalem; before, during, and after the Babylonian exile; following the complete failure and breakdown of the kingdom; and after the loss of state and temple—in short, after the most traumatic series of experiences that could possibly befall a society in those times. The ensuing innovation corresponded in importance and consequence to the gravity of the historical trauma, which far surpassed anything that had previously occurred in Egyptian history.

Using the model of a political alliance as a new form of the relationship between god and man meant the creation of a completely new form of religion, one that proved able to withstand the pressures of political oppression. Biblical texts, especially Deuteronomy, use the language of Assyrian loyalty oaths[22] and vassal treaties.[23] The political theology of Assyria was adopted by way of "subversive inversion" and transformed into the political theology of Israel.[24] Whereas the first stressed the inseparable unity of the divine and the political, the latter stressed the categorical separation of these two spheres.

Following the fall of the northern kingdom, "Israel" had to reinvent itself. The term no longer referred to a political entity. This was the beginning of a process of redefinition that ended up transforming "Israel" into a purely religious term. This goal was only achieved through Saint Paul's radical de-ethnicization of the concept of "Israel." However, the direction was already indicated with this first step taken of transcending the borders of a political "nation." Israel now became "a kingdom of priests," a community of believers and followers of Yahweh, the chosen people of God, a religious entity defined by its exclusive adherence to Yahweh rather than to a political ruler. Thus, the denomination "Israel" was transferable to the kingdom of Judah.[25] Saint Paul did not want to build a new Israel, a new people of God, upon the foundations of the cross and the belief in Jesus' messianic nature and resurrection. He simply wished to redefine and enlarge the notion of "Israel" in order to transcend the borders of ethnicity and the law, which were inseparably intertwined, and to redefine "Israel" to include Jews and gentiles.[26]

It seems obvious to me that there is a direct connection between this distinction and that between religion and politics. Specifically, I am thinking of the separation of religion from the overall system of culture, politics, morality, and law, on the one hand, and the much more general distinction between true and false in the realm of religion—which I have called the "Mosaic distinction," and in which I see the distinctive hallmark of monotheism—on the other.[27] My thesis is that this distinction, rather than the widespread idea of the unity of the divine, was the great innovation that transformed the ancient world in the form of an axial breakthrough. The distinction between true and false was alien to "primary religion,"[28] which was based on distinctions such as pure and impure, sacred and profane. Its introduction signaled a revolutionary step in creating a new type of religion. For the first time—and quite unlike primary religion—this new type sets itself apart not only from other religions, including its own religious tradition, but also from such other spheres of culture as politics, law, and economics. Moreover, it is not only an autonomous sphere but one endowed with superior authority and normativity, forcing the other spheres to come under its spell.

Above all, the Mosaic distinction between true and false meant the distinction between religion and politics, or church and state. Akhenaten had previously drawn the same distinction with regard to the traditional religion of ancient Egypt, which he abolished as false. This step, however, did not lead to a separation between the political and religious spheres. Kingship kept its position as a mediator between god and man even after the Amarna period, during the "Age of Personal Piety"; only its monopoly was dissolved. However, in Egypt the state continued to act simultaneously as a kind of church, being the sole institutionalization of religion. The separation of politics and religion (i.e., *Herrschaft und Heil*) the mundane and the transcendental, was therefore the exclusive achievement of Israel, one that, according to the biblical account, is associated with the name of Moses and with the legend of the Exodus of the children of Israel from Egypt.[29]

The political meaning of the Mosaic Distinction becomes evident in the Exodus tradition. In this context, Egypt appears not so much as the representative of "false religion," that is, paganism and idolatry, but rather as the representative of "false politics," the "house of serfdom."[30] The Exodus from Egypt means leaving the house of oppression and entering the realm of freedom. The latter, to be sure, is not a biblical term and does not occur in this context, but it is obvious that the alliance or covenant with God established at Mount Sinai is presented in the narrative as liberation from serfdom under human rule. Entering into the alliance and the Law did not mean to found a state as much as it did to get rid of the oriental principle of statehood and to found a kind of countersociety in which the principle of statehood or kingship is permitted only minimal importance.[31] It is this antigovernmental impulse that is presented in the narrative as a resistance against Pharaonic oppression. The (trans)formation of the Hebrew tribes into the "people of God" on the basis of a divinely ordained body of legislation meant—perhaps for the first time in history—a clear-cut distinction between state and society. Egypt appeared as the paradigmatic "state" representing both political and divine power and order. By leaving Egypt, Israel separated itself from a political system denounced as false, oppressive, and humiliating. From the viewpoint of the biblical texts—specifically the narrative enactment as the Exodus from Egypt—monotheism appeared as a political movement of liberation from Pharaonic oppression and served as the foundation of an alternative life form where humans are no longer governed by a state and freely consent to enter into an alliance with God and to adopt the stipulations of divine law.[32] In the same way that the people are liberated from political oppression, God emancipates himself from political representation. Religious salvation now becomes the exclusive domain of God, who for the first time takes the initiative of historical action and permanently withdraws the principle of salvation (*Heil*) from political representation and mundane power. The new form of religion meant, first and foremost, a new way of life based on the divine laws of justice and purity rather than on a new belief system.

The story is *set*[33] in Egypt at a time strangely proximate to that of Akhenaten and his monotheistic revolution, that is, in the fourteenth or thirteenth centuries BCE. However, it *was told* at a much later time, in the seventh through fifth centuries, and in Judaea and Babylonia at the time of the Babylonian exile and Persian domination. In terms of historical reality, therefore, the separation of church and state was not achieved until the sixth and fifth centuries BCE, when the political functions of the "state" were absorbed by the Babylonian and Persian empires; this was also the time when Israelites based their identity as the people of God and a kingdom of priests on Torah and temple rather than on king and palace. Henceforth religion and politics, or church and state, would remain separate spheres whose relationship had to be laboriously negotiated and whose reunification could be achieved only through force. Political theology was transformed into a critical discourse that, according to biblical tradition, was critical of government and, based on Greek tradition, was critical of religion. I obviously do not wish to suggest that the systematic distinction between religion and politics had already been achieved as early as the first—let alone the second—millennium BCE. With regard to these ancient times, terms such as "religion," "politics," "church," and "state" are clearly anachronistic. What I mean is that the intellectual foundations for such a terminology were first laid concurrently with the rise of monotheism, which made these distinctions possible. This distinction between and separation of religion and politics have to be regarded as among the most important features of axiality. Subsequent attempts at reuniting and undifferentiating[34] these two spheres may be regarded as shifts toward de-axialization—as in the French tradition of the "rois thaumaturges," Byzantine and French caesaro-papism, totalitarian forms of civil religion,[35] as well as in religious movements that insist on the direct political realization of religious truth.

The anti-Egyptian or, more generally, anti-state character of biblical monotheism and its political theology find their clearest expression in the prohibition of images. Idolatry primarily means the legitimization of the state in terms of divine representation. The state presents itself in its images, symbols, and ceremonies as a representative of the divine. From the viewpoint of the Bible, this is idolatry. From the viewpoint of Egypt, however, it is precisely for this that the state was created.[36] As we have seen the Egyptians believed the gods to be remote and hidden, having withdrawn from earth and made themselves invisible. In lieu of their corporeal presence, they installed the state on earth to represent them in the form of kings, images, and sacred animals. The most important task of the state was to ensure divine presence under the condition of divine absence and to maintain a symbiotic relationship between man, society, and the cosmos. In the Egyptian text from which I quoted earlier,[37] the king acts as representative of the creator, installed on earth "for ever and ever" in order to establish "Ma'at" (true order and justice) and to expel disorder. The king depends on god, whom he imitates and represents, and god depends on the king for maintaining the order of creation on earth among the living. God created the king "in his image," so to speak, and "image of god" is, in fact, one of the most common royal epithets.

Biblical political theology is the exact reverse. From this perspective, it is precisely the category of representation that points up the falseness of Pharaonic politics with respect to religion in its most obvious and abhorrent form, namely, the sphere of kings, images, and sacred animals. The prohibition against images means, in the first place, that the "living God" (*Elohim hayim*) must not be represented.[38] Images contradict the real presence of the divine implied by the idea of the covenant. The latter is a form both political and "living" reflecting God's turning toward the world. Images are media of a "magical" representation of an absent divine power and therefore imply or presuppose the idea of divine absence. The "living God" hides and reveals himself as he chooses and forbids any attempt at a magical summoning of his presence. This is the political meaning of the prohibition against images. The Golden Calf was meant to replace Moses and was the only form in which God had allowed himself to be represented. The Israelites, who believed Moses dead, wanted to replace the representative of God by his representation. The function of the Golden Calf was clearly political, meant to serve not as a cult image but as a political symbol of leadership in the same way that Moses himself did in leading his people out of Egypt. The destruction of the Golden Calf put an end to these attempts at political representation. Images were artificial gods, and the relationship with "other gods" (*elohim aherim*) was forbidden. An alliance was formed with a single overlord. The political meaning of monotheism in its early stage did not deny the existence of other gods. On the contrary, without the existence of other gods the command to remain faithful to the Lord would have been pointless. These "other gods" were not nonexistent, like the gods whose worship Akhenaten abolished, but they were forbidden.

With the radical destruction of representation, the divine or "transcendental" sphere became independent of political institutions and was able to survive the Babylonian exile and the loss of sovereign statehood. Under the Persians the former kingdom of Judah was integrated into the Persian Empire as a province within the satrapy of Transeuphratene. Religion became an autonomous sphere, constituting and consolidating a vantage point from which all other spheres of culture, including the political, could be transformed. Max Weber, in his "Zwischenbetrachtung," identified the tension between religion and other cultural spheres such as economics, politics, aesthetics, the erotic, and the intellectual, as characteristic of religions of salvation or redemption (*Erlösungsreligionen*).[39] Tension presupposes distinction and differentiation, and it is my belief that the process of differentiation—especially with respect to the religious and political spheres—is a characteristic feature of axiality.

Voegelin reconstructed the process leading from the "cosmological societies" of the Ancient Near East to the rise of new, metacosmic or "transcendental" worldviews in Israel and Greece, viewing it as a shift from "compactness" to "differentiation." Compactness is the hallmark of myth and the totalizing tendency of mythical thinking.[40] Differentiation, conversely, may be identified as a hallmark of axiality. However, according to Weber, Habermas, and others, axiality is not to be equated either with antiquity (a certain time period around 500 BCE) or with modernity, for which the differentiation of autonomous spheres is the most characteristic property.[41] Weber and those who followed his lead, including Voegelin and Habermas, interpreted differentiation as a purely mental process and a form of rationalization. What I have attempted to demonstrate in this chapter with respect to ancient Egypt and Israel is the close relationship between historical and intellectual processes. Distinctions and differentiations in the intellectual sphere were brought about and forced upon the human mind by catastrophic and traumatic historical experiences. Although the rise of monotheism in the ancient world undoubtedly had historical consequences,[42] the rise of monotheism may itself be seen as a consequence of historical changes. In this sense, I take the rise of intellectual and religious concepts in ancient Egypt, such as the judgment of the dead and "Personal Piety," to be consequences of or somehow related to historical traumatic events such as the breakdown of the Old Kingdom and the Amarna experience.

The separation between state and religion (*Herrschaft und Heil*) can be identified both as the hallmark of biblical monotheism and simultaneously as "axiality." However, this revolutionary quality of monotheism has historically proven to be the least stable. Christianized and Islamized societies had no difficulty in relapsing into the system of representation. Well-known examples are Byzantine caesaro-papism, the role of the French king as head of the church, and the Arab institution of the caliphate.[43] The originally Egyptian idea of the state as the representation of divine rule on earth could easily be reintroduced into monotheistic religions, and monotheism could easily be reconciled with the claim of a human ruler not only to be obeyed but to be adored as the representative of god.

5

Five Steps toward Canonization

Tradition, Scripture, and the Origin
of the Hebrew Bible

In chapter 4 I tried to place the rise of monotheism in Israel in the broader cultural and intellectual context of transformations that have traditionally been subsumed under the notion of an "Axial Age." Moreover, I tried to place these "Axial" transformations in the context of primarily traumatic historical changes and experiences. In the present chapter I will explore another context that seems to me of equal relevance for those "Axial" transformations—especially with respect to the rise of monotheism, namely, the development of writing and literacy.[1] It never occurred to Jaspers that his theory was based on ancient texts, and that without the use of writing for the codification and ensuing canonization of "transcendental visions," the "Axial Age" could never have occurred. Writing is a necessary, though not sufficient, condition for transformations of "Axial" magnitude and importance. Nor did it occur to students of monotheism that there is not a single monotheistic religion that is not based on a canon of holy writ.[2] The history of media provides an equally important context for the emergence of monotheism as political history. Traditional "pagan" religions also have "sacred texts" whose sacredness rests in their power to create divine presence, the "third dimension" of the divine world, as explained in chapter 1. However, these are never collected into a canon that is simultaneously closed (i.e., excluding the addition of any new texts and the removal of any existing texts) and foundational in providing the basis for the entire life of the community and its individual members.[3]

Though I cannot claim any specific competence concerning biblical history and literature, I am interested in the history and phenomenology of canonization in the context of my theoretical work on "cultural memory."[4] In this context the textual history of the Hebrew Bible represents both a unique and extremely influential instance of the formation and transformation of a canonical tradition. Here one finds—perhaps for the first time in recorded history—a form of codifying cultural memory that changed our world in a most fundamental way, more than all the changes brought about by war or revolution. As was stated earlier, all of the so-called world religions are founded on an architecture of canonized scripture. There seems to exist a necessary connection between "revelation" and "canon," between "secondary religions" (i.e., religions based on the distinction between true and false that reject every older and foreign tradition as falsehood or ignorance),[5] and that specific form of written and highly normative codification of cultural memory called canonization. There is no secondary religion that is not based on a canonized body of scripture serving as a codification of memory. Belonging to such a religion means having learned and more or less internalized this memory recorded as text. It is, moreover, obvious that this preponderance of memory and codification is a necessary correlative of revelation. Revealed knowledge always is (or presents itself as) extraterrestrial, or extramundane. It comes from another world, like "air from other planets blowing," to quote Stefan George. It is not knowledge based on thisworldly experience and accumulated in the course of centuries. Furthermore, it is knowledge that people are not encouraged to expand through their own experience. God is invisible: this is the first and foremost teaching of revealed monotheism. You are not going to see God; you depend on listening to his word in order to get close to him. The concept of revelation is the opposite of what can be called natural evidence. There is no other access to revealed truth other than through Scripture. "Nobody has ever seen God," one reads in the Gospel of John (1:18; cf. First Epistle of John, 4:12, where this phrase is quoted), and Saint Paul teaches us "that we walk in faith and not in clear sight (or evidence)" (2 Cor. 5:7). Faith (Gk. *pistis;* Heb. *emunah*) is just another word for "memory," for it is all about not forgetting what was said to the ancestors and about trusting the authenticity of their experience and testimony. The absence of exterior evidence is compensated for by an interior or spiritual representation, that is, memory and its codification in Scripture. This shift from external evidence to memory and internal trust or certainty has much to do with what Freud called progress in spirituality or intellectuality ("Fortschritt in der Geistigkeit").[6]

The appeal to memory is so decisive that right from the start a religion based on revealed truth has had to have recourse to techniques of recording—that is, to writing—in order to fight the ever-present danger of forgetting. Moreover, it had had to invest writing with the highest authority and to develop a new form of tradition, namely, canonization. It requires not only writing but a very innovative and special form of written tradition—canonized Scripture—to represent the revealed truth that has no natural basis in human experience. Monotheism, therefore, is primarily a matter of memory.[7] This applies not only to the three Western monotheistic religions—Judaism, Christianity, and Islam—but also to Zoroastrianism, Manichaeism, Buddhism, Jainism, Daoism, Confucianism, Mormonism, as well as other religions, some of which may not be classified as monotheism but all of which share the polemical character of biblical monotheism in opposing and rejecting an older religion.

Even "Western culture"—that corpus of literary, aesthetic and scientific works—is based on processes of canonization.[8] The same applies to every national and regional organization of cultural memory. The principle of canonization thus appears to be ubiquitous, natural, and self-evident. This perspective, however, is entirely subjective since we are looking at these developments and their origins from within. The situation appears in a totally different light if viewed from the perspective of ancient Egypt, that is, from a point of view that predates even the early origins of canonization and is external to this development. Seen through the eyes of ancient Egypt, the phenomenon loses its self-evident nature and appears as a virtually inexplicable process resulting from an unpredictable and improbable concatenation of events. Recognizing this change of perspective is one advantage of a remote discipline such as Egyptology and may justify this venture into a field beyond one's professional competence.

The notion of tradition oscillates between two meanings. If one looks at it from the point of view of memory and remembering in the manner of, say, Maurice Halbwachs, tradition appears as the opposite of living, incorporated, and communicated knowledge ("la mémoire vécue").[9] In contradistinction to the fluidity and malleability of what Halbwachs has called "la mémoire collective" and I prefer to call "communicative memory,"[10] tradition appears as externalized, objectified, and institutionalized knowledge, something solid, fixed, and normative. However, if one looks at tradition from the point of view of Scripture, it

is tradition that appears fluid and malleable when compared to the so-
lidity and fixedness of normative Scripture. Seen in this light, tradition
appears as knowledge that is largely implicit and transmitted not only
verbally but also through nonverbal imitation, whereas the transmission
of canonized knowledge operates through verbal teaching and interpretation. The reflections and observations that follow are based on this
second perspective, the opposition of "tradition" and "Scripture."

First of all, one has to realize that there is no natural evolutionary
path that leads from tradition to text. The natural path of tradition leads
toward habituation, toward becoming implicit and even unconscious.[11]
In order to become explicit, a tradition has to confront a crisis or even
a break. Impulses to make tradition explicit, to record or codify it in
textual form, must come from without. Here one encounters the same
connection between "breakdown" and "breakthrough," or trauma and
("axial") transformation, discussed in chapter 4. The present chapter will
identify five such external impulses that helped shape the Hebrew Bible.
There might be more, but it is not the number that matters but rather the
plurality. My thesis is that these impulses are purely contingent; they do
not follow each other based on any logical necessity. After any of these
externally caused changes, the development might have taken quite a
different turn. Just as the transformation of tradition into text is not the
natural evolution of tradition, canonization is not the natural consequence of such text creation. On the contrary, the natural path of textual transmission is deterioration, not an increase but rather a decrease
in normative meaning. In search of normative meaning, philologists
always look for the archetype, the original text, the earliest attestation.
Canonization turns this natural and logical course of textual history on
its head. Normative meaning is to be sought not in the earliest but in the
final stage of textual history. The logic of archaeology must be replaced
by the logic of emergence in order to do justice to the semantics of canonization. Process, tendency, and finality matter, not origin, archetype,
and source criticism.[12] Again, there is no natural path leading from text
to canonization. Impulses must come from without, not from within.

The five steps of canonization are therefore external to the inner dynamics both of tradition and of literary transmission. They come from
outside, from the contingencies of history. The plurality and external
nature of the impulses toward textual recording and canonization are
mirrored in the pluralistic structure and content of the Hebrew canon.
This is its most conspicuous distinctive feature, unlike a more monolithic
canon such as the Qur'an.

The Disembodiment of the Law: The Invention
of a Normative Past

The first step from tradition to Scripture was taken in the context of the codification of law. It can tentatively be dated to the end of the seventh century BCE, to the time of King Josiah. This development has generally been interpreted as the adoption of Mesopotamian forms of legal codification dating back to the third millennium BCE.[13] However, this strikes me as incorrect. In Mesopotamia one is dealing not with law codes but rather with law books or legal literature. This distinction is of decisive importance.[14]

Legal literature ("law books") is a genre of the literary transmission of knowledge (*Wissensliteratur*), which is the great specialty of cuneiform culture. A law book, however, is not a code and has no prescriptive, binding force. It is not "normative" but "informative." Although it conveys the necessary knowledge concerning how to make laws, it does not promulgate and enforce them. Laws are made and enforced by the king. Legal literature may help him and his councilors in this task, but it does not restrict his freedom to legislate. One is dealing here with two fundamentally different functions of writing. One is that of storage in the sense of an extension and externalization of memory.[15] The other is that of publication in the sense of an extension and disembodiment or "excarnation"[16] of voice, of the performative utterance of the law-giving king. The first function is served by legal literature, the second by royal decrees and edicts whose force rarely outlasts the reign of the king who edited them. The first function may be called "informative," the second "performative." The latter performs an act of speech in the medium of writing.[17] The law code belongs to the realm of performative writing in the sense that it produces the legal order it describes. The law books, conversely, are purely descriptive and informative. Although they teach justice, they are never referred to as authoritative sources in lawsuits. The actual law is embodied in the reigning king, who must not be restricted in his legislative capacity by a book. Authority resides not in Scripture but in the king; where there is a king, there is no need for a law code. The wisdom behind this principle of legal kingship, common both to Mesopotamia and Egypt, seems to be that the legal culture of a society must always accommodate itself to the changing circumstances and contingencies of actual history as well as to the specificity of actual cases and problems. Laws cannot be eternally valid; they must constantly conform to the historical circumstances of a changing world. Eternal validity is merely the *idea* of justice that is thought to be embodied in the person of the king. The king is the interface between two different and potentially conflicting principles, namely, law and history. In Hellenistic philosophy, which was already reacting against the rise of codified law, this principle of legislative kingship was termed *nomos empsychos*, or *lex animata* (animated law), the law incarnated in the king.[18] Conversely, the principle of legal codification must be understood as a step toward disembodying the law from its royal incarnation. If a law code is superfluous where there is a law-giving king, the king becomes superfluous where there is a law code. This is the subversive point of the Torah in its incipient stage, its first step toward canonization. Although it has no parallels in Egypt and Mesopotamia, it does in archaic, proto-democratic Greece.[19] The disembodiment of the law has a revolutionary, anti-monarchical tendency.

The Torah replaces the law-giving king in his two aspects, both as the source of the law and as the interface between law and history. This is the specificity of biblical legal codification. In Greece codified law is neither framed by a normative history nor attributed to God as the source of legislation. It is plausible that a connection exists between these two properties of biblical law, its revealed character and its embeddedness in a sacred history (the Exodus from Egypt). The eternal validity of the law requires a timeless normativity of its historical circumstances, that is, the framing by means of a normative past. The master narrative of the Exodus story functions as a recontextualization of the law, which had become decontextualized by its disembodiment. The law-giving king embodies not only the law but also its historical context, its here and now. In the process of disembodiment, the law comes to be re-embodied in the 613 stipulations of the Torah and their "halakhic" proliferation and interpretation; the historical context is re-embodied in the Exodus story, which gives the law its eternal meaning. The law makes sense only in connection with the framing story. If your son asks you, "Why are we doing this?" you respond, "Because we were slaves in Egypt." The Torah does not require blind obedience. On the contrary, you are required to remember the story in order to understand the law and to obey it with an understanding heart. The story explains everything. It serves as determinative for the meaning of each of the various prescriptions. It replaces the actual context of the law as embodied within the person of the reigning king, with its historical context placed in the normative past. The visual evidence of the king and his various representations and representatives is replaced by a text that requires learning and remembering. Once again memory replaces vision.

In Mesopotamia and Egypt kingship was not the embodiment solely of legal authority but also of history, time, and chronological orientation. The king-list provided the only means of reckoning time.[20] The counting of years starts anew with every new king. History is equivalent to the actions of the king; and historiography is the annalistic recording of these actions. During times of interregnum, when there is no king, the years are counted in the Egyptian king-lists as "idle" or "empty" because there are no actions that would fill them. The institution of the king-list is therefore replaced in the Bible with a list of generations (*toledot*). This may be seen as a disembodiment of time and history, formerly embodied in the person of the king and the institution of kingship in the same way that legal codification must be interpreted as the disembodiment of the law.

If one looks for a historical situation that may have provided the decisive impulse in taking this first step of recording a legal tradition in textual form and of canonizing such a legal text, one can point to the time of the young king Josiah, when, according to legend, a book was found during restoration work in the Temple that was written by Moses himself and contained the Law of the Lord (2 Kings 22). This book is generally believed to be Deuteronomy, which is a codification of revealed Law, framed by a recapitulation of the Exodus story. The anti-monarchical tendency of the Deuteronomic school is well known and need not be demonstrated here.[21]

The political theology of the Deuteronomic tradition is subversive in two respects. First, it reduces the position of the Judaean king to that of a keeper of divine law whose legitimacy depends on the strength of his obedience to the law. Second, and even more innovatively, it replaces the traditional dependence of the Judaean king on his Assyrian overlord through the revolutionary idea of an alliance with God himself, not only overriding but even excluding every other alliance.[22] This is the third and most decisive disembodiment. The *Torah* thus replaces the king in three ways: first, as the source of legislation by making God the source of the law and Scripture its "performative" codification; second, as the interface between law and history by embedding the law into a master narrative or a normative past; and third, as the overlord of a political alliance by forming a treaty with God Himself.

Although in its general outlines the origin of this rather subversive political movement date back to the time of the first prophets in the eighth century, its final breakthrough can best be dated around 622 BCE, when there was both a release of Assyrian pressure and a young king ruling Judah who was open to reform. The Josian reform, however, had not only legal but also cultic aspects:[23] One is dealing here not only with politics but also with political theology. The worship of God as political overlord and lawgiver requires a kind of monopolization and exclusivity that must be seen as first steps not only toward canonization but also toward monotheism.

The Disembodiment of Tradition: The Babylonian Situation

The second step toward canonization follows immediately after the first, only without any logical or causal necessity. It is not the consequence of the first but is due to two completely external and contingent historical events: the fall of Jerusalem in 587 BCE and the deportation of the Israelite elite, commonly known as the Babylonian exile. For the Jews this catastrophe meant the rupture of the mimetic chain of tradition and the destruction of its implicit and unconscious dimensions—in short, the loss of everything that was not put into normative writing and learned by heart. Normally a society did not survive such an upheaval in its cultural identity and was assimilated into the larger context of the Assyrian or Babylonian empires. This was the fate, for example, of the ten "lost" tribes of Israel, the kingdom of the north, who were deported to Assyria in 722 BCE. That the Jews deported from Jerusalem managed to retain their cultural and religious identity during the fifty years of Babylonian exile was due to the fact that the first step toward canonization had already been taken, enabling them to go into exile with the Torah, which could already serve as a "portable homeland," in the words of the exiled German Jewish poet Heinrich Heine. Thus, the second step was not caused but rather preconditioned by the first step. Without the first step (the codification of the law) the second step (the codification of tradition) would have taken another form and direction.

Egypt experienced a comparable destruction of lived traditions during the First Intermediate Period (2200–2000 BCE), in the wake of the breakdown of the Old Kingdom. This crisis of social memory led to a comparable shift in the creation of texts and to the rise of wisdom literature.[24] Wisdom literature in ancient Egypt mainly consisted of a codification of social norms, maxims, and axioms. As in the Jewish case, nonverbal imitation and apprenticeship were replaced by explicit learning and interpretation. In Egypt the transition from "lived" to "learned" tradition led to the rise of a school—apparently the achievement of the

Middle Kingdom—intended to train a new elite for the reestablished institutions of a Pharaonic monarchy and its bureaucratic administration. However, in Judah—especially in the case of the Babylonian exile— there was a marked tendency both to democratize and depoliticize tradition. The entire society was transformed into a "learning community,"[25] a "wise and cultured people" (Deut. 4:6: '*am hakham ve-navon*) and a "kingdom of priests."[26]

Such a transformation of tradition into textual form can be interpreted as another type of "disembodiment." What becomes disembodied in this case is the implicit knowledge internalized by the older members of the community and transmitted to the young through silent imitation. The rupture of the chain of imitation occurs in situations of social disintegration. This is the typical environment whereby explicit instructions are put into written form. Helmuth Lethen has provided a vivid description of such a situation in the interval between World Wars I and II: "In moments of social disorganization, when the edifices of traditions crumble and morality loses its persuasiveness, there is a need of instructions of behavior or *Verhaltenslehren* [conduct books] that help to distinguish between one's own and the alien, the internal and external. They help to delimit zones of confidence against spheres of distrust and to determine identity."[27] In the case of the Babylonian exile, the codification of law was enriched with all kinds of traditions and transformed into such a comprehensive body of behavioral instruction. It served not only as a foundation of legal culture but also as a source of general orientation, lifestyle, and confidence—in short of social and cultural identity able to resist the natural drive toward assimilation.

Canon from Above: The Persian Situation

The Persian Empire established its domination over the conquered countries by ruling them according to their native laws.[28] Thus, the Persian kings began collecting and codifying local customs and transformed them into imperial law. In Egypt a commission was appointed "to codify the former law which was valid until the forty-fourth year of Amasis."[29] A learned Egyptian named Udjahorresne got the order to restore the "houses of life," meaning the Egyptian centers of learning, a combination of library and scriptorium.[30] However, the impulse toward collection and codification went far beyond the legal sphere. At Hibis, in Khargeh Oasis, Darius I erected a temple that reflected a new type of temple decoration, wherein all the walls of the edifice, from floor to ceiling, were covered with texts and representations that resembled a comprehensive codification of ritual and theological knowledge.[31] For the first time Egypt entered a period of prolonged foreign domination and was faced with the imminent danger of cultural forgetting. The temple, as a vessel of cultural memory, was a reaction against this danger, a fortress of memory.

The Jewish counterpart of Udjahorresne was Ezra the scribe. A member of the Jewish priestly aristocracy who remained in Babylon, he was sent into the satrapy of Transeuphratene with a similar order, which stated: "For thou art commissioned by the king and the seven councilors and shouldst investigate, according to the law of thy god, which is in thy hand, the state of affairs in Judah and Jerusalem."[32] With Ezra and his law-code[33] the recording in written texts of the normative traditions of Israel entered a new stage, for now the canonized text was complemented by an element that can be identified as the necessary correlative of every canonization, namely, a culture of exegesis. Ezra assembles the Israelites at the water gate of Jerusalem and had the Torah not only read to them but interpreted paragraph by paragraph. As the Jewish historian Yosef Hayim Yerushalmi has noted, for the first time in history a sacred text ceased to be the exclusive property of the priestly class and became the common property of the people. This represented the birth not only of Scripture but also of exegesis.[34]

Again, it is important to realize that the third step toward canonization by no means necessarily follows from the first and second steps. The Persian authorization of local law was not restricted to Judah but had parallels in Egypt and other countries as well. No inner dynamics or evolutionary path led from step two to step three. One is still dealing with external, contingent, totally different impulses. Here the impulse comes "from above," whereas the first step toward canonization under King Josiah must be interpreted as coming "from below" despite royal support. In the first instance the political theology of the Torah was intentionally subversive[35] because it tended to replace the king with the sacred book. Now, given the situation of Persian domination, it appeared to be rather supportive because it favored depoliticizing the Jewish community. The Torah now served as a sub-state organization of Jewish life. There was no need for a Jewish king within a Persian satrapy, and his replacement by a book conformed to the principles of Persian rule.

Moreover, the Persian period signaled the end of prophecy,[36] which added to the authority of the canon. The prophet gave way to the scribe. The interpreter of Scripture replaced the interpreter of the will

of God. Text and professional philological competence replaced authority based on vision and divine commission. In this respect, Judah
came to resemble Egypt more than Israel ever did. The prophet had no
parallel in Egypt, but the *sofer* closely resembled his Egyptian colleague,
the *hierogrammateus*. The fourth step was common to Egypt and to Judah
as well as to many other societies in the ancient world.

The Rise of Textual Communities: Enclave Cultures and Core Libraries

Brian Stock has demonstrated that the heretical movements of the
Middle Ages revolved around a core of highly authoritative texts that
they adopted as their own. He coined the term "textual communities"
to reflect their most characteristic feature.[37] The only way to legitimize
their sectarian dissociation from the official tradition was to point to a
specific (body of) text(s) or a particular interpretation of common texts
whose normative claims and authority could be presented as superior to
the claims of mainstream traditions and institutions. Dissidence requires exegetical authority and philological expertise. Many of the characteristics Stock has shown to be typical of these medieval "textual communities" already existed within similar groups in antiquity—such as
the Orphics, Pythagoreans, Essenes, the Qumran group, Gnostics, Her-
meticists, Christians, and Neoplatonists—which typically assembled
around a core library of normative literature.[38]

The archaeological finds in Qumran, Nag Hammadi, Tebtynis, and
other places give us some idea of what such a core library might have
looked like. Qumran, it is true, also functioned as a center of book pro-
duction and preserved many books that did not play a major role in the
life of the community.[39] Still, it is obvious that these libraries aimed
not at completeness but rather at relevance, normativity, sanctity, and
indispensability. This is best demonstrated if one contrasts these core libraries with palace libraries such as that of Ashurbanipal at Niniveh, the
Peisistratides at Athens, or those at Alexandria and Pergamon. These
were libraries that aimed at completeness and tried to collect everything
written. They became the models of the national libraries of our time.
Their structure was closely related to the idea of empire: to assemble
and represent the entire knowledge of the realm. The idea behind a core
library is totally different. It is about assembling and representing the
distinctive and exclusive knowledge of a group that sees itself as separate
from the rest of the world. Mary Douglas has proposed the following

distinction between several types of socio-intellectual structures. A society centered in a core library closely corresponds to an "enclave culture," the culture of a threatened minority that develops a multitude of contradistinctive customs—such as purity laws—in order not to be swallowed up by the majority culture.[40] The "sectarian" movements in Second Temple Judaism present conspicuous cases of enclave culture.[41] A chain of recurring events—such as the destruction of the First Temple, the Babylonian exile, the Maccabean wars and, still later, the destruction of the Second Temple and the diaspora—transformed Israel, to use Mary Douglas's terminology, from an "individualistic culture" into a "hierarchic culture," and then into an "enclave culture." It is the historical experience and the social structure of an enclave culture that informed the final redaction of the biblical texts. However, one also encounters core libraries in Egypt, where it makes no sense to speak of sectarian movements. Egyptian temple libraries,[42] some of whose catalogues have been preserved in temple inscriptions, show much the same structure and confirm the findings from Elephantine and Tebtynis.[43] Most of the books they contained were doubtlessly the same as in other temple libraries. They thus represented and codified general rather than sectarian knowledge. Nevertheless, it makes perfectly good sense to identify these priestly groups, who not only worked but lived in the temples, as enclave cultures. They formed enclaves of traditional Egyptian knowledge in a Hellenistic and syncretistic environment.

An Egyptian temple library was not only restricted in size but was also organized according to a certain structure or architecture. Clement of Alexandria gives a vivid description of such a library. He speaks of forty-two "indispensable" or "absolutely necessary" (*pany anankaiai*) books that formed the stock of such a core library and were all written by Thot-Hermes himself. The structure of the library resulted from the hierarchical order of the priesthood and the specialization of the different priestly ranks. The priests were not supposed to read and learn all of the books. Rather, they were to specialize in certain groups corresponding to their rank and office. In describing a procession of these priests, Clement shows both the hierarchy of the priesthood and the structure of their library.[44] The *singer* comes first. He carries a musical emblem as a sign of his rank. He is supposed to have memorized two books of Hermes, one containing hymns to the gods and the other a biography of the reigning king. Next comes the *horoscopos*, carrying a palm branch and an astrological emblem. He is supposed to have memorized the four astrological books of Hermes (one dealing with the order of darkness, one with the planets, one with the encounters and appearances of sun and moon, and the last with the risings). Then the *hierogrammateus* comes forth bearing a feather on his head and in his hands a book and the tools of a scribe. He is supposed to know the so-called hieroglyphic books dealing with cosmography and geography: the constellations of the sun, the moon, and the five planets; the soil of Egypt and the nature of the Nile; the structure and equipment of the temples; the grounds allotted to the temples; and the measurements and objects used in the temples. He is followed by the *stolistes*, whose competence lies in ten books dealing with education, cult, and sacrifice. Last comes the *prophetes*, or high priest, who carries a situla of water and is followed by attendants carrying a processional plate with various types of bread. As the chief of the temple priesthood, he has memorized the ten so-called hieratic books concerning the laws, the gods, and everything about priestly education. "The absolutely necessary books of Hermes total forty-two, of which thirty-six, containing the entire philosophy of the Egyptians, are committed to memory by the priests. The remaining six books are learned by the *pastophoroi*. They deal with medicine, specifically with anatomy, disease, the bodily members and organs, drugs, ophthalmology, and gynecology."[45]

We are dealing here with a combination of book culture and memory culture typical of the oriental world. The books are not only meant to be read but to be memorized and mastered. To achieve this goal, the Egyptian priests introduced a partition of labor or expertise corresponding to the interior architecture of the canon of thirty-six or forty-two books, respectively. Both thirty-six and forty-two are sacred numbers. Thirty-six is a celestial number related to time, corresponding to the thirty-six "decan" stars and to the thirty-six "weeks" (decades) of the Egyptian year. Forty-two is a terrestrial number related to space, corresponding to the forty-two "nomes" of Egypt, symbolized by the forty-two bodily parts of Osiris, whose members, according to the myth, were dispersed all over Egypt after he was slain and torn apart by Seth. Thus, just as the number forty-two symbolizes the totality of Egypt, the forty-two books symbolize the totality of Egyptian "philosophy." The same principle applies to the number of books of the Hebrew Bible. Based on modern counting practices, they total thirty-six books, which may reflect Egyptian influence in defining a numerical symbol of totality (the totality of time). According to traditional Jewish counting practices, however, this number is reduced to twenty-two or twenty-four by counting the twelve minor prophets as one book and other constructions. Flavius

Josephus explains these numbers as the sum total of the letters of the Aramaic (24) and Hebrew (22) alphabets, respectively. In view of early Jewish theories concerning the preexistence of the Torah and its role in creation, the number of the letters (Gk. *stoicheia*, or elements) is a much stronger symbol of totality than the number of the decan stars.

Clearly, the Hebrew Bible reflects the structure of such a temple library of indispensable books. It reflects a similar architecture that, in this case, is composed of three stories (instead of five, as in the Egyptian case). The five books of the Torah form the uppermost floor and correspond to the books containing the knowledge of the most normative value to be learned by the high priest. The eight—or, alternatively, nineteen—books of the prophets (*Nevi'im*) occupy the second floor. Last in normativity come the twelve "Writings" (*Ketuvim*) on the ground floor. They represent a stock of comparatively secular literature meant to be read in school and to form a literary canon of Hebrew "classics," like the Alexandrian canon of classical Greek literature.[46]

The Hebrew Bible represents the core library of a particular textual community among other textual communities, such as the Pharisees, the Sadducees, the Essenes, and the Qumran community. It later became the canon of normative Judaism in general and was used by what can be considered a textual community as well as an enclave culture on the larger scale of the Jewish diaspora.

The Concept of Idolatry: The Linguistic Reduction

Whereas the first four impulses toward canonization have many parallels in the ancient world, the fifth is exclusively Jewish. It consists of an act of polemical contradistinction according to which early Judaism sets itself apart from the rest of the world, which it constructs and excludes by this same step as "pagan."[47] This impulse is the most difficult one to grasp. It is not easy to see what canonization and the concept of idolatry could possibly have in common. The condemnation of virtually all visual forms of communication or contact with the divine as "idolatry" and the expulsion of divine presence from everything that was not verbal or scriptural reduced and concentrated all religious experience and expertise to Scripture, transforming the latter into an object not only of study but also of contemplation and worship.[48] Midrashic interpretation seems to me to be a practice of contemplation as well as a hermeneutic methodology. The attitude toward cult images is transferred to Scripture. According to this process, Scripture assumes a new kind of sacredness. Only now does the text become a kind of temple where God resides.

The concept of idolatry—as defined in the second commandment and the story of the golden calf, and as ridiculed by the satirical descriptions of the prophets (e.g., Isa. 44; Jer. 10)[49]—is, of course, much older than the Hellenistic period, when it became for Judaism the central and defining cultural and religious abomination. It is possible that the concept assumed absolute centrality only after the destruction of the Second Temple, when the daily sacrifices and presentations of these offerings and acts of worship could no longer be performed, and when religious life was reduced to reading and studying, preaching and interpreting the sacred books of the canonized core library. The concept of idolatry underwent a considerable change of meaning in the course of its development from early "mono-Yahwism"—the exclusive worship of Yahweh in full recognition of the existence of "other gods," for only thus does the stress on fidelity and on the "jealousy" of God make sense—to pure "monotheism," which categorically negates the existence of other gods.[50] Now the question no longer concerns the Jews' own god and the other gods but truth and falsehood. Images turn into "idols," representing not an existing being but phantasmagorical imaginings. In the light of this distinction between truth and falsehood, which for the first time is introduced into the realm of religion,[51] Scripture assumes the dignity of an exclusive codification of truth compared to which all other representations of the divine are denigrated as expressions of lies, error, or ignorance.

In order to understand what this textual reduction or concentration means, one has to realize what idolatry does *not* mean. It does not include verbal images. There is no problem in calling God king, bridegroom, father, judge, shepherd, or gardener. As long as such images are only verbal, there is nothing wrong with them.[52] Language is acceptable. This means that everything other peoples are displaying in a multitude of symbolic forms must be condensed into Scripture. This is the most radical and comprehensive form of "disembodiment." Written language now represents not only the king but also the priest, the temple, ritual, theater, art, and politics—in short, the world. This leads me back to the reflection with which I began: the correspondence between the concept of revelation, the radical extraworldliness of God, and the concept of canon, the exclusive scriptural nature of his revelation. Living by the canon means living in this world as a stranger. "I am a stranger on earth. Do not take thy commandments from me" (Ps. 119:19).

Christianity did not follow Judaism in its radical emigration from the world into Scripture. Rather, through its theology of incarnation it reopened the door to images, sacramental magic, and other forms of religious life. It was perhaps in contradistinction to emergent Christianity but also, of course, to the "cosmotheism" of late antiquity that Judaism (which in the beginning had also used images in the first synagogues, such as Sepphoris and Dura Europos) grew increasingly severe in its exclusion of images and its abomination of idolatry.

For Judaism this concentration on Scripture provided the means for its survival. Egypt, conversely, clung to temple ritual and cult images. Thus, the destruction of the temples and the discontinuation of ritual put an end to Egyptian culture. The forty-two books of the core library never became a canon in the Hebrew sense because they supported but never replaced the temple ritual.

In conclusion, I again would like to stress the plurality and contingency of the different impulses that led to the formation of the Hebrew canon. Some of them are closely connected to the traumatic experience of a violent disruption of continuity, causing a crisis of cultural memory. This applies most particularly to the second step, the deportation of the Jewish elite to Babylon, which meant a rupture of the "chain of imitation." The fifth step, the shunning of idolatry, can also be interpreted as such a memory crisis because it implied the intentional forgetting of many traditional and familiar forms of religious life. However, each of the five steps involved a reorganization and reorientation of cultural memory in reaction to far-reaching political, cultural, and religious changes.

6

No God but God

Exclusive Monotheism and the Language of Violence

Cultura facit saltus: Introductory Remarks

In chapter 1 I described the many roads that lead from polytheism to monotheism. Polytheism is not a random accumulation of deities, demons, and spirits but a coherent system that may be regarded either as a unified divine world or as an irreducible but structured plurality of deities. Both of these aspects are simultaneously possible. The former presents the divine world as a latent monotheism found, for example, in Egyptian wisdom literature or in the story of the Golden Chain at the beginning of book 8 of the *Iliad*. The latter presents the divine world as a manifest polytheism in its three-dimensionality of cult, cosmos, and sacred language. It is easily understandable why and how polytheism can turn into monotheism. This is just a process of latency turning into manifestation, which can be observed as gradually progressing in all of the great polytheistic religions of the ancient world.

However, there is also a price to pay for this form of inclusive monotheism that sees God in all gods, namely, the loss of personality and closeness with respect to the idea of God. The more all-encompassing the idea of God, the more God tends to fade into the impersonal remoteness of a Supreme Being or even into the abyss of negative theology. Until fairly late in history, people were not willing to pay this price. The cosmic god of the Egyptians and the Alexandrian Greeks was revered simultaneously with the *deus absconditus*, the invisible, ineffable One-and-All, and the powerful, if not omnipotent, god of the magicians, who promised protection against and salvation from every evil. For example, Isis was worshiped both as the deity who incorporated the innumerable deities of all religions in the world and as the tutelary goddess of navigation and rescuer of the shipwrecked. In time, however, the idea of a divine One-and-All became more and more difficult to relate to in terms of cult and personal prayer, and inclusive monotheism evolved into a form of mysticism and esotericism. Only by means of such mystical techniques as deep meditation could individual adepts aspire to connect to the One-and-All at rare moments of illumination.

During the same centuries of late antiquity, when the temples fell into neglect and official cult turned into private mysticism, another, totally different kind of monotheism spread from Judaea—or Palestine, as the region later came to be called—into all the provinces of the Roman Empire. It was not easy for the pagans of that time to tell the two forms of monotheism apart and to comprehend the unbridgeable gulf that separated Jove from Yahweh. Yet for apologetic or propagandistic reasons Jewish writers also indulged in likening their God to the god of the philosophers. Even today many historians of religion are unwilling to see in the rise of biblical monotheism anything but just a general evolution from polytheism to monotheism. However, a process of slow evolution is not the form in which the Bible itself tells the story and recalls the breakthrough toward true monotheism. Biblical monotheism is not the latent monotheism of polytheism finally become manifest under the motto "All gods are one" but rather a totally new form of monotheism that excludes rather than absorbs the other gods under the motto "No other gods!" or "No god but God!" This form of monotheism, which may be called "exclusive," is a matter not of evolution but of revolution.[1]

To be sure, there is a third form of asserting the oneness of God. This is usually understood to be the proper hallmark of monotheism: "God is One!" meaning "the only one." Privileging this form over and against the other two means blurring the decisive differences since this form occurs in all three contexts. First, in the context of polytheism it is frequently used to emphasize the uniqueness or sovereign power of a specific god, especially the creator. There are thus hundreds of assertions such as "Amun [Amun-Re, Re, Ptah, etc.] is one [unique]" in Egyptian texts, and the same applies to Mesopotamian, Anatolian, and Canaanite texts.[2] Second, it occurs in the context of inclusive monotheism (see chapter 3). Lastly, in the context of biblical monotheism the motto *YHWH æchad*, "the LORD is One," of course holds the central place. However, to take this assertion as the distinctive feature of monotheism would be to engage in endless discussions about what the notion of "oneness" could mean in such different contexts as biblical, Mesopotamian, Canaanite, Egyptian, and many other religions where it is equally widespread. One should also realize that there is no such motto as "The gods are many!" which could be opposed to the monotheistic "God is One!" as the polytheistic credo. Polytheism is not a "religion" in the same sense that monotheism is. The truly distinctive, innovative, and revolutionary character of biblical — or, to be more precise, Deuteronomic — religion is expressed in the commandment "[Thou shalt have] No other Gods!" for which there is no parallel in the religions dwelling on the theme of divine oneness.

What would the term "revolution" mean in this context? I am here obviously not speaking of a political revolution, perhaps not even a historical event at all. Rather, one is dealing here with the phenomenon of retrospection (*Nachträglichkeit*), to use the Freudian term, a revolution a posteriori, after the fact; and a feat not of history but of memory. Let me try to clarify this concept by referring to Charles Darwin's motto *Natura non facit saltus* (Nature does not take leaps). Though commonly attributed to Leibniz, the idea goes back to Aristotle. In the *Guide* Maimonides developed this idea in the very context of monotheism and revelation.[3] According to the latter, if one wishes to understand God's workings throughout history, one must study his workings in nature. In this sphere everything proceeds by means of gradual succession and imperceptible transition. Only a sequence of infinitely small steps and complicated deviations leads from one extreme to the other. According to Maimonides, the same applies to God's revelation in history. One must imagine it as a process of sliding change and natural growth. Evolution, not revolution, is the principle both of nature and of history.

Culture, however, follows different laws.[4] Culture does proceed in leaps. It may very well be that long preparatory stages and processes involving tiny transitions are implied even in the great cultural transformations. They are, however, staged, perceived, and, above all, remembered and represented in the cultural memory of a society in terms of leaps, revolutions, and sudden turns. Even biblical monotheism may have slowly evolved out of polytheism.[5] However, in the Hebrew Bible, the codified cultural memory of the Jewish people, successful realization of monotheism is represented as a leap and a revolutionary break as radical as one can possibly imagine. The span of time — more than four hundred years — that the children of Israel spent in Egypt destroyed any continuity with the patriarchal past, as recounted in Genesis. The Exodus from Egypt meant a break with any adopted Egyptian traditions. The gift of the Torah at Mount Sinai meant a radically new beginning, the opposite of any slow evolution. It was a miraculous and extraordinary intervention of God into human history, cutting through the succession of ages and any natural evolution by creating a radically new reality. This is how culture works as far as its self-perception, self-enactment, and, above all, its memory is concerned. *Cultura facit saltus.*

This form of narrative self-representation may also provide the key to the problem with which the present chapter is concerned, namely, exclusive monotheism and the language of violence. Why do the biblical texts use the language and imagery of violence in their narrative representations of the foundation and success of monotheism? Does the idea of monotheism, the exclusive worship of one god instead of a divine world, or the distinction between true and false in religion, in which there is one true god and the rest are false gods, imply or entail violence? Are violence and intolerance, rigor and zealotry the price that exclusive monotheism has had to pay for sticking to the notion of a very personal and passionate God while stressing the idea of Oneness?

Why is this question important and in what context it is it being asked? The interest of the question lies in the wave of religiously motivated violence that is presently descending on the world. One harbors the suspicion that David Hume might have been right after all when he postulated a connection between monotheism and violence in chapter 9 of *The Natural History of Religion* (1757).[6] Thus, the question is whether exclusive monotheism may have social, political, and anthropological consequences, specifically whether there are such things as "monotheistic man" and "monotheistic societies," and, if so, whether they are particularly prone to violence and intolerance. The question is as important as it is dangerous. The danger lies in its implied essentialism. Is there, after all, such a thing as "monotheism?" There are many religions, branches, and sub-branches, so who can tell which ones are to be classified as essentially monotheistic? Given this diversity, how can it be legitimate to classify anyone as "monotheistic man?"

Two modifications or specifications might be helpful in avoiding the pitfalls of essentialism. The first consists in speaking not of "consequences" but rather of "propensities." Consequences are a matter of necessity and inevitability; they will sooner or later become real in one form or another. Propensities, conversely, are a matter of potentiality and probability; they leave us free with respect to how to deal with them. I am therefore not going to discuss any anthropological, sociological, and political consequences that follow necessarily and inevitably from monotheism, nor do I believe that monotheism is inherently or structurally violent and intolerant. I am speaking here only of propensities, which may, under certain historical conditions, lead to violence and intolerance. Precisely because one is dealing with propensities and not with consequences, a reflection upon their origin and structure is important in order to avoid their turning from potentialities into realities of various kinds that have haunted the world and continue to do so. The other specification concerns the very notion of "monotheism." By this I mean simply the principle that there be "no god but God" or, in the form of the first commandment, "[Thou shalt have] no other gods," regardless of any further distinctions between monotheism, henotheism, monolatry and the like. Seen in this light, the danger of essentializing monotheism disappears. It may be true that there is no such thing as pure "monotheism" in the Bible or elsewhere, but no one will deny that the principle of "no other gods!" or "no god but God" is a leading idea in all three of the so-called Abrahamic religions. The violent and intolerant propensities lie in the structure of "counterreligion,"[7] which does not refer to any specific religion existing in historical reality but rather to a theoretical construct or model, like Max Weber's "ideal type," which may be more or less adequately applied to various historical phenomena.

Exclusive monotheism draws new boundaries between God and other gods, truth and untruth, us and them, present and past, the new and the old. In this latter respect, which is perhaps the most important of all, it distinguishes not only between "us" and "them" but draws the boundary even within one's own group or one's own self; it distinguishes between our or my own past and present, our or my old and new selves. By dint of this distinction, exclusive monotheism creates what could be called a logic and a rhetoric of conversion. It is a religion that always conceives of itself as new, as a founded religion. The distinction it introduces calls for a commitment to be made "with all thine heart, and with all thy soul, and with all thy might" (Deut. 6:5). In view of my quest for anthropological implications, I wish to retain this stress on inner man, on individuality and interiority, as a possible first characteristic feature of "monotheistic man."[8]

Violence—always understood as propensity and not as consequence—is inherent not in the idea of the One God but in the exclusion of other gods, not in the idea of truth but in the persecution of untruth. There is no logical necessity for the distinction between true and untrue to turn violent. The implication turns real only if the distinction between truth and untruth or "us" and "them" is interpreted in terms of friend and foe.

As an Egyptologist, I am concerned with the innovative—even revolutionary—newness of monotheism, with origins, first occurrences, beginnings. That is why I have chosen to focus my analysis on the Hebrew Bible. Only here does one deal with a monotheistic movement that had no model,[9] whereas such other religious movements as Christianity and Islam were preceded by the Jews and their Bible. In this respect, it is important to stress the fact that among the three so-called Abrahamitic religions, Judaism is the only one that has never turned the implications of violence and intolerance into historical reality precisely because it has relegated the final universalizing of truth to eschatology and not to history.

Canaanophobia: Idolatry as Abomination

Bearing in mind these preliminary precautions, I wish to turn to the Bible and recall—among up to six hundred passages mentioning internecine violence[10]—some of the typical scenes of violence that orchestrate the institution of monotheism. These all too familiar passages have often been quoted with polemical intentions, first by the church fathers in order to fabricate a case against Judaism, then by critics of religion—especially in the eighteenth century—to do the same against the Judeo-Christian tradition in general. Reciting them here might seem like a mere renewal of stale polemics. I am not quoting these passages in order to build up a case against monotheism, let alone Judaism.[11] This was part of the agenda of the Enlightenment 250 years ago and is now becoming part of a Jewish discourse on the biblical roots of religious violence, especially in the more recent works of Regina Schwartz[12] and Jonathan Kirsch.[13] I do not wish to accuse or criticize but merely to understand. Moreover, it seems inappropriate to cite these passages in arguing against Judaism or Christianity because in neither do they play any considerable role. They are neither taught in a Jewish yeshiva nor preached from a Christian pulpit. Their interest is purely historical, in that they testify to the self-representation of the new religion in its incipient stages. However, my interest in these texts is not historical but "mnemo-historical." The question I wish to pose is not "Why has monotheism been instituted with so much violence?" but rather "Why has the story of its institution been told and remembered in the Bible in so many scenes of violence? Why do the central texts that proclaim the exclusive Oneness of god use the language of violence?" Violence is not an element of a hostile view toward monotheism from without but rather the self-portrait of monotheism as seen from within. The aim of this chapter is to answer the following question: Why does biblical monotheism see itself as violent?

Where to begin? The accounts of the Exodus from Egypt, violently forced upon Pharaoh by God-sent plagues—and even more so the conquest in Canaan—depict the birth of the Israelite nation and the rise of monotheism (these two events being two aspects of the same process) in terms of extreme violence. Even if one assumes that these events never actually occurred in chronological history and view them as myths and legends—by means of which a society reconstructs its past, which provides direction and perspective to its present goals and problems—the question of their meaning becomes all the more urgent. These scenes seemingly deal with external violence directed at other peoples, such as the Egyptians and the Canaanites. A closer reading of the biblical texts, however, reveals that internal violence directed against one's own group, or even against one's own self, plays a much more important role. In several (though not all) respects "Canaan" can be understood as a symbolic representation of Israel's own pagan past and persisting pagan or syncretistic traditions. As far as its biblical self-portrait is concerned, monotheism is a religion with propensities toward internal rather than external violence. This is what makes the study of pertinent texts so interesting despite the fact that they have lost interest in the context of Jewish and Christian exegesis. I shall quote the texts in the excellent new translation by Robert Alter.[14]

The beginning consists of the story of the Golden Calf. The Israelites relapse into idolatry. They cannot stand the long absence of their leader, Moses, on Mount Sinai and believe him dead. They ask Aaron to fashion an image in order to replace God's representative, Moses, with a representation that will walk before them and lead them through the desert. As an atonement and a punishment, Moses initiates a punitive action that is described in Exodus as follows:

> Then Moses stood at the gate of the camp and said, "Whoever is for the LORD—to me!" And the Levites gathered round him. And he said to them, "Thus says the LORD God of Israel: Put every man his sword on his thigh, and cross over and back from gate to gate in the camp, and each man kill his brother, and each man his fellow, and each man his kin." And the Levites did according to the

word of Moses, and about three thousand men of the people fell on that day. (Exod. 32:27–28)

Decisive are the words "each man kill his brother, and each man his fellow, and each man his kin" (*ish 'et-achîw w^e'ish 'et-re'éhu w^e'ish 'et-q^erobô*). Here violence explicitly turns within and severs the most intimate human bonds. The commitment that God demands of each individual person and the covenant that he extends overrides and breaks all human bonds and obligations. One may compare and complement this with an equally famous passage from Deuteronomy:

> Should your brother, your mother's son, or your son or your daughter or the wife of your bosom or your companion who is like your own self [*'achîkha ben-'immekha 'ô-binkha 'ô-bitt^ekha 'o 'eshet-chêqékha 'o re'akha asher k^enafsh^ekha*] incite you in secret, saying, "Let us go and worship other gods," that you did not know, neither you nor your fathers, from the gods of the people that are all around them, the ones close to you or the ones far from you from the end of the earth to the end of the earth, you shall not assent to him and you shall not heed him, and your eye shall not spare him and you shall not pity and shall not shield him. But you shall surely kill him. Your hand shall be against him first to put him to death and the hand of all the people last. And you shall stone him and he shall die, for he thought to thrust you away from the LORD your God.[15]

In this case one can trace this language of violence to Assyrian loyalty oaths.[16] The Assyrian Empire demanded absolute loyalty from its vassals, including such forms of thought control as spying on one's friends and neighbors and denouncing and prosecuting them in the event that they expressed disloyal thoughts. How is it possible to connect such a language with the biblical idea of God? How is it possible that people see their god as wishing them to denounce and kill their friends, companions, and neighbors? It is easy to retrace the ways in which Assyrian texts and concepts were translated into Hebrew and even entered the Bible since some of the kings of Judah had to use such language in swearing a loyalty oath to the Assyrian king. However, it is not easy to understand how these political concepts could possibly get translated into theological ones and how God came to play the role of an Assyrian despot. Perhaps the idea was to get rid of the Assyrian and any other dependency by entering into a similar kind of dependency with God by forming with God the very same treaty that the Assyrian king had imposed. In transforming Assyrian politics into biblical theology, the Israelites may have hoped to transform politics into religion and thereby to be liberated from politics altogether, to become independent of, or at least indifferent to, any further forms of political oppression. Did they not, perhaps, pay too high a price in taking the Assyrian idea of political exclusivity—you shall not have other overlords besides me—as a model of religious exclusivity and thereby politicizing both the concept of god and the new idea of religion? As a possible solution, Old Testament scholar Othmar Keel proposes to ascribe these concepts not to monotheism proper but rather to a preliminary stage that may be called monolatry or even mono-Yahwism, which is not to be confused with mature monotheism.[17] The message is that one must not blame monotheism for intolerance and violence. Keel further asserts that the god of true monotheism is free of jealousy because he has no rivals.

I totally agree that one is dealing here with a form of monotheism that still has to be "humanized," to be developed into a less violently exclusive form. The various traditions of the Jewish exegesis, in particular, show the ways in which such a sublimation and humanization has been achieved. Concerning the biblical self-portrait of monotheism, however, the distinction between immature and true monotheism, or monolatry and monotheism, does not apply. It may very well be true that true monotheism does not know jealousy. The God of the covenant, however, is a jealous god, *El Qanna'*, who distinguishes between friend and foe, reckoning the crime of the fathers, who are his foes, with the children unto the third and fourth generations, but showing mercy to thousands of generations of his friends, who love him and obey his commands. Perhaps this is not real, mature monotheism, but it is the centerpiece of covenant theology and therefore central to the cultural semantics under analysis. It forms the very foundation of our intellectual and spiritual tradition. Deuteronomy is not to be isolated and marginalized. Rather, it belongs to the absolutely central texts not only of Jewish but also of Christian tradition. It is correct to state that there is no such thing as "the" biblical monotheism, that the Bible contains many different traditions and, correspondingly, many varieties of monotheism or monolatry, and that one is dealing here with something rather special that may be called "Deuteronomism." However, one must also recognize that Deuteronomism, or covenant theology, has proven enormously influential in the course not only of Jewish but also of Christian—especially Protestant—history. I totally agree with Stephen Geller, who has stated that biblical religion "is truly monotheistic only in its Deuteronomic form [and] that this is as close to monotheism as one could get in antiquity."[18] Correspondingly, the "jealousy" of God belongs within the core semantics of monotheism and cannot be split off and isolated without severely distorting the historical phenomenology of biblical monotheism. This semantic core of the prophetic and Deuteronomic movements is not so much concerned with the unity of God as it is with the exclusion of other gods as false or forbidden. Thus, these movements—which came to be subsumed under the rubric "Yahve-alone-movement"[19] following the groundbreaking work of Morton Smith—should instead be called "No-other-Gods-movement" since this, and not the Yahweh-alone-predication, is what sets them apart from all other religious practices inside and outside the Hebrew world. Exclusive (exclusivist) monotheism typically reckons with other gods, that is, with rival claims for power and truth, which it rejects as incompatible with its own truth.[20]

Zeal: Killing and Dying for God

What makes the theme of divine jealousy particularly important in the quest for anthropological and social implications of monotheism is the fact that it has a human counterpart, namely, "to be zealous" for God. Divine jealousy and human zeal have their lexical counterparts in the Hebrew *qin'ah* (zeal, jealousy) and *qanna'* (jealous, said only of God; *qana'* applies to human beings). This theological and anthropological concept of "zeal" seems to me to be another characteristic feature of the new concept of man. The model of all those who are zealous for god is Phinehas, son of Eleazar. The story is told in chapter 25 of Numbers. As in the story of the golden calf, one is dealing with a case of unfaithfulness or disloyalty, here with obvious sexual connotations.

> Now Israel stayed at Shittim, and the people began to go whoring with the daughters of Moab. And they called the people to the sacrifices of their gods, and the people ate and bowed down to their gods. And Israel clung to Baal Pe'or, and the LORD's wrath flared against Israel.
> And the LORD said to Moses, "Take the chiefs of the people and impale them to the LORD before the sun, that the LORD's flaring wrath may turn away from Israel." And Moses said to the judges of Israel, "Each of you kill his men who cling to Baal Pe'or."
> And look, a man of the Israelites came and brought forth to his kinsmen the Midianite woman before the eyes of Moses and before the eyes of the whole community of Israelites as they were weeping

at the entrance to the Tent of Meeting. And Phinehas son of Eleazar son of Aaron the priest saw, and he rose from the midst of the
community and took a spear in his hand.

And he came after the man of Israel into the alcove and
stabbed the two of them, the man of Israel and the woman, in her
alcove and the scourge was held back from the Israelites. And those
who died in the scourge came to twenty-four thousand. And the
LORD spoke to Moses, saying:

"Phinehas son of Eleazar son of Aaron the priest, turned away
My wrath from the Israelites when he zealously acted for My zeal
in their midst, and I did not put an end to the Israelites through my
zeal."[21]

What, precisely, was the sin of the people, for which twenty-four
thousand had to die in the scourge, and who knows how many by being
impaled before the sun? They had befriended the Moabites, who invited
them to participate in feasting and thus seduced them into worshiping
their gods. This was indeed inevitable. In the ancient world the only
legitimate excuse for consuming meat was through sacrifice, which involved arranging a feast, consecrating the animal to be slaughtered to
a deity (Baal Pe'or in this case), and enjoying the meal together. To
slaughter meant to sacrifice. Every meal involving the consumption of
meat was a sacrificial meal and a religious feast. Eating meat with other
people amounted to worshiping their gods, which meant violating the
first commandment concerning exclusive monotheism, namely, to admit
of no other gods. The distinction between slaughter and sacrifice that
Deuteronomy introduces (12:13–19) is yet another revolutionary feature
of the new religion.

It bears repeating that these cruel stories stem from an early phase of
monotheism, when the gods were still conceived of as actual rivals of
Yahweh and not as fictitious, imagined entities. In this period the exclusive worship of the One God was primarily a matter of absolute and
unconditional loyalty and faithfulness. Even in later times, when people
were convinced that there was only a single God, monotheism did not
cease to be a matter of loyalty and faithfulness. The Hebrew word *emunah*, which corresponds to our notion of faith, means "firmness," "fidelity," "steadiness." The device "No other gods!" remained valid even in
times when such other forces as the devil, materialism, sexuality, and
secular enticements replaced the pagan gods as competition to the
uniqueness of God.

The language of violence is somehow connected to notions of jealousy and loyalty, as well as conjugal fidelity with respect to the fear of seduction and the terrible punishment meted out for unfaithfulness and adultery. The laws concerning engaging in commerce with the peoples living in the countries to be conquered bespeak the same fear of seduction and enticement. One reads in Exodus (34:12–17):

> Watch yourself, lest you seal a covenant with the inhabitant of the land against which you come, lest he be a snare in your midst. For their altars you shall shatter and their pillars you shall smash and their cultic poles you shall cut down. For you shall not bow to another god, for the LORD, His name *is* Jealous, a jealous God he is. Lest you seal a covenant with the inhabitant of the land, and they whore after their gods and sacrifice to their gods, and he call you and you eat of his sacrifice, and you take from his daughters for your sons, and his daughters whore after their gods and make your sons whore after their gods.[22]

Stipulations concerning how to deal with enemy cities may also be seen in this context. Deuteronomy draws an important distinction here derived from the spirit of exclusive monotheism and its underlying distinction between true and false in matters of religion:

> When you approach a town to do battle against it, you shall call to it for peace. And it shall be if it answers you in peace and opens to you, all the people found within it shall become forced labor for you and serve you.
>
> And if it does not make peace with you, and does battle with you, you shall besiege it. And when the LORD your God gives it into your hand, you shall strike down all its males with the edge of the sword.
>
> Only the women, and the little ones, and the cattle, and everything that is in the town, all its booty you shall plunder for yourself; and you shall consume the booty of your enemy that the LORD your God gives to you.[23]

Up to this point the text corresponds closely to the usual practice of those times. However, there now follows the introduction of a quite novel distinction:

> Thus you shall do to all the towns far distant from you, which are not of the towns of these nations.
>
> Only, of the towns of these people that the LORD your God is about to give you in estate, you shall let no breathing creature live,

but you shall surely put them under the ban: the Hittite and the Amorite, the Canaanite and the Perizzite, the Hivite and the Jebusite, as the LORD your God has charged you, so that they will not teach you to do according to do all the abhorrent things that they did for their gods, and you would offend the LORD your God.[24]

Distant cities may be conquered and pillaged "normally." With respect to the cities of Canaan, however, the *herem* ban has to be executed, leaving nothing alive.[25] For the cities of Canaan are not foreign cities and towns but rather the Israelites' own towns that have not yet joined the new religion, converted to monotheism or, worse still, relapsed into worshiping other gods. The symbol "Canaan" refers to Hebrew paganism, midway between pagan and Jew, and therefore an object regarded with fear and abomination, like all in-between things.[26] From the denomination "Canaan," according to Othmar Keel, "the Deuteronomic texts construe a foreign, pre-Israelite population [*Vorbevölkerung*] against which Israel distinguishes itself essentially."[27] This distinction, however, is specific to biblical semantics. The term *herem* refers to a form of sacrifice and belongs to traditions of ritualized warfare that were not specific to ancient Israel but were also practiced in such neighboring countries as Moab[28] and Assyria.[29] Archaeology has shown that the vast majority of Israelites had always lived in the country and that no traces exist of a major invasion, destruction, and superimposition, which should have been the case if the biblical stories had any "historical truth" beyond their "narrative truth."[30] To be sure, one ought not to think that the purely fictitious and utopian Deuteronomist martial law was ever put into practice at the time of the kings of Judah.[31] It is, however, part of the cultural semantics of monotheism and consequently always has the potential of actualization, of being transformed into historical reality.

This may have already been the case in the sixties of the second century BCE, when Judas Maccabee based his resistance movement against Antiochus IV Epiphanes, the ruler of the Seleucid Empire, on Deutoronomic martial law. The case warrants a closer look.[32] The historical situation was in some respects similar to the century of oppression under Assyrian and Babylonian hegemony. Both periods were characterized on the Jewish or, rather, Judaic side by opposition and symbolic counterviolence.

According to I Maccabees, the ruler Antiochus IV devised a plan to transform his empire into a national state. He "issued a decree that there should be only one people," meaning that the various peoples living in his realm should not live according to their own laws and religions but according to a single unified imperial law. His means of bringing about national unity consisted of cultural rather than ethnic cleansing. There was to be only one culture, one law, and one religion in his realm. Within the framework of this new ideology, Jews who lived according to their own traditional law were not tolerated.[33]

Again according to 1 Maccabees, as a reaction to the scenes of forced assimilation, the priest Mattathias "was seized with the passionate zeal for the Law and he did what one Phinehas did to Simri, the son of Salu" (2:24). This scene in Numbers 25 served as a model for the Maccabean resistance. However, the Maccabean uprising was not only a movement of resistance against the Seleucid tyrant but also a civil war directed against the "Hellenists," or reformers, among the Maccabees' own people. Under Seleucid pressure, the Jewish population was split into two parties that fought with equal zeal, one for and the other against the Law.[34] Given this situation, the Jews had to decide whether to be for or against the Law since there was no third option. Tradition turned into a matter of choosing between life and death, similar to the choice Moses had presented to the children of Israel when he presented the Law:

> I call both heaven and earth to witness this day against you. I have set before you life and death, the blessing and the curse: choose thou life, that thou and thy seed may live.[35]

The Maccabees did not just defend themselves against the troops of Antiochus IV. They are recorded as having extinguished the life of entire Jewish towns and cities that had adopted the Hellenistic way of life according to the treatment that Deuteronomy prescribed for Canaanite and Israelite towns that had relapsed by adopting pagan rites:

> Should you hear in one of your towns which the LORD your God is about to give you to dwell there saying "Let us go and worship other gods" that you do not know. And you seek and inquire and ask well, and, look, the thing is true and well-founded, this abhorrence has been done in your midst, you shall surely strike down the inhabitants of that town by the edge of the sword, putting it under the ban, it and everything in it, and its beasts, by the edge of the sword. And all its booty you shall collect in the middle of its square and burn in the fire—the town and all its booty—altogether to the LORD your God, and it shall be an everlasting mound, it shall never be rebuilt.[36]

Judas Maccabee used this law as a script for his guerrilla warfare "that the scriptures may be fulfilled" (*hina plerothôsin hai graphai*).[37] "You shall conquer them and utterly destroy them. You shall make no covenant with them nor show mercy to them [*lo tekhonnem*]."[38] This is zealotry in its purest form of total engagement for God and his law (Heb. *qin'a* and Gk. *zelos*). In its literalism, it even foreshadows a fundamentalist attitude.

Even this may be pure literature, pure memory, like other scenes of violence in the biblical narrative. The books of Maccabees, compiled two generations after the event, codify the memory of the Hasmonaeans, the victorious party. The latter had good reason to present themselves as extraordinarily loyal to the law since they had themselves become assimilated, adopting Greek names, titles, dress, and manners.[39] If one is, in fact, dealing with literature here, it is a type based on an older and highly normative literature. This is not only the report of a series of events but also a quotation: the report of an event that reenacts a literary narrative. This seems to me to imply an element of fundamentalism. The most revolutionary innovation of biblical monotheism is perhaps its claim of regulating life in its entirety and not merely in terms of cult, ritual, and feast.

The Fulfillment of Scripture

This might be the right place to mention writing and literacy. Earlier I stated that Judas Maccabee based his warfare on Deuteronomy. This principle may be generalized. In the time of the Maccabees pious Jews based their entire lifestyles on the Scriptures.[40] The Torah, with its 613 commandments and prohibitions—including a growing system of interpretations and applications—served as a script for leading one's life, running one's business, performing the rituals, ruling the community—in short regulating every aspect of individual and collective existence. This was a new phenomenon in the history of writing as well as that of religion and civilization generally. Never before had writing served such comprehensive functions. One may call this new form of writing and literacy "canon."[41] In chapter 5 I distinguished between an informative and a performative use of writing. An example of the informative mode is the warning on a cigarette box stating: "Smoking may be hazardous to your health." A performative illustration might be the sign: "No Smoking." Whereas the warning provides the potential user with relevant knowledge, the sign expresses a prohibition. If I ignore the warning, I am running a personal risk. If I ignore the sign, I am committing an offense and may be punished. The new form of religion that made its first literary appearance in the Hebrew Bible used the performative mode of writing in order to influence the entire individual and collective life of human beings. No pagan religion had ever made similar claims. Religion had previously regulated commerce between human beings and divine or numinous powers, but not the entire realm of human action, experience, and thought. This totalizing claim on human life was the hallmark of the new religion that, for brevity's sake, is called monotheism and is realized by means of performative or canonized writing.[42]

As I demonstrated in chapter 5, the Torah does not inform us concerning how to administer justice; rather, it administers justice itself. Its performative claim does not stop at jurisdiction but extends to all aspects of life. It is this intensified form of writing, with its scriptural quality, that I call "canon." It is expressed in Deuteronomy in terms of two formulas. The first reads:

> You shall not add to the word that I charge you, and you shall not subtract from it. (4:2)

The second occurs two chapters later:

> And these words that I charge you today shall be upon your heart.
> You shall rehearse them to your sons and speak of them when you sit in your house and when you go on the way and when you lie down and when you rise (6:6–7).

In the first formula the script is closed; nothing may be added or subtracted. In the second the script must be reincarnated, internalized, and constantly taught and discussed by everyone. A life according to the script is required, a "life in quotations" (*zitathaftes Leben*, to use Thomas Mann's expression).[43] For every situation, every decision in life, you have to find and follow the appropriate verse. Life is fulfillment of Scripture. To be sure, in this extreme form the principle applies only to Judaism. Yet it is important to bear in mind that every religion of the new type — not only the monotheistic varieties but also Buddhism — is based on a canon. All of them share in common the performative mode of writing, the claim to regulate the entire individual and collective life according to a canon of sacred texts codifying the will of God. This principle of a Scripture-based way of life — what Max Weber has referred to as "methodische Lebensführung" (a methodical conducting of one's life) — seems to me a third characteristic of "monotheistic man."

At the time of the Maccabees, the emerging canon was already exerting its life-forming and transforming influence. People had begun to "live in quotations," as in the story of Phinehas, son of Eleazar, or the martial law of Deuteronomy 20. Some were even "dying in quotations." The Maccabean wars not only provide the first instances of religious warfare, or zeal, but also the purest form of passive zealotism, namely, martyrdom.[44] The readiness to die for the law is the expression of the same kind of zeal as the readiness to kill for it. The Hebrew term for martyrdom is *qiddush ha-shem* (hallowing the name), which corresponds to the very first request in the Christian Lord's Prayer: "Hallowed be thy name." The ideal form of dying for God or for the Law is to die with a scriptural quotation on one's lips.[45]

Martyrdom evolved as an extreme form of a lifestyle based on the law of living (and dying) "in quotations," and it did so simultaneously with the formation of a belief in the immortality of the soul and of rewards and punishments in the hereafter. This belief was contested among the Sadducees and the Pharisees, with the Pharisees' view persisting in Christianity and Rabbinic Judaism as well as in Islam. The martyr acts as a citizen of the "coming world" (*olam ha-bah* in Jewish terminology or the "kingdom of God" in Christian terminology). The Jewish term refers to Apocalypticism, a religious orientation that arose within Judaism at the time of the Maccabean wars. The days of this world, in which injustice and oppression prevail, are numbered. The signs point to a fall and a new beginning. The dawn of the world to come appears precisely during the worst period of suffering. Such language may express the new apocalyptic atmosphere that in those days inspired not only Jews but also many circles and movements in the ancient world, from China and Persia to Egypt, Rome, and beyond. Apocalypticism and oppression go hand in hand. Apocalypticism is a form of religious and intellectual resistance, and martyrdom requires violent oppression and persecution in order to exist. Martyrdom is a religious response to violence. It is true that martyrs are murdered not for religious but for political reasons; they are treated as rebels, not as heretics. In their own minds, however, they die for a religious principle. This idea is only possible within the framework of the new religion, with its motto "no other gods," because it is a matter of refusing to worship idols and to eat sacrificial meat, that is, to commit actions deemed incompatible with the Law, with true religion and the life based on it. This category of religious incompatibility and the distinction between true and false on which it is based is the hallmark of the new form of religion called monotheism. This distinction generates a cultural semantics that, in its turn, generates such new forms of human action as religiously motivated killing and martyrdom, its passive counterpart.

The Rhetoric of Conversion

The language of violence as such is nothing new in the ancient world. Its natural home or framework is the royal inscription, where it fulfills a well-defined function based on the principle that, to quote Niklas Luhmann, "Politics and law are only possible if they are able to use physical violence for their enforcement and to efficiently exclude counterviolence."[46] The empires of the ancient Near East are therefore based on a cultural semantics aimed at uniting and controlling great masses of subjects and vassals under one system of government. The aim of biblical monotheism, conversely, is the unequivocal liberation first of the chosen people and then of mankind from such all-encompassing claims of political power as are symbolically represented by Pharaonic Egypt in the house of serfdom. Israel obviously had to move away from these oppressive systems of political violence, but why did it have to adopt motifs of violence in its own foundational cultural semantics? It is useless to object that violence plays only a marginal role since God shows mercy to thousands who love him and visits the iniquities of those who hate him onto only three or four generations. Behind this opposition between love and hatred there is the distinction between friend and foe that is fundamental to the language of violence. Even more useless and mistaken, it would appear, is the conventional Christian opposition between the "jealous and vengeful God of the Old Testament" and the Christian "God of love." The jealousy of God derives from his love. It is a loving God, a God passionately inclined toward humankind and his chosen people, who makes the distinction between friend and foe. Not coincidentally, this distinction appears in the context of the prohibition against images, in which the motto "No other gods" finds its clearest expression.

> You shall make you no carved likeness, or image of what *is* in the heavens above or what *is* on the earth below or what *is* in the waters beneath the earth.
> You shall not bow to them and you shall not worship them, for I am the LORD your God, a jealous God, reckoning the crime of fathers with sons, and with the third generation and with the fourth, for My foes, and doing kindness to the thousandth generation for My friends and for those who keep My commands.[47]

It should now be clear how the language of violence and the de-
mand "No other gods!" are connected in the Hebrew Bible. The boundary drawn here between the One God and the other gods shares with
politics and law the principle that it must be "able to use physical violence . . . and to efficiently exclude counterviolence."[48] All this is easily
understandable in a context in which these other gods, whose worship
was prohibited, were still acknowledged in terms of their existence and
power to attract. For this reason exclusive monotheism had to draw on a
semantics of breaking away, of exclusion, of conversion.

I wish to return to Canaan and the peculiar role it plays in the
Deuteronomic tradition as a symbol of Hebrew paganism. The Hebrew
Bible is the document of a society that underwent a cultural metamorphosis under extreme political pressure, which was unique and unprece-
dented at the time. This metamorphosis is quite insufficiently described
in terms of a progression "from polytheism via monolatry to monotheism." One is dealing here not with a development following evolutionary
lines for which parallels and regularities might be adduced, but rather
with a revolutionary process that, on the plane of individual experience,
can be compared only to a conversion. The converts must not forget their
past. They must remain aware of their old form of existence in order to
retain their new identity all the more resolutely and steadily and to steer
clear of any form of relapse. In this respect, assimilation is the opposite of
conversion in the sense that it requires complete oblivion of one's original identity. These psychological mechanisms are clearly expressed in
biblical writings, specifically in Deuteronomy, which is dominated by a
single concern, namely, the preservation of memory and the concomi-
tant fear of forgetting.[49] It repeatedly impresses on its readers the warning against forgetting. Forgetting, in this case, is the same as assimilation
or relapse: assimilation to, or relapsing into, the customs of Canaan, the
country to conquer and to possess. If one realizes that Canaan is just a
cipher for one's own pagan past and that of one's neighbors, who did
not yet undergo the same metamorphosis, one understands that assimilation or forgetting is tantamount to relapsing into one's former existence, which is the fear of all converts. At the root of the pronounced
anti-Canaanism of Deuteronomy and its language of violence lies the
pathos of conversion: the passion of a life-changing commitment, the
fear of relapse, and the resolve to exterminate the pagan within.

Like martyrdom and religiously motivated warfare, conversion is one
of those phenomena that are possible only in the sphere of exclusive
monotheism, as expressed in the motto "no other gods!" Conversion to
pagan religions is not possible.[50] This is primarily due to the fact that the

new form of religion is not just a question of cult and worldview but requires the commitment of the entire human being, the whole of one's life, during feast days and every day of the year. Secondarily it is due to the category of incompatibility and of exclusion implicit in this motto. We are dealing here with a new, intensified, emphatic notion of truth that does not permit any compromise with what it excludes as untrue. Here one must commit oneself. Here, within the constraint to make such a commitment, the duty to remember, the fear of forgetting, the compulsion of constant internal awareness—all are sources of the motifs of violence deeply rooted in the cultural semantics of monotheistic religions. In this context it is important to realize that violence is not inherent in the distinction between true and false in religion in the sense of a necessary consequence. Rather, it is just a potential implication and a possibility that could turn into reality under certain historical circumstances, especially in situations involving fear and uncertainty. Why can the distinction between true and false lead to violence? The language of violence is exploited as a resource in the political struggle for power in order to stir up fear and hatred and to win mass acceptance. It is therefore necessary to historicize these motives by tracing them to their origins. One must uncover their genesis in order to restrict their validity.

Cultura facit saltus: biblical memory represents the reception of the Torah and monotheism as such a cultural leap of primary importance. Who can say whether we ourselves, as we reflect on monotheism, are not involved in a development that, in retrospect, will perhaps be represented as a leap of comparable magnitude? Perhaps it is this postmodern consciousness, on the threshold of a new digital age of globalism, that urges us to render an account to ourselves concerning the Mosaic foundations of our world.

If the violent potential of its semantic implications remains the price of monotheism, it is also important to remember for what this price has been paid. Monotheism means exodus, that is, enlightenment. It means the liberation of mankind from the constraints of the powers of this world, of the given. It means the discovery of an alternative realm of human commitment and investment beyond the traditional realms of state, society, and nature. It means the discovery of the inner man and new dimensions of subjectivity. As a final consequence, the distinction between true and false means the distinction between God and world.[51] If this distinction enables man to go beyond the given powers of cosmos and politics in his search for God, it pushes us to go beyond even the sacred texts and truths of traditional religion. This is the message of monotheism in its most radical expression. Take, for example, Arnold

Schoenberg's opera *Moses und Aron*. Schoenberg places the biblical depiction of God as a jealous God of love and wrath, of mercy and justice, into the mouth not of Moses but of Aron, thereby debunking it as just another image, as false as an image can be (*falsch wie ein Bild nur sein kann*). There is no end to the search for truth since there is no end to interpretation. To repeat, Judaism can teach us a lesson concerning how to deal with the language of violence. Othmar Keel may be right after all in drawing the distinction between "immature" and "true" monotheism. Judaism somehow "matured" and went beyond a theology of jealousy and zealotry at the same time that the ideal of zeal, of dying for God, was being adopted by the early Christians. The biblical texts quoted earlier were in a sense placed into "cold storage." Although they retained their place in the textual tradition, they did not do so in the cultural memory of Judaism. They are not assigned in the Talmudic education provided in the yeshiva and play no role in modern Jewish discourse.[52] Rabbinic Judaism managed to overcome and leave behind the concept of "zeal" that had motivated the sectarian movements of the Second Temple period and their inner strife, defusing the overheated atmosphere of apocalyptic thought and transforming antagonism (with its severe social and political consequences) into dispute and dialogue, however controversial.[53] The rabbis deliberately overlooked "the passages that call on a faithful Jew to take up arms against the 'abominations' of paganism."[54]

I have demonstrated that the language of violence and intolerance in the Hebrew Bible is a feat of memory and not of history. It belongs to the ways in which biblical monotheism represents and remembers its installation and not to the ways it has actually been installed. Since it belongs to memory, it has as much to do with forgetting as with remembering. We cannot change history, but we can change the myths into which history is continuously transformed through collective memory. This is the road that should be taken. Monotheism itself pushes us to go beyond the logic of exclusivity and the language of violence. Those who believe in revelation must realize that the latter has put humankind on a new path toward truth but not in the possession of "the" truth. The truth of any concrete religion will always remain relative not in relation to any other concrete religion—which would end up by reducing both truth and religion to banality—but in relation to absolute Truth, which is the transcendent and necessarily hidden goal of every religion.

Conclusion

The Mosaic Distinction

The Mosaic Distinction, as I defined it over a decade ago,[1] is the distinction between true and false in religion. This proposal has met with many objections from biblical scholars,[2] who insist that this distinction was certainly not one of Moses' crucial concerns when he led his people out of Egypt. He was concerned with freedom and slavery, justice and injustice, good and evil rather than with questions of religious truth, let alone orthodoxy. This view is correct and remains so even when one replaces the "historical" Moses with the "symbolic" Moses, that is, with Moses as a figure not of history but of memory. What biblical tradition ascribes to Moses has little to do with theology but rather more with ethics, politics, law, behavior, dietary rules, social organization, ritual observances, and abstention from worshiping other gods or God in the wrong way. All of these things concern questions not of "truth" but of loyalty and correctness. Moses did not leave Egypt because of its wrong or false religion. The terms "true" and "false," my critics insist, refer to philosophy rather than religion. This latter distinction has been considered only by Greek philosophers, but not by Moses. It should consequently be dubbed the "Parmenidean" distinction. This is again correct, and it explains why Moses has been hailed by many Greek writers as a philosopher, a forerunner of Plato, who in turn came to be recognized as a Greek Moses.[3] Strabo wrote that Moses was an Egyptian priest who left Egypt with a group of followers out of dissatisfaction with Egyptian polytheism.[4] Three hundred years earlier, Hecataeus of Abdera praised Moses for the purity of his concept of God.[5] To impute to Moses the distinction between true and false in religion is to perpetuate this misunderstanding

127

and to turn the god of Abraham, Isaac, and Jacob into the god of the philosophers.

Still, there is much that Moses—always to be understood in the sense of "what the name 'Moses' stands for" and not "what the (historical) 'man Moses' did and believed"—rejected with regard to Egypt, and even more so with regard to "Canaan." These often violent rejections were based on a single underlying, decisive distinction that called for commitment and conversion. It is this underlying distinction that generated not only rejections, "abominations," and exclusions of all sorts but also social distinctions that led to the formation of segregative communities, or "enclave cultures," to use Mary Douglas's terminology. Although I do not insist on the determination of this distinction in terms of "true" and "false," I emphasize the distinction as such, which I hold to be an innovative cultural event of the highest importance.

Perhaps the best way to deal with the distinction I have in mind is not to determine it at all but rather to take it as a kind of deep-structure concept that, on the surface of articulate speech, may be realized in terms of good and evil, just and unjust, pure and impure, freedom and slavery, loyalty and disloyalty, religion and idolatry, orthodoxy and heresy. Eventually it may even be realized in terms of truth and untruth, god and world, spirit and matter, as well as other more philosophical categories. Many of these "surface" distinctions (with the exception of religion and idolatry, orthodoxy and heresy) are to be found in other religions and cultural contexts as well, but they are not related to the same deep-structure distinction that calls for commitment and conversion. The new form of religion based on this distinction creates a frame of communal and individual life that is clearly set off from other forms of life—so clearly and distinctly, in fact, that entering it amounts to a complete transformation or "conversion;" while leaving it amounts to "apostasy," defection, or desertion, and defending it may involve either killing or dying for it.

The Biblical Theory of Paganism

If one looks carefully at some of the biblical texts in which the distinction between the true God and the other gods, or true belief and idolatry, is stressed, one sees that idolatry is not only associated with such evils as injustice, lawlessness, oppression, violence, murder, and fornication but above all with a lack of insight, a failure to recognize the truth.

Selecting Psalm 82 as an example, here the distinction between true and false appears in the distinction between justice and its opposites, namely, oppression, exploitation, violence, and lawlessness. Surprisingly, the distinction also appears in the form of a distinction between "God" and "the gods."

A PSALM BY ASAPH
God presides in the great assembly.
    He judges among the gods.

"How long will you judge unjustly,
    and show partiality to the wicked?" Selah.

"Defend the weak, the poor, and the fatherless.
    Maintain the rights of the poor and oppressed.
Rescue the weak and needy.
    Deliver them out of the hand of the wicked."

They don't know, neither do they understand.
    They walk back and forth in darkness.
All the foundations of the earth are shaken.

I said, "You are gods,
    all of you are sons of the Most High.
Nevertheless you shall die like men,
    and fall like one of the rulers."

Arise, God, judge the earth,
    for all the nations are your inheritance.

Ps. 82:1–7

There are several speech constellations involved in this psalm. Verse 1 is spoken by an anonymous speaker who addresses no one in particular. Verses 2–4 are spoken by "God" (YHWH replaced by Elohim) addressing the other gods within the assembly of gods. Although verse 5 is again formulated impersonally, it is also spoken by God, who, in verse 6, refers to himself as "I" and once again addresses the other gods in announcing their imminent death. The last verse is again spoken by an anonymous speaker (most likely the same one who uttered verse 1), who this time addresses God and bids him to rule over the nations, which, following the demise of their gods, have fallen to his lot.

The theme of this seemingly polytheistic text, which reckons with a world full of gods, is the relationship between the only true God and the other gods, that is, between monotheism and paganism. The other gods represent the other religions, whose "paganism" is bluntly denounced as wickedness, partiality, injustice, and oppression of the poor and needy. Pagan gods typically side with the mighty because the system of paganism knows no distinction between state and religion. Paganism reflects worship of political power, wealth, and physical strength. Only "God" sides with the poor, the widowed, and the orphaned. He represents the sole power that breaks the "law of the fishes," as it is called in Indian tradition, according to which the big fish eat the little ones. Verse 5 makes clear that paganism is a matter of cognition. Paganism implies the inability to recognize the truth, leading to injustice, lawlessness, and oppression. It is a state of stupidity and madness. The psalm announces the death not of God but of the gods. On this day God will "inherit" the whole earth and bestow his justice upon it.

Obviously this is not an early, polytheistic psalm but a rather late one reflecting on the relation between monotheism and paganism. The latter is criticized here not for its "idolatry" but for its injustice, the same criticism that Exodus applies to Pharaonic Egypt.

In order to criticize the "idolatry" of the pagans, biblical literature uses another genre, namely, the satire of trades.[6] This well-known literary genre is frequently attested in ancient Egypt. Its method is to depict the specific activity of a member of a given profession or trade in isolation, abstracted from all significant frames and contexts reflecting the social division of labor. A specialized profession is shown as consisting of an absurd hustling and bustling without any meaningful purpose and result, in an atmosphere similar to that encountered in the works of Samuel Beckett or Franz Kafka.[7] It is with a similar intentionally uncomprehending gaze that the caricatures of this genre regard the rites of foreign religions.

In reading some of these texts, one immediately becomes aware of their interdependence. It seems obvious that one is dealing with examples of a rather tightly defined genre, or with texts following a common model. In the first two examples one encounters similar confrontations between the God of Israel and the gods of the "nations," who are here demoted from the rank of *elohim* to mere "idols."

> Why should the nations say,
> "Where is their God, now?"
> But our God is in the heavens.
> He does whatever he pleases.
> Their idols are silver and gold,

the work of men's hands.
They have mouths, but they don't speak.
They have eyes, but they don't see.
They have ears, but they don't hear.
They have noses, but they don't smell.
They have hands, but they don't feel.
They have feet, but they don't walk,
neither do they speak through their throat.
Those who make them will be like them;
yes, everyone who trusts in them.
Israel, trust in Yahweh!
He is their help and their shield.

Psalm 115:2–9

Hear the word which Yahweh speaks to you, house of Israel!

Thus says Yahweh, "Don't learn the way of the nations, and don't be dismayed at the signs of the sky; for the nations are dismayed at them or the customs of the peoples are vanity; for one cuts a tree out of the forest, the work of the hands of the workman with the axe.

They deck it with silver and with gold; they fasten it with nails and with hammers, that it not move.

They are like a palm tree, of turned work, and don't speak: they must be carried, because they can't go. Don't be afraid of them; for they can't do evil, neither is it in them to do good."

There is none like you, Yahweh; you are great, and your name is great in might.

Who should not fear you, King of the nations? For it appertains to you; because among all the wise men of the nations, and in all their royal estate, there is none like you.

But they are together brutish and foolish: the instruction of idols! it is but a stock.

There is silver beaten into plates, which is brought from Tarshish, and gold from Uphaz, the work of the artificer and of the hands of the goldsmith; blue and purple for their clothing; they are all the work of skilful men.

But Yahweh is the true God; he is the living God, and an everlasting King: at his wrath the earth trembles, and the nations are not able to abide his indignation.

You shall say this to them: The gods that have not made the heavens and the earth, these shall perish from the earth, and from under the heavens.

He has made the earth by his power, he has established the

world by his wisdom, and by his understanding has he stretched
out the heavens:

when he utters his voice, there is a tumult of waters in the heavens, and he causes the vapors to ascend from the ends of the earth;
he makes lightnings for the rain, and brings forth the wind out of
his treasuries.

Every man is become brutish and is without knowledge; every
goldsmith is disappointed by his engraved image; for his molten
image is falsehood, and there is no breath in them.

They are vanity, a work of delusion: in the time of their visitation they shall perish.

The portion of Jacob is not like these; for he is the former of all
things; and Israel is the tribe of his inheritance: Yahweh of Armies
is his name. (Jeremiah 10:1–16)

The following chapter from (Deutero-)Isaiah comes particularly
close to the Egyptian "satire of trades." This is the text that represents
the locus classicus of the genre of religious satire:

Everyone who makes an engraved image is vain.
The things that they delight in will not profit.
Their own witnesses don't see, nor know, that they may be disappointed.
Who has fashioned a god,
or molds an image that is profitable for nothing?
Behold, all his fellows will be disappointed;
and the workmen are mere men.
Let them all be gathered together. Let them stand up.
They will fear. They will be put to shame together.
The blacksmith takes an axe, works in the coals,
fashions it with hammers, and works it with his strong arm.
He is hungry, and his strength fails;
he drinks no water, and is faint.
The carpenter stretches out a line.
He marks it out with a pencil. He shapes it with planes.
He marks it out with compasses, and shapes it like the figure of a man,
with the beauty of a man, to reside in a house.
He cuts down cedars for himself,
and takes the cypress and the oak,
and strengthens for himself one among the trees of the forest.
He plants a fir tree, and the rain nourishes it.
Then it will be for a man to burn;
and he takes some of it, and warms himself.
Yes, he burns it, and bakes bread.

Yes, he makes a god, and worships it;
he makes it an engraved image, and falls down to it.
He burns part of it in the fire.
With part of it, he eats meat.
He roasts a roast, and is satisfied.
Yes, he warms himself,
and says, "Aha! I am warm. I have seen the fire."
The rest of it he makes into a god,
even his engraved image.
He bows down to it and worships,
and prays to it, and says, "Deliver me; for you are my god!"
They don't know, neither do they consider:
for he has shut their eyes, that they can't see;
and their hearts, that they can't understand.
No one thinks, neither is there knowledge nor understanding to say,
"I have burned part of it in the fire.
Yes, I have also baked bread on its coals.
I have roasted meat and eaten it.
Shall I make the rest of it into an abomination?
Shall I bow down to a tree trunk?"
He feeds on ashes.
A deceived heart has turned him aside;
and he can't deliver his soul,
nor say, "Isn't there a lie in my right hand?"

Isaiah 44:9–20

By far the longest and most elaborate specimen of religious satire is to be found in the apocryphal Wisdom of Solomon, a text probably dating from the first century BCE (quoted below in the King James version). It is obviously based on Isaiah 44 but takes (Deutero-)Isaiah's arguments much further. The argument against idolatry unfolds in three long chapters (13–15). Chapter 13 distinguishes between two groups among the idolaters: those who worship cosmic elements, thus confusing creator and creation; and those who worship the works of their own hands. Both are mistaken forms of "false religion," although the first is less so and remains closer to true religion than the second one.

> *1:* Surely vain are all men by nature, who are ignorant of God, and could not out of the good things that are seen know him that is: neither by considering the works did they acknowledge the workmaster; *2:* But deemed either fire, or wind, or the swift air, or the circle of the stars, or the violent water, or the lights of heaven, to be the gods which govern the world. *3:* With whose beauty if they

being delighted took them to be gods; let them know how much better the Lord of them is: for the first author of beauty hath created them. *4:* But if they were astonished at their power and virtue, let them understand by them, how much mightier he is that made them. *5:* For by the greatness and beauty of the creatures proportionably the maker of them is seen. *6:* But yet for this they are the less to be blamed: for they peradventure err, seeking God, and desirous to find him. *7:* For being conversant in his works they search him diligently, and believe their sight: because the things are beautiful that are seen. *8:* Howbeit neither are they to be pardoned. *9:* For if they were able to know so much, that they could aim at the world; how did they not sooner find out the Lord thereof? *10:* But miserable are they, and in dead things is their hope, who call them gods, which are the works of men's hands, gold and silver, to shew art in, and resemblances of beasts, or a stone good for nothing, the work of an ancient hand. *11:* Now a carpenter that felleth timber, after he hath sawn down a tree meet for the purpose, and taken off all the bark skilfully round about, and hath wrought it handsomely, and made a vessel thereof fit for the service of man's life; *12:* And after spending the refuse of his work to dress his meat, hath filled himself; *13:* And taking the very refuse among those which served to no use, being a crooked piece of wood, and full of knots, hath carved it diligently, when he had nothing else to do, and formed it by the skill of his understanding, and fashioned it to the image of a man; *14:* Or made it like some vile beast, laying it over with vermilion, and with paint colouring it red, and covering every spot therein; *15:* And when he had made a convenient room for it, set it in a wall, and made it fast with iron; *16:* For he provided for it that it might not fall, knowing that it was unable to help itself; for it is an image, and hath need of help; *17:* Then maketh he prayer for his goods, for his wife and children, and is not ashamed to speak to that which hath no life. *18:* For health he calleth upon that which is weak: for life prayeth to that which is dead; for aid humbly beseecheth that which hath least means to help: and for a good journey he asketh of that which cannot set a foot forward; *19:* And for gaining and getting, and for good success of his hands, asketh ability to do of him, that is most unable to do any thing. (Solomon 13:1–19)

Chapter 14 at first continues this line of argumentation, pointing to the inability of idols to save the needy in situations involving turmoil and danger, but then proceeds to formally curse both the idol and its maker.

1: Again, one preparing himself to sail, and about to pass through the raging waves, calleth upon a piece of wood more rotten than the vessel that carrieth him. *2:* For verily desire of gain devised that, and the workman built it by his skill. *3:* But thy providence, O Father, governeth it: for thou hast made a way in the sea, and a safe path in the waves; *4:* Shewing that thou canst save from all danger: yea, though a man went to sea without art. *5:* Nevertheless thou wouldest not that the works of thy wisdom should be idle, and therefore do men commit their lives to a small piece of wood, and passing the rough sea in a weak vessel are saved. *6:* For in the old time also, when the proud giants perished, the hope of the world governed by thy hand escaped in a weak vessel, and left to all ages a seed of generation. *7:* For blessed is the wood whereby righteousness cometh. *8:* But that which is made with hands is cursed, as well it, as he that made it: he, because he made it; and it, because, being corruptible, it was called god. *9:* For the ungodly and his ungodliness are both alike hateful unto God. *10:* For that which is made shall be punished together with him that made it. *11:* Therefore even upon the idols of the Gentiles shall there be a visitation: because in the creature of God they are become an abomination, and stumbling blocks to the souls of men, and a snare to the feet of the unwise. *12:* For the devising of idols was the beginning of spiritual fornication, and the invention of them the corruption of life. *13:* For neither were they from the beginning, neither shall they be for ever. *14:* For by the vain glory of men they entered into the world, and therefore shall they come shortly to an end. (Solomon 14:1–14)

The second part of the chapter presents a highly interesting theory about the twofold origin of idol-making, namely, death and dominion. The idol compensates for absence by representing both the deceased, who is missed by the surviving family, and the ruler, who is absent from his distant subjects. Out of these relatively "innocent" origins, however, paganism developed as a false religion, taking these images for gods.

15: For a father afflicted with untimely mourning, when he hath made an image of his child soon taken away, now honoured him as a god, which was then a dead man, and delivered to those that were under him ceremonies and sacrifices. *16:* Thus in process of time an ungodly custom grown strong was kept as a law, and graven images were worshipped by the commandments of kings. *17:* Whom men could not honour in presence, because they dwelt far off, they took the counterfeit of his visage from far, and made an express image of a king whom they honoured, to the end that by this their forwardness they might flatter him that was absent, as if he were present. *18:* Also the singular diligence of the artificer did help to set forward the ignorant to more superstition. *19:* For he, peradventure willing to please one in authority, forced all his skill to make the resemblance of the best fashion. *20:* And so the multitude, allured by the grace of the work, took him now for a god, which a little before was but honoured. *21:* And this was an occasion to deceive the world: for men, serving either calamity or tyranny, did ascribe unto stones and stocks the incommunicable name. (Solomon 14:15–21)

The last part of the chapter again falls into debunking and cursing the idolaters in the strongest terms.

22: Moreover, this was not enough for them, that they erred in the knowledge of God; but whereas they lived in the great war of ignorance, those so great plagues called they peace. *23:* For whilst they slew their children in sacrifices, or used secret ceremonies, or made revellings of strange rites; *24:* They kept neither lives nor marriages any longer undefiled: but either one slew another traitorously, or grieved him by adultery. *25:* So that there reigned in all men without exception blood, manslaughter, theft, and dissimulation, corruption, unfaithfulness, tumults, perjury, *26:* Disquieting of good men, forgetfulness of good turns, defiling of souls, changing of kind, disorder in marriages, adultery, and shameless uncleanness. *27:* For the worshipping of idols not to be named is the beginning, the cause, and the end, of all evil. *28:* For either they are mad when they be merry, or prophesy lies, or live unjustly, or else lightly forswear themselves. *29:* For insomuch as their trust is in idols, which have no life; though they swear falsely, yet they look not to be hurt. *30:* Howbeit for both causes shall they be justly punished: both because they thought not well of God, giving heed unto idols, and also unjustly swore in deceit, despising holiness. *31:* For it is not the power of them by whom they swear: but it is the just vengeance of sinners, that punisheth always the offence of the ungodly. (Solomon 14:22–31)

Chapter 15 ends the invective against idolatry as the epitome of false religion by stressing the difference between idolatry and true religion.

1: But thou, O God, art gracious and true, longsuffering, and in mercy ordering all things, *2:* For if we sin, we are thine, knowing thy power: but we will not sin, knowing that we are counted thine. *3:* For to know thee is perfect righteousness: yea, to know thy power is the root of immortality. *4:* For neither did the mischievous invention of men deceive us, nor an image spotted with divers colours, the painter's fruitless labour; *5:* The sight whereof enticeth fools to lust after it, and so they desire the form of a dead image, that hath no breath. *6:* Both they that make them, they that desire them, and they that worship them, are lovers of evil things, and are worthy to have such things to trust upon. *7:* For the potter, tempering soft earth, fashioneth every vessel with much labour for our service: yea, of the same clay he maketh both the vessels that serve for clean uses, and likewise also all such as serve to the contrary: but what is the use of either sort, the potter himself is the judge. *8:* And employing his labours lewdly, he maketh a vain god of the same clay, even he which a little before was made of earth himself, and within a little while after returneth to the same, out when his life which was lent him shall be demanded. *9:* Notwithstanding his care is, not that he shall have much labour, nor that his life is short: but striveth to excel goldsmiths and silversmiths, and endeavoureth to do like the workers in brass, and counteth it his glory to make counterfeit things. *10:* His heart is ashes, his hope is more vile than earth, and his life of less value than clay: *11:* Forasmuch as he knew not his Maker, and him that inspired into him an active soul, and breathed in a living spirit. *12:* But they counted our life a pastime, and our time here a market for gain: for, say they, we must be getting every way, though it be by evil means. *13:* For this man, that of earthly matter maketh brittle vessels and graven images, knoweth himself to offend above all others. *14:* And all the enemies of thy people, that hold them in subjection, are most foolish, and are more miserable than very Babes. *15:* For they counted all the idols of the heathen to be gods: which neither have the use of eyes to see, nor noses to draw breath, nor ears to hear, nor fingers of hands to handle; and as for their feet, they are slow to go. *16:* For man made them, and he that borrowed his own spirit fashioned them: but no man can make a god like unto himself. *17:* For being mortal, he worketh a dead thing with wicked hands: for he himself is better than the things which he worshippeth: whereas he lived once, but they never. *18:* Yea, they worshipped those beasts also that are most hateful: for being compared together, some are worse than others. *19:* Neither are they beautiful, so much as to be desired in respect of beasts: but they went without the praise of God and his blessing. (Solomon 15:1–19)

Of course, this is an apocryphal text that must not be taken as representative of monotheistic intolerance. The sages were undoubtedly right in excluding this text with its stark polemics from the canon and in denying it any normative authority. However, this text could never have been written except in a monotheistic context. It may not represent but is certainly expressive of attitudes that were not uncommon among Jews and Christians.

One of the most interesting aspects of this polemical construction of the other religion as "idolatry" is the combination of ignorance (not knowing the truth), evil (not knowing the good and just), sexual offense, defilement, and physical repulsion. Idols and idolatrous rites become the object of "abomination." The Hebrew term *to'ebah* has strong physical connotations and closely corresponds to the concept of "abjection" and the "abject" as defined and analyzed by Julia Kristeva.[8]

Is Tolerant Monotheism Possible?

This monotheistic concept of religion probably did not emerge in its pure form until late antiquity in the struggles for contradistinctive self-definition involving Judaism, Christianity, and Gnosticism.[9] Even if Moses—the "symbolic Moses"—is not to be associated with that emergence, the concept of the "Law" and of entering the Law by way of commitment and conversion, which is precisely what the name Moses stands for, he nevertheless laid the groundwork. It created a new form of normative identity based not on birth, place, descent, citizenship, or other biological and/or political ties but on adherence to a complex of laws, rules, and beliefs. Although it is true that Judaism never overcame the ethnical or biological determinators of belonging and identity, and that only Christianity broke with these ties, the original impulse to make identity rather than biology or politics a question of commitment, formation, memory, and obedience or observance can be traced back to the Deuteronomistic concept of "Moses."

This impulse is part of that greater move of "staying back and looking beyond" which is the hallmark of the "Axial Age" or, to use Benjamin Schwartz's phrase, the "Age of Transcendence,"[10] the act of going beyond the given. Polytheism, or "Cosmotheism," may be characterized as a theory of the given capable of making people feel totally at home in the world. It was this principle of "feeling at home" that made poets, artists, and philosophers of the eighteenth century look back nostalgically to paganism and that is already prominent in the Hermetic text I quoted at the end of chapter 2. Monotheism laid the foundations for an alternative principle of "naturalization," or feeling at home in an invisible world that was not "given" but rather promised and mysteriously emergent. This holds true both for "inclusive" (all gods are One) and "exclusive" (no god but God) monotheism. Monotheism is the response to experiences of estrangement and alienation that made people lose their sense of feeling at home in a world that had turned hostile and inhospitable. These were people who had been deported from their home countries; oppressed by foreign domination; and had suffered various injustices, including corruption, exploitation, wars, conquests, political and economic crises, and instability.[11] Hegel's dictum that the periods of happiness constitute the empty pages in the book of history holds true not only for political history but also for the history of religion.[12] The Bible, it is true, is full of praise for the beauties of the world, which bespeak the greatness of its creator. Moreover, the notion of nature as the other book of God had been prominent in Christian tradition since the twelfth century. There is much to be said in support of even biblical religion being concerned with making human beings feel at home in the world, placing them—being fashioned in the image of God—above all other creatures. The Hebrew Bible is polyphonic, a book of many voices, and the origins of monotheism constitute only one of these voices. It is this voice, however, that changed the Western world and constitutes the greatest cultural event in its long history.

Whenever its idea of truth is conceived of as something both absolute and scripturally revealed, that is, "given," the intolerance inherent in monotheism is irreducible. The concepts of the "absolute" and the "given" are mutually exclusive. Anything "absolute" is categorically transcendent and hidden, and anything "given" is categorically relative and open to transformation. Concrete religions such as Judaism, Christianity, Islam, Buddhism, and Hinduism belong within the sphere of the "given" and draw their legitimacy not from their (exclusive) possession of but rather from their (common) relation or aspiration toward Truth. This concept approximates the eighteenth-century concept of *religio duplex*, the distinction between popular (exoteric) and elite (esoteric) religion. In its modern form, the position of popular religion is held by the various concrete religions, with their irreducible and irreconcilable differences. The position of elite religion is held by various forms of highly compatible, albeit nonconvergent, forms of religious "wisdom" or "deep religion," as represented by such sages as Albert Schweitzer, Mahatma Gandhi, and Rabindranath Tagore. There are many concrete, or "surface," religions but only one "deep" religion. This attitude toward religious truth roughly corresponds to the eighteenth-century ideal of tolerance as expressed, for instance, in Lessing's parable of the three rings in *Nathan der Weise*. However, Christian theologians such as Karl Barth and Dietrich Bonhoeffer—who rejected the term "religion" altogether as applied to Christianity because of its inherent plurality and ensuant relativism—claimed for Christianity itself the status of deep religion. The latter, however, can never assume the form of an articulate system of norms and dogmas. Deep religion focuses on a point beyond the Mosaic Distinction between true and false religion. Surface, or concrete, religions always exist in the plural. There is no "one religion" any more than there is "one civilization" or "one language"—and the extant religions must acknowledge their status. The partial analogy of language may prove helpful. Although there is no single human language but rather a plurality of concrete human languages (Fr. *langues*), there is only a single human capacity for speech (Fr. *langage*). Correspondingly, although there will always be an irreducible plurality of human religions, there is only one common human capacity for religion and one common search for universal truth.

In his influential book *Jerusalem, or, Religious Power and Judaism* (1783), Moses Mendelssohn rejects the concept of "revealed truth" with regard to Judaism:

> I believe that Judaism knows nothing of a *revealed religion*, in the sense in which it is taken by Christians. The Israelites have a divine legislation: laws, commandments, statutes, rules of life, instruction in the will of God, and lessons how to conduct themselves in order to attain both temporal and spiritual happiness: those laws commandments, etc., were revealed to them through Moses, in a miraculous and supernatural manner; but no dogmas, no saving truths, no general self-evident propositions: Those the Lord always reveals to us, the same as to the rest of mankind, by *nature*, and by *events;* but never in *spoken* or *written* words [of revelation].[13]

He goes on to distinguish between three kinds of truth:

> 1. Religious dogmas and propositions of immutable truths of God, of his government providence, without which man can neither be enlightened nor happy. These were not forced on the belief of the people, by threats of eternal or temporal punishment, but suitably to the nature and evidence of immutable truths, recommended for rational consideration. They needed not be suggested by direct revelation, or promulgated by words or writing, which are understood only in this or that place, at this or that time. The Supreme Being revealed them all to all rational beings, by events

and by ideas, and inscribed them in their soul, in a character legible and intelligible at all times, and in all places.

2. Historical truths, or accounts of the occurrences of the primitive world, especially memoirs of the lives of the first ancestors of the nation; of their knowledge of the true correction immediately following thereon; of the covenant which God entered into with them, and his frequent promise to make their descendants a nation dedicated to himself. These historical truths, contain the groundwork of the national union; and, as historical truths, they cannot, according to their nature, be received otherwise than *on trust;* authority alone gives them the necessary evidence. And they were, moreover, confirmed to the nation by miracles, and supported by an authority which sufficed to place *faith* beyond all doubt and hesitation.

3. Laws, judgments, commandments, rules of life, which were to be peculiar to that nation; and by observing which, it was to arrive at national—as well as every single member thereof, at individual—happiness. The lawgiver was God himself; God, not in his revelations as Creator and Preserver of the universe, but God, as Lord Protector and ally of their forefathers; as the liberator, founder, and leader, as the king and ruler of that people. And he gave the laws a sanction, than which nothing could be more solemn; he gave them publicly, and in a marvellous manner never before heard of, whereby they were imposed on the nation, and on their descendants for ever, as an unalterable duty and obligation. These laws were *revealed,* that is, they were made known by the Lord, by *words* and *in writing.* Still, only the most essential part thereof was entrusted to letters; and without the unwritten laws, without explanations, limitations, and more particularly definitions, even these written laws are mostly unintelligible, or must become so in the course of time; since neither any words or written characters whatever retain their meaning unaltered, for the natural age of man. (90–95; summary and italics mine)

Mendelssohn reserves the concepts of revelation and exclusive truth for the last type of truth, the specific rules of Jewish life. This corresponds to what I call "concrete religion." In addition to the irreducible plurality of concrete religions, there is one general human religion based on the natural revelation of immutable truths common "to all rational beings," corresponding to my concept of "deep religion."

How can "deep religion" be practiced in modern life, and how may human beings relate to it? Certainly the eighteenth century's way of translating the distinction between surface religion and deep religion into the concept of *religio duplex*—with its distinction between the popular or public religion of the church and the elite religiosity of secret societies— is no longer viable. Lessing was a freemason, and his parable of the rings is based on the Masonic experience. Nevertheless, it seems fully applicable to our modern civilization, which lacks secret societies—at least in the eighteenth-century sense. What we need is a form of "wisdom" that enables us to look past the surface forms of concrete religions, with their irreducible differences and distinctions, and focus upon that transcendental point beyond these distinctions in relation to which true tolerance—that is, recognizing relativity without resorting to banality— becomes possible. God is different not only from "gods" but also from any representation that any concrete religion can produce. It is this absolute divine difference that precludes any intolerant insistence on the exclusive possession of truth. However, one must not forget that it was biblical monotheism that taught Westerners the divine difference.

Toward a Critique of Religious Violence

I would like to conclude some general remarks concerning the origin and nature of religious violence. In order to arrive at a better understanding of this specific form of violence, it is necessary to draw several distinctions. First, one must distinguish between power, violence, and constraint. Violence is physical violence. Johan Galtung's notion of "structural violence" refers to constraints related to power rather than actual violence.[14] By not drawing this distinction, one is unable to understand the character and specific power of nonviolent action. Second, one must follow the example of Walter Benjamin, who in his essay "Zur Kritik der Gewalt" distinguished between two types of violence— which he terms "divine" and "mythical"—and acknowledge the existence of different forms of violence that must be kept apart.[15]

Unlike Benjamin, I distinguish not two but five forms of violence. The first type I call raw, or "affective," violence. This violence, which Benjamin for some obscure reason calls "divine violence," springs from three affective sources, namely, anger, greed, and fear. Violence motivated by anger typically manifests itself as revenge, violence out of fear expresses itself as self-defense or preemptive action, and violence motivated by greed is usually masked as "might is right," for which the Melian Dialogue in Thucydides' *History of the Peloponnesian War* may serve as a particularly impressive example. All three are forms of raw violence, which is typically used in one's own name and for one's own sake, in contrast to the remaining forms of violence, which are executed in the name of another, higher authority.

The second form of violence, legal violence, is pitted against raw violence. This is the foundation of states and legal institutions that Benjamin calls "mythical violence." Legal violence is counterviolence. Unlike raw violence, legal violence distinguishes between just and unjust. The aim of legal violence is the creation of a sphere of law and justice in which raw violence is excluded. Within this sphere violence must never be used to further one's own interests. Personal aims must be pursued exclusively by legal means. Violence without legal support will be criminalized, but the law, in turn, has to form an alliance with violence in order to become "enforced." This "force" consists in credibly announced sanctions. Legal violence, unlike raw violence, is always used vicariously for the sake of a plaintiff. It is therefore separated from its affective basis. It is undesirable for the judge or executioner to become angry or fearful or greedy in order to form and execute a sentence.

A third form of violence is political violence, which should be distinguished from legal violence, because in a state of emergency it turns against the institutionalized law and suspends a greater or lesser part of civil rights. In its extrovert form it rests on the distinction not of just and unjust but of friend and foe. This distinction does not generally define the sphere of the political at large, as Carl Schmitt claims,[16] but rather the sphere of political violence, that is, violence in the name of the state. Political violence ignores the separation from its affective ground, which is constitutive of legal violence. On the contrary, political violence, which aims at preserving power internally and depends on stirring up a love for the state and hatred of its internal and external enemies—a fact evident throughout the modern world. This hatred may be nourished by anger, greed, or fear. In this context, the estrangement of the other in terms of race, class, or religion—what Erik H. Erikson has called "pseudospeciation"[17]—play an important role.

There are, however, two remaining forms of violence. It is only through them that one enters the realm of religion. The fourth type I call ritual violence. We have lost sight of this form because it has almost vanished from the domain of modern world religions. In early, or "pagan," religions all violence that is exerted in the name of religion is ritual violence. Here the law stating "thou shalt not kill" applies even to animals, only with the following restriction: "You may only kill what is to be offered in sacrifice." Animals that are to be killed in order to be eaten must first be offered up as a sacrifice. Biblical monotheism had abolished this archaic link between slaughtering and sacrifice: "But thou shalt kill according to all thy desire, and shalt eat flesh according to the blessing of the LORD thy God, which he has given thee in every city; the unclean that is within thee and the clean shall eat it on equal terms, as the doe or the stag" (Deut. 12:15). Moreover, it has emphatically turned its back on human sacrifice. The abolition of human sacrifice, however, appears to be a general phenomenon that occurs in most ancient religions and is not specific to monotheism.

The fifth and final form of violence I call religious violence, meaning violence with reference to the will of God. My thesis is that this form of violence occurs only in monotheistic religions. I do not wish to claim that monotheism is responsible for violence in general and am fully aware that the professed aims of monotheism are peace and justice. It is therefore important to distinguish between different forms of violence. Monotheism is responsible only for religious violence. The ancient world in which this new form of religion first appeared was, of course, full of violence. The Egyptians, Assyrians, Babylonians, Persians, Greeks, and Romans employed much violence in creating and expanding their empires. However, these entities were states, not religions, and the violence they employed should be classified as raw, legal, and political rather than religious. These political systems also contained cults as part of their culture. This, however, is totally different from those new religions that spread transnationally and instilled a transnational identity. However, it must also be mentioned that this new structure of world religions was only rudimentarily expressed in Judaism and only became fully realized in Christianity and Islam.

What, then, is religious violence? By this term I mean a kind of violence that stems from the distinction between friend and foe in a religious sense. The religious meaning of this distinction rests on the distinction between true and false. Ritual violence rests on the distinction between pure and impure. Only the pure may be offered up in sacrifice. The distinction between true and false does not play any role here. Religious violence, conversely, is directed against pagans, unbelievers, and heretics, who either would not convert to the truth or have defected from it and are therefore regarded as enemies of God.

In wondering about the origins of religious violence, my purpose was to deconstruct, by means of genealogical reconstruction, the connection between religion and violence. To me this connection is not only disastrous but also contradictory. My search for origins has led me to the political sphere, that is, to legal and political violence. Religious violence is nothing original, nothing necessarily implied in the idea of monotheism. Monotheism originally meant the liberation of man from the omnipotence of political power. This was at first conceivable only as counterviolence, religious violence against political violence. Essentially this is a question not of violence against violence but of power against power. The basic idea behind biblical monotheism is to erect a counterpower against the all-encompassing power of the political. Religion can exert its counterpower against the political only if it has recourse to totally different means and values. The truth of this lesson, which is implied in many of Jesus' words and actions, has been demonstrated in modern times by Mahatma Gandhi, who based his nonviolent but extremely powerful actions on the religious idea of "truth."[18] It has by now become imperative to dissociate religion from violence. Violence belongs to the sphere of the political, and a religion that uses violence fails to fulfill its proper mission in this world and remains entangled in the sphere of the political. The power of religion rests on nonviolence. Only through a complete rejection of violence is monotheism able to fulfill its liberating mission of forming an alternative counterpower to the totalizing claims of the political.

I am not suggesting that one return to "Egypt," to the polytheistic system of mutual translatability and recognition, but rather that one step forward toward a religion that clings to the idea of the unity of God and commits itself to the moral commandments, while at the same time returning to a weak notion of truth in the sense expressed by Lessing and Mendelssohn: a truth that exists beyond the absolute knowledge of human beings, one that can only be aimed at but never possessed.

NOTES

Introduction

1. Smith, *The Early History of God*. This book provides an excellent survey (xii–xli) of recent developments in the field, including a plethora of bibliographic references.

2. Smith, *The Origins of Biblical Monotheism*.

3. Moor, *The Rise of Yahwism*.

4. Albertz, *A History of Israelite Religion in the Old Testament Period;* Patrick D. Miller, *The Religion of Ancient Israel*.

5. See, in addition to Smith, Keel and Uehlinger, *Gods, Goddesses, and Images of Gods in Ancient Israel*.

6. See the classic work by Morton Smith entitled *Palestinian Parties and Politics That Shaped the Old Testament*.

7. Armstrong, *A History of God*. For a very different approach, see Miles, *God: A Biography*.

8. This point was made clear by Peter Schäfer in his response to my book *Die Mosaische Unterscheidung* [The Mosaic Distinction]. See Schäfer, "Das jüdische Monopol: Jan Assmann und der Monotheismus."

9. Voegelin, *Das Volk Gottes* [The People of God].

10. See especially Voegelin, *Der Gottesmord* [The Murder of God].

11. In "Die heilige Gewalt" Peter Schäfer characterized Freud's view of monotheism as typical of nineteenth-century liberal Protestantism and not of "true" monotheism; see also his book *Der Triumph der reinen Geistigkeit*. The same applies to Max Weber's concept of monotheism as rationalization and "disenchantment of the world." Schäfer is certainly right to locate these ideas in late-nineteenth-century Protestantism. Nevertheless, it is undeniable that the impulse toward "Geistigkeit" or ethics and the rejection of magic is central to the biblical project.

12. I am thinking here only of the critical debate on monotheism, not of the equally heated but purely historical debate about the early history of monotheism in ancient Israel. For an excellent overview of this debate from 1990 until 2002, see Smith, *The Early History of God*, xii–xxxviii.

147

13. Yerushalmi, *Freud's Moses*.

14. See the critiques included in my book *Die Mosaische Unterscheidung* and, more recently, Schäfer, "Das jüdische Monopol," 12.

15. See Polymnia Athanassiadi and Michael Frede, introduction to *Pagan Monotheism in Late Antiquity*, 4–9. Cf. Tertullian's definition of "pagans" as "deorum falsorum multorumque cultores" (*Cor. Mil.* 11).

16. I would especially like to thank Steven Aschheim, who opened my eyes to some unwanted implications that were still sensitive even in my Jerusalem lectures. In another sense, I am equally grateful to Peter Schäfer for his harsh critique, which helped me to clarify my points.

17. Armstrong, *The Great Transformation*.

Chapter 1. Understanding Polytheism

1. See, however, Burkhard Gladigow ("Polytheismus und Monotheismus"), who provides an excellent survey of the various forms in which ancient "pagan" religions were studied and conceived of, as opposed to biblical monotheism, especially in the eighteenth and nineteenth centuries. Francis Schmidt's edited volume *The Inconceivable Polytheism* likewise focuses more on the "reception history" of ancient polytheism than ancient religion itself.

2. "Gott," in Helck and Otto, *Lexikon der Ägyptologie*, 2:756–86.

3. Assmann, *Ägypten: Theologie und Frömmigkeit einer frühen Hochkultur* [*The Search for God in Ancient Egypt*].

4. See Boyarin, "The Christian Invention of Judaism"; Susanna Elm, "Hellenism and Historiography."

5. Quoted in Assmann, *Egyptian Solar Religion in the New Kingdom*, 19–20.

6. See, e.g., The Wisdom of Solomon.

7. Assmann, *Ma'at*.

8. See Assmann, "Das ägyptische Prozessionsfest."

9. See Assmann, "Kultlied." For a selection of festival songs celebrating the "union of heaven and earth," see Assmann, *Liturgische Lieder an den Sonnengott*, 254–60.

10. These events are dealt with in a mythological composition, edited by Erik Hornung, entitled *Der ägyptische Mythos von der Himmelskuh*.

11. Quoted in Erman and Grapow, *Wörterbuch der ägyptischen Sprache*, 3:418n8.

12. See Assmann, "Stadtgötter und Gottesstädte," in my *Ägypten: Theologie*, 25–35.

13. See Dihle, "Die Theologia tripertita bei Augustin."

14. For this distinction see Fishbane, *Biblical Myth and Rabbinic Mythmaking*, 134.

15. Josephus, *Contra Apionem*, Book I, secs. 38–41.

16. See Hornung, *Geschichte als Fest;* idem, "Zum altägyptischen Geschichtsbewusstsein." See also Redford, *Pharaonic King-Lists, Annals, and Day-Books*. For a

discussion of the change in this general attitude in the Ramesside Age (thirteenth century BCE), see my chapter "Die Entdeckung der Vergangenheit: Innovation und Restauration in der ägyptischen Literaturgeschichte," in Assmann, *Stein und Zeit*, 303–13.

17. See Assmann, *Zeit und Ewigkeit im alten Ägypten;* idem, "Das Doppelgesicht der Zeit im altägyptischen Denken," in my book *Stein und Zeit*, 32–58.

18. See Eliade, *Le Mythe de l'éternel retour.*

19. See Assmann, *Ma'at*, 252–67.

20. *Instruction for King Merikare*, 136–37; see Quack, *Studien zur Lehre für Merikare*, 78–79.

21. See Assmann, "Altorientalische Fluchinschriften und das Problem performativer Schriftlichkeit."

22. See Griffiths, *The Divine Verdict.*

23. See Falkenstein, "Fluch über Akkade."

24. See Wilcke, "Die sumerische Königsliste und erzählte Vergangenheit," esp. 133.

25. See Albrektson, *History and the Gods.*

26. See Bottéro, "Symptomes, signes, écritures."

27. See Assmann, *Ma'at*, 252–72; idem, "State and Religion in the New Kingdom."

28. For an overview of Hittite historiography, see the following: Götze, *Die Annalen des Mursilis;* idem, "Die Pestgebete des Mursilis"; Güterbock, "The Deeds of Suppiluliuma," 41–50, 59–68, 75–85, 90–98, 107–30; Hoffner, "Propaganda and Political Justification in Hittite Historiography"; idem, "Histories and Historians of the Near East"; Cancik, *Grundzüge der hethitischen und alttestamentlichen Geschichtsschreibung.*

29. See Baltzer, *Das Bundesformular.*

30. See Götze, *Hattusilis.*

31. See Hillers, *Treaty-Curses and the Old Testament Prophets.* On antique treaties in general, see Canfora, Liverani, and Zaccagnini, *I Trattati nel Mondo Antico.* For parallels between biblical and oriental treaties, see Weinfeld, *Deuteronomy and the Deuteronomic School*, 116ff.; idem, "The Common Heritage of Covenantal Traditions in the Ancient World," in Canfora, Liverani, and Zaccagnini, *I Trattati nel Mondo Antico*, 175–91; and McCarthy, *Treaty and Covenant.*

32. See Tadmor, "Autobiographical Apology in the Royal Assyrian Literature."

33. See the classical work by John van Seters, *In Search of History.*

34. See Fishbane, *Biblical Myth and Rabbinic Mythmaking.*

Chapter 2. Seth the Iconoclast

1. Luhmann, "Rechtszwang und politische Gewalt," 154; quoted in Conrad, "Der Begriff des Politischen," 77–78.

2. See Cogan, *Imperialism and Religion*.

3. Quoted in Luckenbill, *Ancient Records of Assyria and Babylonia*, 2:245. This reference was brought to my attention by Yoram Cohen (Tel Aviv).

4. By "system" I refer not to religions but, more generally, to constructions of reality and their rules of inclusion and exclusion.

5. See "Translating Gods" in chapter 3 of the current book. For a discussion of the concept of intercultural translatability, see Budick and Iser, *Translatability of Cultures*.

6. For a discussion of this notion, see "Toward a Critique of Religious Violence" in the conclusion of the current book.

7. See Römer, "Le Sacrifice humain en Juda et Israël."

8. For a discussion of human sacrifice in ancient Greece, see the following: Hughes, *Human Sacrifice in Ancient Greece;* Bonnechère, *Le Sacrifice humain en Grèce ancienne;* Georgoudi, "À propos du sacrifice humain en Grèce ancienne."

9. See Albert and Midant-Reynes, *Le Sacrifice humain en Egypte ancienne et ailleurs.*

10. Burkert, *Homo Necans*, 2–3; see also Kirsch, *God against the Gods*, 52.

11. Nietzsche, *On the Genealogy of Morals*, 60–61. For a different translation see *On the Genealogy of Morality*, 41.

12. The distinction between orthodoxy and heresy seems to have been introduced by Christian writers of the second century CE and adopted by early rabbinic scholars. See Boyarin, *Borderlines*, 37–86. Until then the term "hairesis" had referred to one movement in relation to other "sectarian" movements but not in relation to "orthodoxy."

13. Iamblichus, *De mysteriis Aegyptiorum*, 187–88.

14. Ramses IV text Kairo JE [Journal d'entrée, Cairo Museum] 48 831. Mariette, *Abydos* II, 54; Korostovtsev, "La Stèle de Ramses IV"; Kees, *Lesebuch,* 16. Kitchen, *Ramesside Inscriptions*, 6:23, line 13.

15. Kitchen, *Ramesside Inscriptions*, 6:23, lines 8–9.

16. Quoted in Streck, *Assurbanipal und die letzten assyrischen Könige*, 2:119–20.

17. *De Iside et Osiride*, 31.9.363C–D = Babbitt, *Plutarch's Moralia*, 5:76–77; Griffiths, *Plutarch's De Iside et Osiride*, 418–19.

18. See Stern, *Greek and Latin Authors on Jews and Judaism*, 1:97–98. For the motif of the ass cult, see Stricker, *Asenarii* I; *Asenarii* II; *Asenarii* III; and *Asenarii* IV. See also Bickerman, "Ritualmord und Eselskult"; Bori, *The Golden Calf and the Origins of the Anti-Jewish Controversy*, 102–13; Schäfer, *Judeophobia*, 56–57.

19. See Gager, *Moses in Greco-Roman Paganism*, 30–31.

20. I am here using the Loeb edition of *Manetho*, trans. W. G. Waddell. See Schäfer, *Judeophobia*, 17–21.

21. For a discussion of this point, see my *Moses the Egyptian*, 57–59.

22. See Meyer, *Aegyptische Chronologie*, 92–95; Krauss, *Das Ende der Amarnazeit;* Redford, "The Hyksos Invasion in History and Tradition"; idem, *Pharaonic King-Lists, Annals, and Day-Books*, 293; Loprieno, *La Pensée et l'écriture*, 110–15. This

interpretation is now generally accepted by Egyptologists, together with the inclusion of other memories such as those of the Hyksos, the Assyrians, and the Persians.

23. Douglas, *In the Wilderness,* 148.

24. See Schott, *Urkunden mythologischen Inhalts,* 1:15–16.

25. Papyrus Sallier I, 1.2–3. See Gardiner, *Late-Egyptian Stories,* 85; Goedicke, *The Quarrel of Apophis and Seqenenre,* 10–11. See also Goldwasser, "King Apophis of Avaris and the Emergence of Monotheism." (I owe this reference to Israel Knohl.) Goldwasser holds that the "sin" of the Hyksos king Apophis could not have been his worship of Seth—the latter was considered a great god in the Ramesside era—but rather the exclusivity of this worship. She goes so far as to attribute to Apophis the first introduction of monotheism and the "Mosaic distinction." I do not concur with this interpretation because the Hyksos kings do not seem to have persecuted traditional Egyptian religion, and this, not the exclusivity of worship, is the hallmark of the Mosaic distinction.

26. Papyrus Louvre 3129 J, 38–57; Papyrus BM 10252 II, 3–34; Schott, *Urkunden mythologischen Inhalts,* 2:120–29.

27. Ovid, *Metamorphoses,* bk. 3, no. 5. See also Störk, "Die Flucht der Götter."

28. Nikandros apud Antoninus Liberalis, *Transformationes* 28, see Hopfner, *Fontes historiae religionis aegypticaoe,* 81. See also Apollodorus, *Bibliotheca* I, 6.3; Hyginus, *Astronomia* (ed. Bernhardt Bunte) II, 28 (cf. *Fabulae* 196); Josephus, *Contra Apionem,* Book II, 128–29; Lucian, *De sacrificiis,* 14; *Mythographus Vaticanus* I, 1, 11, and 86; Nigidius Figulus, *Sphaera Graecanica* (ed. Anton Swoboda), 122–25; Porphyrius, *De Abstinentia* III, 16; Servius, comm. in Vergil, *Aeneid* VIII, 698; Suidas s.v. Typhos. All quotations are from Smelik and Hemelrijk, "Who Knows Not What Monsters Demented Egypt Worships?"; see esp. 1904–5n342.

29. Diodorus of Sicily, *Bibliotheca Historica* I.86.

30. See Tasinato, *Sulla curiosità: Apuleio e Agostino.*

31. See Merkelbach, *Isis-Regina, Zeus Sarapis,* 417–34 (on Lucius's curiosity and his transformation), 266–303 (on his liberation and initiation).

32. See Schott, *Urkunden mythologischen Inhalts,* 1:5.

33. Papyrus Jumilhac XVII.19–XVIII, 11. This brief quote is part of a much longer elaboration of the connection between ritual and political order. See Vandier, *Le Papyrus Jumilhac,* 129–30.

34. Asclepius 24–26, in Nock, *Corpus Hermeticum II,* 326–29; coptic version: Nag Hammadi Codex VI, 8.65.15–78.43, in Krause and Labib, *Gnostische und hermetische Schriften aus Codex II und Codex VI,* 194–200. See also Colpe and Holzhausen, *Das Corpus Hermeticum Deutsch,* 1:287–88; Fowden, *The Egyptian Hermes,* 39–43; Mahé, *Hermès en Haute-Égypte,* 2:69–97; Frankfurter, *Elijah in Upper Egypt,* 188–89.

35. Fishbane, *Biblical Myth and Rabbinic Mythmaking.*

Chapter 3. All Gods Are One

1. Lewis, *The Allegory of Love*, 57.
2. Cudworth, *The True Intellectual System of the Universe*, 194. See my *Moses the Egyptian*, 80–90.
3. See my article "Translating Gods." My argument here is that this principle of religious translatability was blocked by the Mosaic Distinction. This idea has been taken up by Ronald Hendel in his *Remembering Abraham*. I owe this last reference to Mark Smith.
4. Voegelin, *Order and History*.
5. See Litke, *Reconstruction of the Assyro-Babylonian God-lists*.
6. See Mitchell, "The Cult of Theos Hypsistos between Pagans, Jews, and Christians."
7. Ps. Just. Cohort. ad Gent. 15 = Orph.fr. 239. Macrobius, *Saturnalia* I, chap. 18, sec. 17, quotes the first verse. On these kinds of "theological oracles" see Nock, "Oracles théologiques."
8. Macrobius, *Sat.* I, chap. 18, sec. 20. See the following: Peterson, *Heîs Theós*, 243–44; Hengel, *Judentum und Hellenismus*, 476–77. On the inscription *Heîs Zeùs Sérapis Iaó* [CIL II Suppl. 5665] see Dunand, "Le Syncrétisme isiaque à la fin de l'époque hellénistique," 170n.
9. See the following: Peterson, *Monotheismus als politisches Problem*, 45–147; Schindler, *Monotheismus als politisches Problem;* Momigliano, "The Disadvantages of Monotheism for a Universal State"; Fowden, *Empire to Commonwealth*.
10. Ausonius Epigrammata no. 48, in White, *Ausonius*. Lucaniacus was Ausonius's estate.
11. Augustin, *De consensu evangelist.* 1, 22, 30 and 23, 31 PL 34, 1005f = Varro fr. I, sec. 58b; see Hengel, *Judentum und Hellenismus*, 472.
12. This view was expressed in a letter to Anebo, quoted by Iamblichus, *De mysteriis Aegyptiorum*, chap. 7, sec. 5; see Des Places, *Les Mystères d'Egypte*, 193.
13. Quoted in Chuvin, *A Chronicle of the Last Pagans*, 58.
14. Origen C. Cels. I 24, V 41 (45); see Hengel, *Judentum und Hellenismus*, 476.
15. Plutarch, *De Is.*, chap. 67; see Griffiths, *Plutarch's De Iside and Osiride*, 223–24.
16. Seneca, *Ad Lucilium Epistulae morales*, 492–95.
17. Mark Smith, *The God in Translation* (quoted with author's permission). In a footnote Smith refers to H. Rackham's comment that "different races have different names" (*Pliny*, 178–79).
18. Santner, *On the Psychotheology of Everday Life*, 3–6.
19. For a précis of this queen, see van den Hout, "Khattushili III of Khattusha."
20. ANET 393, quoted in Smith, *The God in Translation;* see also Singer, "'The Thousand Gods of Hatti,'" 90.
21. Quoted with permission of the author.

22. See Bonnet, "Zum Verständnis des Synkretismus"; idem, "Egyptian Deities in Context," esp. 31–36.

23. See Kurth, "Götter determinieren Götter." Kurth derives the concept of "determination" from one of the functions of hieroglyphic scripts, the "determinatives" or classifiers, signs that have no sound value but determine the meaning of a word by allocating it to a specific semantic class. In a similar fashion divine names are added to another name in order to "determine" its meaning.

24. Homer, *Iliad*.

25. See Parpola, "Monotheism in Ancient Assyria."

26. *Enuma Elish*, Tablets VI and VII. See Bottéro, "Les Noms de Marduk."

27. Quoted in Craig, *Assyrian and Babylonian Religious Texts*, 1:29, line 3. See Livingstone, *Court Poetry and Literary Miscellanea*, no. 2, 1.3 (on p. 7). For an English translation see Foster, *Before the Muses*, 2:720–24, esp. 720, line 3. I owe these references to Nils Heessel.

28. Quoted in Ebeling, *Keilschrifttexte aus Assur religiösen Inhalts*, 25, col. 2, lines 3–24; see also Krebernik, "Vielzahl und Einheit im altmesopotamischen Pantheon," 45.

29. For Egyptian traditions of reflecting on the Oneness of the Divine, see Hornung, "Das Denken des Einen im alten Ägypten." See also Baines, "Egyptian Deities in Context."

30. *Instruction for King Merikare*, 130–38; my translation throughout unless otherwise noted. Volten, *Zwei altägyptische politische Schriften*, 73–78.

31. See Posener, "Sur le monothéisme dans l'ancienne Égypte."

32. Ogden Goelet in Goelet and Levine, "Making Peace in Heaven and on Earth," 273.

33. Baruch A. Levine in Goelet and Levine, "Making Peace in Heaven and On Earth," 282–91. Levine actually proposes two alternative interpretations in addition to this one: "an impersonal power that governs matters" and "a supreme, international unnamed deity who adjudicates between the chief deities of the parties." I think the differences between these interpretations appear as such only in the light of biblical and Western theology. I owe these references to Mark Smith, who in his study *God in Translation* (forthcoming) adds: "Parenthetically, I would note that Levine's unnamed supreme god who mediates between the chief gods of two empires, though possible, sounds to me like Jan Assmann's single god (or god-ness) for the Late Bronze Age. . . . Both sound to me more like the Greco-Roman period idea of a single god that informs or underlies all divinity." For examples from the Greco-Roman period compare Xenophanes' "true god," who is "One god among gods and men [the] greatest / Neither in form nor in thought resembling human beings" (translated in Versnel, "Thrice One," 93). I agree with Smith but would add that with Ramesside theology we are already on a path that will eventually lead to Greco-Roman concepts.

34. Papyrus Boulaq 17 = Papyrus Cairo CG 58038 IV, 3–5. See Assmann, *Re und Amun*, 176–77 (*Egyptian Solar Religion*, 125). See also *Instruction for King*

Merikare, 130–38; Assmann, *Re und Amun*, 168–69 (*Egyptian Solar Religion*, 119–20); Assmann, *Ma'at*, 234–35.

35. See Zandee, *De Hymnen aan Amon van Papyrus Leiden I 350*, 20–21, pl. 4; see also Assmann, *Ägyptische Hymnen und Gebete* [*ÄHG*], no. 139.

36. Zandee, *Hymnen*, 75–86; *ÄHG*, no. 138.

37. Stele Leiden V 70 = *ÄHG*, no. 90; Leiden K 11 = Kitchen, *Ramesside Inscriptions*, 3:175, lines 2–5.

38. Sandman, *Texts from the Time of Akhenaten*, 95, lines 12–13. Regarding this passage, see Fecht, "Frühformen der Amarna-Religion," 33; Assmann, *Sonnenhymnen in Thebanischen Gräbern* [*STG*], text 54 (x).

39. Sandman, *Texts*, 15, lines 1–9; cf. *STG*, text 253 (s).

40. Zandee, *Hymnen*, 75–86. See *ÄHG*, 318, no. 138.

41. On the concept of the limitlessness of god, cf. "who concealed himself, whose limits cannot be attained." Papyrus Leiden I 344 vso. II, 8–9; see Zandee, *Der Amunshymnus des Papyrus Leiden I 344*, 2:120–26. See also Papyrus Berlin 3049, 16, 6; Sethe, *Thebanische Tempelinschriften aus griechisch-römischer Zeit*, 116: "whose circuit has no limits."

42. Papyrus Mag. Harris IV, 1–2 = Hibis 32, 1; see *ÄHG*, no. 129, 1–6.

43. Papyrus Leiden I 344 vso. III, 2–3 (Zandee, *Amunshymnus*, 3:168–76).

44. Chassinat, *Le Temple d' Edfou*, 3:34, lines 9–10.

45. *ḫprw.f m ḥḥw:* stela of Ramesses III = Kitchen, *Ramesside Inscriptions*, 6: 452, line 8.

46. Sethe, *Thebanische Tempelinschriften*, sec. 138b, p. 110. Of Yahweh, on the contrary, it is said: "'One' is his name" (Zech. 14:9). All biblical quotes are from the *English Standard Version* unless otherwise noted.

47. On this meaning of *ḥḥw*, see *STG*, text 149 (c).

48. Hymn to the primeval god in the "Livre que mon fleurisse" in Papyrus Berlin 3030 VIII–IX; Papyrus Louvre 3336 I, 1–16; Papyrus Brussels, published in Speelers, "Un papyrus funéraire," 28.

49. Jean Claude Goyon, in Parker, Leclant, and Goyon, *The Edifice of Taharqa*, 69–79; 40–41; pl. 27. See also *ÄHG*, no. 128. A parallel demotic text has been published by Mark Smith: "Louvre E3229: A Demotic Magical Text."

50. A graphic illustration of the otherwise largely unpublished representation of the ten Ba's of Amun in the crypt of the Ptolemaic Opet Temple at Karnak may be found in Traunecker, *Les Dieux de l'Égypte*, 97, fig. 8.

51. See Sauneron, *Le Papyrus Magique Illustré de Brooklyn*, 23, plate IV, fig. 3 (facing p. 13).

52. See Sethe, *Thebanische Tempelinschriften*, sec. 1g. See also Sethe, *Amun*, sec. 202.

53. See *Reliefs and Inscriptions at Karnak I*, pl. 23; see also *ÄHG*, no. 196.

54. *ÄHG*, no. 143, 111–24.

55. *STG*, no. 88, 124–25.

56. See Festugière, *La Révélation d'Hermès Trismégiste*, vol. 2, *Le Dieu cosmique*.

57. See Merkelbach and Totti-Gemünd, *Abrasax*, 1:136–37; for similar Greek texts, and for their striking parallels with Ramesside theology, see also 1: 127–34.

58. Mahabharata III, V, verses 1296off., quoted in Widengren, *Religionsphänomenologie*, 94.

59. Bhagavad Gita, canto 11, quoted in Widengren, *Religionsphänomenologie*, 95.

60. Mundaka-Upanishad II, 3, 4, quoted inWidengren, *Religionsphänomenologie*, 97.

61. For the history of this formula, see my *Moses the Egyptian*, 204–7.

62. *Te tibi, una quae es omnia, dea Isis, Arrius Balbinus v(oti) c(ompos)*, which translates as "Arrius Balbinus dedicates you [i.e., your statue] to you, goddess Isis, who being One are All, for my wish is fulfilled." Quoted in Merkelbach, *Isis Regina, Zeus Sarapis*, 98.

63. Macrobius, *Saturnalia* I, 20, 16–17; see R. van den Brook, "The Sarapis Oracle in Macrobius." See also Merkelbach, *Isis Regina, Zeus Sarapis*, 129–30.

64. The term "cosmotheism" was coined by Lamoignon de Malesherbes with reference to the antique, especially Stoic worship of the *cosmos* or *mundus* as Supreme Being. In his 1782 edition of Pliny the Elder's *Natural History* Lamoignon commented on one of the most typical passages of this religion (*mundum, et hoc quodcumque nomine alio coelum appellare libuit, cujus circumflexu teguntur cuncta, numen esse credi par est*) by proposing to call Pliny "non un Athée, mais un *Cosmothéiste*, c'est à dire quelqu'un qui croit que l'univers est Dieu" (not an atheist, but a cosmotheist, that is, someone who believes the universe to be god). The term has nothing whatsoever to do with the "Cosmotheism church" founded in 1978 by William L. Pierce (1933–2002), a radical fascist, racist, and member of the American Nazi group National Alliance. No one would think of such horrible associations were it not for the Internet, which indiscriminately brings together what would otherwise never converge.

65. See Liebeschuetz, "Significance of the Speech of Praetextatus."

66. In this respect, Dale B. Martin's important remarks (*Inventing Superstition*, 13–16) concerning the absence in Greek and Latin vocabulary and thought of any notion of the "supernatural" should be modified. Preatextatus's notion of "hypercosmic" gods clearly implies a concept of the supernatural and Plato's concept of a reality "beyond Being" seems to have laid the groundwork for such distinctions between the immanent and the transcendent.

67. See Zandee, *Hymnen*, 75–86; *ÄHG*, no. 138.

68. On this concept see Hornung, *Conceptions of God in Ancient Egypt*, 219–21.

69. Commentarium in somnium Scipionis, 1.2, 13–15, quoted in Liebeschuetz, "Praetextatus," 186.

Chapter 4. The Axial Age and the Separation of State and Religion

1. An earlier version of this chapter appeared as "Axial 'Breakthroughs' and Semantic 'Relocations' in Ancient Egypt and Israel." I wish to thank Jóhann Árnason for permission to reprint part of the text in the present book.

2. Here is the context in which the phrase appears: "If there is some common underlying impulse in all these 'axial' movements, it might be called the strain towards transcendence . . . a kind of standing back and looking beyond—a kind of critical, reflective questioning of the actual and a new vision of what lies beyond." Schwartz, "The Age of Transcendence," 3–4.

3. Whitehead and Whitehead, "cong yishi dao liangzhi."

4. See Metzler, "A. H. Anquetil-Duperron und das Konzept der Achsenzeit."

5. The debate on the "Axial Age" continued in the 1970s in the American journal *Daedalus*, whose most pertinent issue appeared in 1975. Since then Shmuel N. Eisenstadt has organized a series of conferences whose papers have been published under the following titles, all edited by Eisenstadt unless noted: *The Origin and Diversity of Axial Civilizations; Kulturen der Achsenzeit: Ihre Ursprünge und ihre Vielfalt; Kulturen der Achsenzeit II: Ihre institutionelle und kulturelle Dynamik;* and *Axial Civilizations and World History*, ed. Árnason, Eisenstadt, and Wittrock. See also Schluchter, *Religion und Lebensführung*.

6. See my book *Herrschaft und Heil*.

7. For the history of this idea, see Griffiths, *The Divine Verdict*. For its application to Egypt, see chapter 3 of my *Tod und Jenseits im Alten Ägypten*.

8. Stele London UC 14333; see Goedicke, "A Neglected Wisdom Text," 26. See also Schenkel, "Eine neue Weisheitslehre?" esp. 11–12.

9. For this interpretation, see chapter 5 of my book *Ma'at*.

10. See my book *Herrschaft und Heil*. Jóhann Páll Árnason has suggested the English translation "relocation."

11. See chapter 4 of my book *Ägypten: Eine Sinngeschichte* [*The Mind of Egypt*]. The term "Persönliche Frömmigkeit" was coined by Adolf Erman in 1910 and translated as "Personal Piety" by James Henry Breasted, who identified this concept as the hallmark of an entire period of Egyptian history, specifically the Ramesside age (1300–1100 BCE).

12. Stele des Antef Chicago OIM 14053; see *STG*, 228–30; *ÄHG*, no. 75.

13. O. Cairo CG 12217 recto; see Posener, "La piété personelle avant l'age amarnien," 206–7.

14. See my essay "Weisheit, Loyalismus und Frömmigkeit."

15. See Sandman, *Texts*, 97, lines 11–12.

16. Among more recent literature on Akhenaten are the following: Hornung, *Akhenaten;* Montserrat, *Akhenaten;* and Reeves, *Akhenaten*.

17. Cf. verse 64 of the "Great Hymn": *pȝ nṯr wꜥ nn kjj wp ḥr.k* ("O sole god,

beside whom there is none!"), see Sandman, *Texts*, 94, line 17; cf.: *nn kjj wp ḥr.f* ("there is no other except him"), 7, lines 7–8.

18. Ibid., 86, lines 15–16.

19. Breasted, *Development of Religion and Thought in Ancient Egypt*, 344–70.

20. Cf. *ÄHG*, no. 173.12–13, 42–43, 62–63, 102; no. 177.5–11.

21. Quoted by Abdel-Qader Mohammed in *Annales du Service des Antiquités de l'Égypte* 59 (1966): pl. 48. See also Wilson, "The Theban Tomb of Si-Mut, Called Kiki"; *ÄHG*, no. 173.

22. See Otto, *Das Deuteronomium*, and Steymans, *Deuteronomium 28*.

23. Baltzer, *Das Bundesformular*.

24. Eckart Otto, "Political Theology in Judah and Assyria."

25. See the excellent article by Uwe Becker: "Von der Staatsreligion zum Monotheismus."

26. I am grateful to Dale Martin for many stimulating discussions about Paul and his concept of "Israel."

27. See my book *Moses the Egyptian*, 1–8.

28. On the distinction between "primary" and "secondary" religions, see Sundermeier, "Religion, Religionen"; idem, *Was ist Religion?*

29. Rodney Needham and Louis Dumont have demonstrated that a similar distinction underlies the Indian system of "Dual Sovereignty," that is, of religious (Brahmin) and political (Kshatriya) leadership. In fact, the duality of religious and military leadership seems rather widespread even among tribal societies and has little to do with what I described as the political implications and consequences of the "Mosaic Distinction."

30. See Kessler, *Die Ägyptenbilder der Hebräischen Bibel*, esp. 9–14.

31. For a discussion of the theory of the weak state, see the following: Malamat, "The Kingdom of Judah between Egypt and Babylon"; Handel, *Weak States in the International System*. For an analysis of the concept of *Kontrastgesellschaft* (countersociety), see Lohfink, "Der Begriff des Gottesreichs vom Alten Testament her gesehen," esp. 44. In another essay, Lohfink applies the concept *Kontrastgesellschaft* to early Israelite society; see "Der gewalttätige Gott des Alten Testaments," esp. 119ff. A similar concept is presented by Pierre Clastres in *La Société contre l'état* [*Society against the State*].

32. For bibliographical details, see my book *Herrschaft und Heil*, 46–52.

33. I obviously do not mean the historical sense of "what really happened" but rather in the narratological sense of narrated time. The biblical narrative is located in Egypt sometime during the fifteenth through thirteenth centuries.

34. This is an admittedly poor translation of the Nazi-era term *Gleichschaltung*.

35. See Voegelin, *Die politischen Religionen*.

36. For a more detailed treatment of this topic, see my article "State and Religion in the New Kingdom."

37. See chapter 1, p. 11.

38. On the prohibition of images, see the following works: Dohmen, *Das Bilderverbot;* Mettinger, *No Graven Image?;* Uehlinger, "Du culte des images à son interdit"; Berlejung, *Die Theologie der Bilder;* Dick, "Prophetic Parodies of Making the Cult Image"; and Keel, "Warum im Jerusalemer Tempel kein anthropomorphes Kultbild gestanden haben dürfte."

39. Weber, *Gesammelte Aufsätze zur Religionssoziologie,* 1:536–73.

40. On this point, see especially the work of Claude Lévi-Strauss. See also Godelier, "Mythos und Geschichte"; and Habermas, *Theorie des kommunikativen Handelns,* 1:72–113.

41. I would like to thank Jóhann Páll Árnason for drawing my attention to the problem of reconciling my concept of "distinction and differentiation" with Weber's theory of the separation of cultural spheres, which is closely related to his concepts of occidental rationalization and modernization. I think it is important to distinguish between "axiality" and "modernity," especially if one considers axiality a nonevolutionary concept (i.e., the "axial paradigm" rather than the "axial age").

42. See Stark, *One True God.*

43. See Al-Azmeh and Bak, *Monotheistic Kingship.*

Chapter 5. Five Steps toward Canonization

1. The present chapter is a slightly revised version of my 1998 Münster Theological Lecture, published as "Fünf Wege zum Kanon."

2. On the distinction between "primary" and "secondary" religions, see Theo Sundermeier, "Religion, Religionen." See also his *Was ist Religion?*

3. The Rgveda may be called an orally transmitted "canon," but in this case memory is transformed—through the extreme use of mnemotechnique— into a kind of writing. Moreover, the Rgveda is not concerned with the entire life form of a community but with the correct performance of rituals.

4. See Assmann, *Das kulturelle Gedächtnis.*

5. See note 2 above.

6. Freud, *Moses and Monotheism,* 142–47.

7. See Smith, *The Memoirs of God.* Although Smith conveys the impression that our views about the rise of monotheism "vastly differ" (ix and 121), I cannot help but feel inclined to agree with his line of reasoning.

8. See Assmann and Assmann, *Kanon und Zensur.*

9. See Halbwachs, *La Mémoire collective* [*The Collective Memory*]. See also Halbwachs, *On Collective Memory;* A. Assmann, *Erinnerungsräume,* 130–33; and Smith, *The Memoirs of God,* 127–29.

10. See my book *Das Kulturelle Gedächtnis,* 48–66.

11. For the process of habitualization, see Bourdieu, *Zur Soziologie der symbolischen Formen,* 125–58. For the process of becoming unconscious, see Erdheim, *Die gesellschaftliche Produktion von Unbewußtheit;* idem, *Die Psychoanalyse und das Unbewußte in der Kultur.*

12. One of the principal representatives of "Canon Hermeneutics" is James A. Sanders; see his *Torah and Canon, Canon and Community* and *From Sacred Story to Sacred Text.*

13. For references to the pertinent literature, see Kippenberg, *Die vorderasiatischen Erlösungsreligionen,* 157–65.

14. See Gehrke, *Rechtskodifizierung und soziale Normen.*

15. See Leroi-Gourhan, *Le Geste et la parole,* vol. 2, *La Mémoire et les rhythmes.*

16. See A. Assmann, "Exkarnation."

17. See Assmann, "Inscriptional Violence and the Art of Cursing."

18. On the doctrine of the ruler as "animated law," see Ehrhardt, *Politische Metaphysik von Solon bis Augustin I,* 168–75; Goodenough, "Die politische Philosophie des hellenistischen Königtums."

19. See Hülkeskamp, "Written Law in Archaic Greece."

20. For Egypt, see Redford, *Pharaonic King-Lists, Annals, and Day-Books.*

21. See Crüsemann, *Die Tora* [*The Torah*]. See also Weinfeld, *Deuteronomy and the Deuteronomic School* and, more recently, Otto, *Das Deuteronomium.*

22. See Otto, *Das Deuteronomium.*

23. See Crüsemann, *Die Tora,* 235–322.

24. See Assmann, "Die Verschriftlichung rechtlicher und sozialer Normen im Alten Ägypten."

25. See Braulik, "Das Deuteronomium und die Gedächtniskultur Israels," quoted from Lohfink, "Der Glaube und die nächste Generation." See also my chapter "Religion als Erinnerung."

26. $w^{e\,\prime}$ *attem tikyû-lî mamlekhet kohonîm* $w^e g \hat{o} y$ *qadôs* (Exod. 19:6).

27. Lethen, *Verhaltenslehren der Kälte,* 7 (my translation).

28. Hans G. Kippenberg ("Die jüdischen Überlieferungen als patrioi nomoi") defines this procedure as a general principle of imperialistic politics: "Wenn Kolonisatoren aus den von ihnen eroberten Territorien ein Imperium machen wollen, dann müssen sie sich zu Beschützern oder geradezu zu Erfindern der Traditionen der unterworfenen Ethnien machen" (51). See also the following: Grevemeyer, "Im Windschatten des Widerstands"; Leclerc, *Anthropologie und Kolonialismus;* Frei and Koch, *Reichsidee und Reichsorganisation im Perserreich;* Kratz, *Translatio imperii,* 161ff., 225ff.

29. Spiegelberg, *Die sogenannte Demotische Chronik,* 30–32. See also Meyer, *Ägyptische Dokumente aus der Perserzeit.*

30. See Lloyd, "The Inscription of Udjahorresnet."

31. See "Der Spätzeittempel als Kanon" in my book *Das kulturelle Gedächtnis,* 177–95.

32. Esra 7:14. For a discussion of the mission of Ezra, see the following: Donner, *Geschichte des Volkes Israel,* 2:416–30; Crüsemann, "Der Pentateuch als Tora"; and Steck, *Der Abschluß der Prophetie im Alten Testament,* 13–21.

33. The Persian title of Ezra was "Scribe of the Law of the God of Heaven." Hans Heinrich Schaeder (*Ezra der Schreiber*) saw Ezra as a Persian secretary of state and commissioner for Jewish affairs.

34. See Yerushalmi, "Réflexions sur l'oubli," esp. 15.

35. See Lohfink, "Der Begriff des Gottesreichs vom Alten Testament her gesehen." See also Assmann, *Politische Theologie zwischen Ägypten und Israel*, 73–80.

36. On this point see the following: Blenkinsopp, *Prophecy and Canon*, and Lang, "Vom Propheten zum Schriftgelehrten." See also Leiman, *The Canonization of Hebrew Scripture*, and Steck, *Der Abschluß der Prophetie im Alten Testament*. On the concept of an end to prophecy, Josephus (*Contra Apionem*, Book I, secs. 38–41) wrote that the history from Moses until Artaxerxes was written by Moses and the prophets "in thirteen books. The remaining four books contain hymns to god and [prescriptions for leading a good] life." He went on to explain that from Artaxerxes to our times exists a tradition that, however, does not enjoy similar appreciation, because the line of the prophets was discontinued. Only what they left us do we regard and worship as our scripture.

37. Stock, "Textual Communities."

38. See Sanders, *Jewish and Christian Self-Definition*.

39. See Stegemann, *Die Essener, Qumran, Johannes der Täufer und Jesus*, 121.

40. Douglas, *In the Wilderness*.

41. See Baumgarten, "Literacy and Its Implications."

42. Egyptian libraries (*pr mdзt*, "house of scrolls," *hierá bibliothéke*, according to Diodor I, 49.3) were affiliated with the temples and contained those books and writings deemed necessary for the functioning of the temple and the performance of cultic activities. See Burkard, "Bibliotheken im alten Ägypten."

43. For a discussion of these catalogues, see the following: Grimm, "Alt-ägyptische Tempelliteratur," 168–69; Redford, *Pharaonic King-Lists, Annals, and Day-Books*, 214–30. From Tebtunis come rituals; hymns; cosmographical and geographical books; works on astronomy, magic, wisdom literature, dream-books; medical books; books about the construction, decoration, and administration of temples; onomastica, etc. See Tait, *Papyri from Tebtunis*; Reymond, *From the Contents of the Libraries of the Suchos Temples in the Fayyum*, pt. 2, *From Ancient Egyptian Hermetic Writings*; Fowden, *The Egyptian Hermes*.

44. Clement of Alexandria, *Stromateis* VI, chap. 4, secs. 35–37. See also Fowden, *The Egyptian Hermes*, 58–59.

45. Clement of Alexandria, *Stromateis* VI, chap. 4, sec. 37.

46. See Lang, "The 'Writings'."

47. See Colpe, "Die Ausbildung des Heidenbegriffs."

48. For this aspect of canon as an all-encompassing foundation of lifestyle and collective identity, see Halbertal, *People of the Book*.

49. See Dick, "Prophetic Parodies of Making the Cult Image."

50. See Loretz, *Des Gottes Einzigkeit*.

51. See my *Moses the Egyptian* and *Die Mosaische Unterscheidung*.

52. See Halbertal and Margalit, *Idolatry*, 37–66.

Chapter 6. No God but God

1. The distinction between "exclusive" and "inclusive" monotheism corresponds *grosso modo* to what John Dillon has called "hard" and "soft" monotheism. See his essay "Monotheism in the Gnostic Tradition."

2. See esp. Loretz, "Die Einzigkeit eines Gottes im Polytheismus von Ugarit"; idem, *Des Gottes Einzigkeit.*

3. Maimonides, *Moreh Nebuchim* III, chap. 32.

4. See A. Assmann, *Zeit und Tradition,* 47–53.

5. For a discussion of the history rather than the memory of monotheism, see the following: Krebernik and van Oorschot, *Polytheismus und Monotheismus;* Porter, *One God or Many?;* and Dietrich and Klopfenstein, *Ein Gott allein?*

6. Hume, "Comparison of these Religions [viz. polytheism and monotheism], with Regard to Persecution and Toleration." In several of his writings Schopenhauer carried the argument even further. For modern critiques of religion along these lines see Schwartz, *The Curse of Cain.* See also Kirsch, *God against the Gods.*

7. For a discussion of this term, see my book *Moses the Egyptian,* 269.

8. See Assmann and Sundermeier, *Die Erfindung des inneren Menschen.* See also Geller, "The God of the Covenant," 287, 296–302, 310–15.

9. The immediately eradicated and long-forgotten monotheistic episode in Egyptian history, namely, the religion of the "sun-disk" instituted by King Akhenaten in the middle of the fourteenth century BCE, did not serve as a model for the prophets. These two movements were only associated much later, in Manetho's account of the iconoclastic assault on Egyptian religion by the "lepers," or "impure ones," under the leadership of "Osarsiph, who took on the name of Moses." See chapter 2 of my *Moses the Egyptian.* See also Schäfer, *Judeophobia.*

10. See Schwager, *Brauchen wir einen Sündenbock?*

11. This is how my book *Moses the Egyptian* has been understood by a number of critics. I have reprinted the most important of these critical responses in my book *Die Mosaische Unterscheidung,* where I attempt to answer my critics.

12. See Schwartz, *The Curse of Cain.*

13. See Kirsch, *God against the Gods.*

14. Alter, *The Five Books of Moses.*

15. Exod. 32:26–28 and Deut. 13:7–10, respectively.

16. See the following: Weinfeld, *Deuteronomy and the Deuteronomic School;* idem, *Deuteronomy 1–11;* Levinson, "'But you shall surely kill him'"; Steymans, *Deuteronomium 28 und die adê zur Thronfolgeregelung Asarhaddons;* Otto, *Das Deuteronomium.*

17. Keel, "Monotheismus." See also Keel's brilliant article *Kanaan—Israel—Christentum.*

18. Geller, "The God of the Covenant," 324.

19. See Smith, *Palestinian Parties and Politics That Shaped the Old Testament.* See also Lang, *Der Einzige Gott.*

20. Even Saint Paul admits that "there are many gods and many lords," adding that "for us there is one God, the Father, of whom are all things, and we for Him; and one Lord Jesus Christ, through whom are all things, and through whom we live" (1 Cor. 8:5). This is the basis of the distinction, commitment, and required loyalty at stake in the new form of religion described as biblical monotheism.

21. Num. 25:1–11.

22. Cf. Exod. 23:31–32: "And I will fix its borders from the Red Sea to the sea of the Philistines, and from the wilderness to the Euphrates, for I shall give into your hand the inhabitants of the land, and you will drive them out before you. You shall not make a pact with them or with their gods. They shall not dwell in your land, lest they cause you to offend Me, for should you worship their gods, it will be a snare for you." The destruction of holy places is also mentioned in Deuteronomy (12:2–3): "You shall utterly destroy all the places where the nations whom you are to dispossess worshipped their gods—on the high mountains and in the valleys and under every lush tree. And you shall smash their altars and shatter their sacred pillars, and their cultic poles you shall burn in fire; and the images of their gods you shall chop down and you shall destroy their name from that place."

23. Deut. 20:10–14.

24. Deut. 20:15–18.

25. This term denotes a form of sacrifice. See Stern, *The Biblical Herem*. See also Niditch, *War in the Hebrew Bible*. The *herem* concept and its application to a conquered town is no Israelite invention; see note 28 below.

26. See the following: Kratz, *Reste hebräischen Heidentums am Beispiel der Psalmen*; Keel, *Kanaan—Israel—Christentum*; Uehlinger, "The 'Canaanites' and Other 'Pre-Israelite' Peoples." Earlier studies in this area include Halpern, *The Emergence of Israel in Canaan*, and Levenson, "Is There a Counterpart in the Hebrew Bible to New Testament Antisemitism?"

27. Keel, *Kanaan—Israel—Christentum*, 5. Keel stresses the "violence" of this separation, by means of which "Israel" cuts itself off from its own origins. Ronald Hendel deals at great length with the stress biblical texts place on the difference between Israel and "the peoples." See his *Remembering Abraham*.

28. Cf. the Mesha Inscription: "And the men of Gad lived in the land of Atarot from ancient times; and the king of Israel built Atarot for himself; and I fought against the city and captured it. And I killed all the people of the city as a *ryt* (satiation-offering?) for Kemosh and for Moab. And I brought back *'r'l dwdh* from there; and I brought it before the face of Kemosh in the Qiriath, and I made the men of Sharon live there, as well as the men of Maharit. And Kemosh said to me, 'Go, take Nebo from Israel.' And I went in the night and fought against it from the daybreak until midday, and I took it and I killed the whole population: seven thousand male subjects and aliens, and female subjects, aliens, and servant girls. For I had put it to *hrm* (the ban) for Ashtar Kemosh. And from

there I took *'r'ly* (or *'t kly,* 'vessels') of YHWH and I presented them before the face of Kemosh" (11.11–17). Quoted in Albright, "The Moabite Stone," with adaptations by Hanson, "The Mesha Stele," and by Ross, "The Stela of Mesha."

29. See Younger, *Ancient Conquest Accounts,* 98.

30. See the following: Halpern, *The Emergence of Israel in Canaan;* Finkelstein, *The Archaeology of the Israelite Settlement;* and Spence, *Narrative Truth and Historical Truth.*

31. For the presumably fictional and literary character of the *herem* Ban on the Canaanites, see the following: Weinfeld, "The Ban on the Canaanites"; Braulik, "Die Völkervernichtung und die Rückkehr Israels ins Verheißungsland"; and Geller, "The Rape of Dinah."

32. I have mainly based my reading of Maccabees on Hengel, *Judentum und Hellenismus,* and Gruen, *Heritage and Hellenism.* See also Kirsch, *God against the Gods,* 78–82.

33. 1 Macc. 1:43–56.

34. This, at least, is the thesis put forward by Elias Bickerman in his book *Der Gott der Makkabäer* [*The God of the Maccabees*]. This thesis was further developed by Hengel; see his *Judentum und Hellenismus,* 503–70.

35. Deut. 30:19.

36. Deut. 13:13–17.

37. Mark 14:49.

38. Deut. 7:2.

39. See Kirsch, *God against the Gods,* 82. There can be little doubt, however, that the forced circumcision and conversion of the Idumaeans following the conquest of their territory by Johannes Hyrkanos, as recounted by Josephus Flavius (*Ant.* 13, 257–58, cf. 13, 318), corresponds to historical fact. See Keel, *Kanaan—Israel—Christentum,* 7.

40. See Agus, *The Binding of Isaac and the Messiah.*

41. See Assmann and Assmann; chapter 3 in Assmann, *Das kulturelle Gedächtnis.* See also chapter 5 in the present book.

42. This is also the reason why the term "religion" should not be applied to pagan and monotheistic religions alike. Religion in the sense of the Deuteronomic revolution is as much of an innovation as the belief in a single God. This is the origin of our notion of religion not as a mere system of divine cult and communication but as the foundation of every aspect of collective and individual life.

43. On Thomas Mann, see my chapter "Zitathaftes Leben" ["A Life in Quotation"]. See also Fishbane (*Biblical Interpretation in Ancient Israel*), who repeatedly uses the phrase "Zitathaftes Leben" with reference both to Thomas Mann and the Bible.

44. On martyrdom, see Boyarin, *Dying for God.*

45. This principle is best illustrated by the martyrdom of Hannah and her seven sons as recounted not in 2 Maccabees but in the Midrash on Lamentations (Threni Rabbah); see Agus, *The Binding of Isaac and the Messiah,* 17–20.

46. Luhmann, "Rechtszwang und politische Gewalt," 154 (my translation), quoted in Conrad, "Der Begriff des Politischen, die Gewalt und Gandhis gewaltlose politische Aktion," 77–78.

47. Exod. 20:5–6 = Deut. 5:9–10.

48. See n.17.

49. See chapter 5 of my book *Das kulturelle Gedächtnis*.

50. See Brelich, "Politeismo e soteriologia."

51. The late Fritz Stolz characterized monotheism as the "Unterscheidung von Gott und Welt." See chapter 8 in his *Weltbilder der Religionen*, 139–212.

52. This fact was pointed out to me in discussions with Aviezer Ravitzky. However, one should recall the use to which the Amalek quotation has been put on the monument of the unknown Jewish martyr in Paris. The Hebrew inscription opens with a quotation from Deuteronomy, "Remember what things Amalek did to thee" (*Zakhor et-asher-asah le-kha Amalek*), continuing: "the Amalek of our time who extinguished 6 millions lives, bodies and souls, without there having been war" (25:17). The texts are there and only God knows what use later generations will make of them under changing situations.

53. See Baumgarten, "Toleranz im Rabbinischen Judentum."

54. Kirsch, *God against the Gods*, 89.

Conclusion

1. Assmann, "The Mosaic Distinction."

2. Some of the more important objections appear in my book *Die Mosaische Unterscheidung*.

3. Cf. Numenios of Apamea: "What is Plato other than a Moses speaking Greek?" (Clement of Alexandria, *Stromateis* I, chap. 22, sec. 150).

4. See Strabo of Amaseia, *Geography* XVI, ch. 2, secs. 35–36, in Stern, *Greek and Latin Authors on Jews and Judaism*, 1:115. See also Schäfer, *Judeophobia*, 24–26.

5. Hecataeus of Abdera, apud Diodorus Siculus, *Bibliotheca Historica* 40, ch. 3, secs. 1–3, in Stern, *Greek and Latin Authors on Jews and Judaism*, 1:11. See also Schäfer, *Judeophobia*, 15–17.

6. The pertinent texts have been collected and analyzed by Preuss, *Verspottung fremder Religionen im Alten Testament*. For a convincing criticism of Preuss's theological approach, see Keel, *Kanaan—Israel—Christentum*, 7–8.

7. In his magisterial study of ancient Egyptian examples of satire, Peter Seibert has analyzed the specific devices of satirical distortion, defamiliarization, or "estrangement." See his book *Die Charakteristik*.

8. See Kristeva, *Les Pouvoirs de l'horreur* [*Powers of Horror*].

9. See Boyarin, "The Christian Invention of Judaism"; idem, *Borderlines*.

10. Schwartz, "The Age of Transcendence," 3–4.

11. For a discussion of *contemptus mundi*, including its long history beyond antiquity, and the ambivalence toward "world" in ancient Christian thinking,

see Wimbush, "Ascetic Impulse in Ancient Christianity." He refers in particular to Jean Delumeau's *Sin and Fear: The Emergence of a Western Guilt Culture*.

12. Here is the original German: "Die Weltgeschichte ist nicht der Boden des Glücks. Die Perioden des Glücks sind leere Blätter in ihr; denn sie sind die Perioden der Zusammenstimmung, des fehlenden Gegensatzes." Hegel, *Vorlesungen über die Philosophie der Geschichte*, 71.

13. Mendelssohn, *Jerusalem oder religiöse Macht und Judentum*, 90 (my translation; italics in original).

14. Galtung, *Strukturelle Gewalt*.

15. Benjamin, "Zur Kritik der Gewalt." See also Derrida, *Gesetzeskraft*.

16. Schmitt, *The Concept of the Political*.

17. Erikson, "Ontogeny of Ritualization in Man."

18. See Conrad, *Gandhi und der Begriff des Politischen*.

BIBLIOGRAPHY

Agus, Aharon. *The Binding of Isaac and the Messiah*. Albany: State University of New York Press, 1988.

Al-Azmeh, Aziz, and János M. Bak, eds. *Monotheistic Kingship: The Medieval Variants*. Budapest: Central European University Press, 2004.

Albert, Jean-Pierre, and Beatrix Midant-Reynes, eds. *Le Sacrifice humain en Égypte ancienne et ailleurs*. Paris: Soleb, 2006.

Albertz, Rainer. *A History of Israelite Religion in the Old Testament Period*. London: SCM Press, 1994.

Albrektson, B. *History and the Gods: An Essay on the Idea of Historical Events as Divine Manifestations in the Ancient Near East and in Israel*. Lund, Sweden: Gleerup, 1967.

Albright, W. F. "The Moabite Stone." In *Ancient Near Eastern Texts Relating to the Old Testament*, ed. James P. Pritchard, 320–21. 3rd ed. Princeton, N.J.: Princeton University Press, 1969.

Alter, Robert. *The Five Books of Moses*. New York: Norton, 2004.

Armstrong, Karen. *The Great Transformation: The Beginning of Our Religious Traditions*. New York: Knopf, 2006.

———. *A History of God: The 4,000-Year Quest of Judaism, Christianity, and Islam*. New York: Ballantine Books, 1993.

Árnason, Jóhann Páll, S. N. Eisenstadt, and Björn Wittrock, eds. *Axial Civilizations and World History*. Leiden: Brill, 2005.

Assmann, Aleida. *Erinnerungsräume: Formen und Wandlungen des kulturellen Gedächtnisses*. Munich: C. H. Beck, 1999.

———. "Exkarnation: Über die Grenze zwischen Körper und Schrift." In *Interventionen*, ed. Alois M. Müller and J. Huber, 159–81. Basel: Stroemfeld, 1993.

———. *Zeit und Tradition: Kulturelle Strategien der Dauer*. Cologne: Böhlau, 1999.

———, and Jan Assmann, eds. *Kanon und Zensur*. Munich: Fink, 1987.

Assmann, Jan. *Ägypten: Eine Sinngeschichte*. Munich: Hanser, 1996. Translated by Andrew Jenkins as *The Mind of Egypt* (New York: Metropolitan Books, 2002; Cambridge, Mass.: Harvard University Press, 2003).

———. *Ägypten: Theologie und Frömmigkeit einer frühen Hochkultur.* 2nd ed. Stuttgart: Kohlhammer, 1991. Translated by David Lorton as *The Search for God in Ancient Egypt* (Ithaca, N.Y.: Cornell University Press, 2001).

———. *Ägyptische Hymnen und Gebete [ÄHG].* Zurich: Artemis, 1975.

———. "Das ägyptische Prozessionsfest." In *Das Fest und das Heilige: Religiöse Kontrapunkte zur Alltagswelt,* ed. Jan Assmann and Theo Sundermeier, 105–22. Gütersloh: Gütersloher Verlagshaus, 1991.

———. "Altorientalische Fluchinschriften und das Problem performativer Schriftlichkeit." In *Schrift,* ed. Hans Ulrich Gumbrecht and Karl Ludwig Pfeiffer, 233–55. Munich: W. Fink, 1993.

———. "Axial 'Breakthroughs' and Semantic 'Relocations' in Ancient Egypt and Israel." In *Axial Civilizations and World History,* ed. Johann P. Arnason, S. N. Eisenstadt, and Björn Wittrock, 133–56. Boston: Brill, 2005.

———. *Egyptian Solar Religion in the New Kingdom: Re, Amun, and the Crisis of Polytheism.* Translated by Anthony Alcock. London: Kegan Paul International, 1995. Originally published as *Re und Amen: Die Krise des polytheistischen Weltbilds im Ägypten der 18.–20. Dynastie* (Freiburg: Universitätsverlag, 1983).

———. "Fünf Wege zum Kanon: Tradition und Schriftkultur im alten Israel und frühen Judentum." In *Wissensbilder: Strategien der Überlieferung,* ed. Ulrich Raulff and Gary Smith, 13–31. Berlin: Akademie Verlag, 1999. Translated by Rodney Livingstone as "Five Stages on the Road to the Canon: Tradition and Written Culture in Ancient Israel and Early Judaism," in Assmann, *Religion and Cultural Memory,* 63–80.

———. *Herrschaft und Heil: Politische Theologie in Altägypten.* Munich: Hanser, 2000.

———. "Inscriptional Violence and the Art of Cursing: A Study of Performative Writing." *Stanford Literature Review* 9 (1992): 43–65. German version in *Schrift,* ed. Hans Ulrich Gumbrecht and K. Ludwig Pfeiffer, 233–56 (Munich: W. Fink, 1993).

———. "Kultlied." In Helck and Otto, *Lexikon der Ägyptologie,* 3:852–55.

———. *Das kulturelle Gedächtnis: Schrift, Erinnerung und politische Identität in frühen Hochkulturen.* 3rd ed. Munich: C. H. Beck, 1999.

———. *Liturgische Lieder an den Sonnengott.* Berlin: Hessling, 1969.

———. *Ma'at: Gerechtigkeit und Unsterblichkeit im alten Ägypten.* Munich: C. H. Beck, 1990.

———. "The Mosaic Distinction: Israel, Egypt, and the Invention of Paganism." *Representations* 56 (1996): 48–67.

———. *Die Mosaische Unterscheidung oder der Preis des Monotheismus* [The Mosaic Distinction]. Munich: Carl Hanser, 2003.

———. *Moses the Egyptian.* Cambridge, Mass.: Harvard University Press, 1997.

———. *Politische Theologie zwischen Ägypten und Israel.* 3rd ed. Munich: Carl Friedrich von Siemens Stiftung, 2006.

———. "Religion als Erinnerung: Das Deuteronomium als Paradigma kultureller Mnemotechnik." In Assmann, *Das kulturelle Gedächtnis,* 212–28.

———. *Religion and Cultural Memory.* Stanford: Stanford University Press, 2006.

———. *Re und Amen: Die Krise des polytheistischen Weltbilds im Ägypten der 18.–20. Dynastie.* Freiburg: Universitätsverlag, 1983.

———. *Sonnenhymnen in Thebanischen Gräbern [STG].* Mainz: Philipp von Zabern, 1983.

———. "State and Religion in the New Kingdom." In *Religion and Philosophy in Ancient Egypt,* ed. James P. Allen et al., 55–88. New Haven, Conn.: Dept. of Near Eastern Languages and Civilizations, Yale University, 1989.

———. *Stein und Zeit: Mensch und Gesellschaft im alten Ägypten.* Munich: W. Fink, 1991.

———. *Tod und Jenseits im Alten Ägypten.* Munich: C. H. Beck, 2001.

———. "Translating Gods: Religion as a Factor of Cultural (In)Translatability." In Budick and Iser, *Translatability of Cultures,* 25–36.

———. "Die Verschriftlichung rechtlicher und sozialer Normen im Alten Ägypten." In Gehrke, *Rechtskodifizierung und soziale Normen,* 61–85.

———. "Weisheit, Loyalismus und Frömmigkeit." In *Studien zu altägyptischen Lebenslehren,* ed. Erik Hornung and Othmar Keel, 11–72. Freiburg: Universitätsverlag, 1979.

———. *Zeit und Ewigkeit im alten Ägypten: Ein Beitrag zur Geschichte der Ewigkeit.* Heidelberg: C. Winter, 1975.

———. "Zitathaftes Leben: Thomas Mann und die Phänomenologie der kulturellen Erinnerung." In Assmann, *Religion und kulturelles Gedächtnis,* 133–58. Munich: C. H. Beck, 2000. Translated by Rodney Livingstone as "A Life in Quotation: Thomas Mann and the Phenomenology of Cultural Memory," in Assmann, *Religion and Cultural Memory,* 155–77.

———, and Theo Sundermeier, eds. *Die Erfindung des inneren Menschen.* Gütersloh: Gütersloher Verlagshaus, 1993.

Athanassiadi, Polymnia, and Michael Frede, eds. *Pagan Monotheism in Late Antiquity.* Oxford: Oxford University Press, 1999.

Babbitt, Frank Cole, trans. *Plutarch's Moralia.* 15 vols. Cambridge, Mass.: Harvard University Press, 1962.

Baines, John. "Egyptian Deities in Context." In Porter, *One God or Many?* 9–78.

Baltzer, Klaus. *Das Bundesformular.* 2nd ed. Neukirchen-Vluyn: Neukirchener Verlag, 1964.

Baumgarten, Albert I. "Literacy and Its Implications." In his *The Flourishing of Jewish Sects in the Maccabean Era: An Interpretation,* 114–36. Leiden: Brill, 1997.

———. "Toleranz im Rabbinischen Judentum: Eine Fallstudie aus der Antike und ihr Ertrag für die Gegenwart." In *Konstruktive Toleranz—Gelebter Pluralismus: Erfahrungen mit dem Zusammenleben von Religionen und Kulturen,* ed. Andreas Feldtkeller, 53–69. Frankfurt: Lembeck, 2001.

Becker, Uwe. "Von der Staatsreligion zum Monotheismus." *Zeitschrift für Theologie und Kirche* 102 (2005): 1–16.

Benjamin, Walter. "Zur Kritik der Gewalt." In *Gesammelte Schriften,* 7 vols., ed.

Rolf Tiedemann and Hermann Schweppenhäuser, vol. 2, part 1, 179–203. Frankfurt: Suhrkamp, 1974.

Berlejung, Angelika. *Die Theologie der Bilder: Herstellung und Einweihung von Bildern in Mesopotamien und die alttestamentliche Bilderpolemik.* Freiburg: Universitätsverlag, 1998.

Bickerman, Elias. *Der Gott der Makkabäer.* Berlin: Schocken, 1937. Translated by Horst R. Moehring as *The God of the Maccabees* (Leiden: Brill, 1979).

———. "Ritualmord und Eselskult." In his *Studies in Jewish and Christian History,* 3 vols., 2:225–55. Leiden: Brill, 1980.

Blenkinsopp, Joseph. *Prophecy and Canon.* Notre Dame, Ind.: University of Notre Dame Press, 1977.

Bonnechère, Pierre. *Le Sacrifice humain en Grèce ancienne.* Athens: Centre international d'étude de la religion grecque antique, 1994.

Bonnet, Hans. "Egyptian Deities in Context." In Porter, *One God or Many?* 9–78.

———. "Zum Verständnis des Synkretismus." *Zeitschrift für ägyptische Sprache und Altertumskunde* 75 (1939): 40–52. Translated by John Baines as "On Understanding Syncretism," *Orientalia* 68 (1999): 181–99.

Bori, Pier Cesare. *The Golden Calf and the Origins of the Anti-Jewish Controversy.* Atlanta, Ga.: Scholars Press, 1990.

Bottéro, Jean. "Les Noms de Marduk, l'écriture et la 'logique' en Mésopotamie ancienne." In *Essays on the Ancient Near East in Memory of Jacob Joel Finkelstein,* ed. Maria de Jong Ellis, 5–28. Hamden: Connecticut Academy of Arts and Sciences, 1977.

———. "Symptomes, signes, écritures." In *Divination et Rationalité,* ed. Jean Pierre Vernant et al., 70–198. Paris: Seuil, 1974.

Bourdieu, Paul. *Zur Soziologie der symbolischen Formen.* Frankfurt: Suhrkamp, 1974.

Boyarin, Daniel. *Borderlines: The Partition of Judaeo-Christianity.* Philadelphia: University of Pennsylvania Press, 2004.

———. "The Christian Invention of Judaism: The Theodosian Empire and the Rabbinic Refusal of Religion." *Representations* 85 (2004): 21–57.

———. *Dying for God: Martyrdom and the Making of Christianity and Judaism.* Stanford: Stanford University Press, 1999.

Braulik, Georg. "Das Deuteronomium und die Gedächtniskultur Israels: Redaktionsgeschichtliche Beobachtungen zur Verwendung von *lamad.*" In *Biblische Theologie und gesellschaftlicher Wandel: Für Norbert Lohfink SJ,* ed. Georg Braulik, Walter Groß, and Sean McEvenue, 9–31. Freiburg: Herder, 1993.

———. "Die Völkervernichtung und die Rückkehr Israels ins Verheißungsland: Hermeneutische Bemerkungen zum Buch Deuteronomium." In *Deuteronomy and Deuteronomic Literature: Festschrift C. H. W. Brekelmans,* ed. M. Vervenne and J. Lust, 3–38. Leuven, Belgium: Peeters, 1997.

Breasted, John Henry. *The Development of Religion and Thought in Ancient Egypt.* 1912. Reprint, Philadelphia: University of Pennsylvania Press, 1972.

Brelich, Angelo. "Politeismo e soteriologia." In *The Saviour God: Comparative*

Studies in the Concept of Salvation, ed. S. G. F. Brandon, 37–50. Manchester, Eng.: Manchester University Press, 1963.

Budick, Sanford, and Wolfgang Iser, eds. *Translatability of Cultures: Figurations of the Space Between.* Stanford: Stanford University Press, 1996.

Burkard, Günter. "Bibliotheken im alten Ägypten." *Bibliothek, Forschung und Praxis* 4, no. 2 (1980): 79–115.

Burkert, Walter. *Homo Necans: The Anthropology of Ancient Greek Sacrificial Ritual and Myth.* Translated by Peter Bing. Berkeley: University of California Press, 1983.

Cancik, Hubert. *Grundzüge der hethitischen und alttestamentlichen Geschichtsschreibung.* Wiesbaden: Harrassowitz, 1976.

Canfora, Luciano, Mario Liverani, and Carlo Zaccagnini, eds. *I Trattati nel Mondo Antico: Forma, Ideologia, Funzione.* Rome: "l'Erma" di Bretschneider, 1990.

Chassinat, Emile. *Le Temple d' Edfou.* 14 vols. Cairo: Imprimerie de l'Institut français d'archéologie orientale, 1928.

Chuvin, Pierre. *A Chronicle of the Last Pagans.* Translated by B. A. Archer. Cambridge, Mass.: Harvard University Press, 1990.

Clastres, Pierre. *La Société contre l'état.* Paris: Éditions de minuit, 1974. Translated by Robert Hurley as *Society against the State* (New York: Zone Books, 1989).

Cogan, Mordechai. *Imperialism and Religion: Assyria, Judah and Israel in the Eighth and Seventh Centuries BCE.* Missoula, Mont.: Society of Biblical Literature, 1974.

Colpe, Carsten. "Die Ausbildung des Heidenbegriffs von Israel zur Apologetik und das Zweideutigwerden des Christentums." In *Die Restauration der Götter: Antike Religion und Neo-Paganismus*, ed. Richard Faber and Renate Schlesier, 61–87. Würzburg: Königshausen & Neumann, 1986.

———, and Jens Holzhausen, eds. *Das Corpus Hermeticum Deutsch.* 2 vols. Stuttgart–Bad Cannstatt: Frommann-Hozboog, 1997.

Conrad, Dieter. "Der Begriff des Politischen, die Gewalt und Gandhis gewaltlose politische Aktion." In *Kultur und Konflikt*, ed. Jan Assmann and Dietrich Harth, 72–112. Frankfurt am Main: Suhrkamp, 1990.

———. *Gandhi und der Begriff des Politischen: Staat, Religion und Gewalt.* Munich: W. Fink, 2006.

Craig, James Alexander. *Assyrian and Babylonian Religious Texts.* 2 vols. Leipzig: J. C. Hinrichs, 1895–97.

Crüsemann, Frank. "Der Pentateuch als Tora." *Evangelische Theologie* 49 (1989): 250–67.

———. *Die Tora: Theologie und Sozialgeschichte des alttestamentlichen Gesetzes.* Munich: Chr. Kaiser, 1992. Translated by Allan W. Mahnke as *The Torah: Theology and Social History of Old Testament Law* (Minneapolis: Fortress Press, 1997).

Cudworth, Ralph. *The True Intellectual System of the Universe.* London: Printed for Richard Royston, 1678.

Delumeau, Jean. *Sin and Fear: The Emergence of a Western Guilt Culture, 13th–18th Centuries.* New York: St. Martin's Press, 1990.

Derrida, Jacques. *Gesetzeskraft: Der "mystische Grund der Autorität."* Translated by Alexander García Düttmann. Frankfurt: Suhrkamp, 1991.

Des Places, Edouard, ed. and trans. *Les Mystères d'Egypte.* Paris: Les Belles Lettres, 1993.

Dick, Michael B. "Prophetic Parodies of Making the Cult Image." In *Born in Heaven, Made on Earth: The Making of the Cult Image in the Ancient Near East,* ed. Michael B. Dick, 1–54. Winona Lake, Ind.: Eisenbrauns, 1999.

Dietrich, Walter, and Martin A. Klopfenstein, eds. *Ein Gott allein?* Freiburg: Universitätsverlag, 1994.

Dihle, Albrecht. "Die Theologia tripertita bei Augustin." In *Geschichte, Tradition, Reflexion: Festschrift für Martin Hengel zum 70. Geburstag,* ed. Hubert Cancik et al., 183–202. Tübingen: Mohr, 1996.

Dillon, Josh. "Monotheism in the Gnostic Tradition." In Athanassiadi and Frede, *Pagan Monotheism in Late Antiquity,* 69–79.

Dohmen, Christoph. *Das Bilderverbot.* 2nd ed. Frankfurt: Beltz Athenäum, 1987.

Donner, Herbert. *Geschichte des Volkes Israel und seiner Nachbarn in Grundzügen.* 4 vols. Göttingen: Vandenhoeck & Ruprecht, 1986.

Douglas, Mary. *In the Wilderness: The Doctrine of Defilement in the Book of Numbers.* Oxford: Oxford University Press, 2001.

Dunand, Francoise. "Le Syncrétisme isiaque à la fin de l'époque hellénistique." In *Les Syncrétismes dans les religions grecque et romaine,* ed. F. Dunand and P. Lévêque, 79–93. Proceedings of the Bibliothèque des Centres d'Études supérieures spécialisés, Strasbourg, June 9–11, 1971. Paris: Presses universitaires de France, 1973.

Ebeling, Erich. *Keilschrifttexte aus Assur religiösen Inhalts.* Leipzig: J. C. Hinrichs, 1915–1923.

Ehrhardt, Arnold A. T. *Politische Metaphysik von Solon bis Augustin I.* Tübingen: Mohr, 1959.

———, ed. *Kulturen der Achsenzeit II: Ihre institutionelle und kulturelle Dynamik.* 3 vols. Frankfurt: Suhrkamp, 1992.

———, ed. *The Origin and Diversity of Axial Civilizations.* Albany: SUNY Press, 1986.

Eisenstadt, Shmuel N., ed. *Kulturen der Achsenzeit: Ihre Ursprünge und ihre Vielfalt.* 2 vols. Frankfurt: Suhrkamp, 1987.

Eliade, Mircea. *Le Mythe de l'éternel retour.* Paris: Gallimard, 1949. Translated by Günther Spaltmann as *Kosmos und Geschichte* (Reinbek: Rowohlt, 1966) and by Willard R. Trask as *The Myth of the Eternal Return: Or, Cosmos and History* (Princeton, N.J.: Princeton University Press, 1971).

Elm, Susanna. "Hellenism and Historiography: Gregory of Nazianzus and Julian in Dialogue." *Journal of Medieval and Early Modern Studies* 33 (2003): 493–515.

Erdheim, Mario. *Die gesellschaftliche Produktion von Unbewußtheit.* Frankfurt: Suhrkamp, 1984.

————. *Die Psychoanalyse und das Unbewußte in der Kultur.* Frankfurt: Suhrkamp, 1988.

Erikson, Erik H. "Ontogeny of Ritualization in Man." *Philosophical Transactions of the Royal Society* (1966): 251 B, 337–49.

Erman, Adolf, and Hermann Grapow, eds. *Wörterbuch der ägyptischen Sprache.* 7 vols. Leipzig: Hinrichs, 1926. Reprint, Berlin: Akademie Verlag, 1953.

Falkenstein, Adam. "Fluch über Akkade." *Zeitschrift für Assyriologie* 57 (1965): 43–124.

Fecht, Gerhard. "Frühformen der Amarna-Religion." *Zeitschrift für Ägyptische Sprache* 94 (1967): 25–50.

Festugière, André-Jean. *La Révélation d'Hermès Trismégiste.* Vol. 2, *Le Dieu cosmique.* Paris: Les Belles Lettres, 1949.

Finkelstein, Israel. *The Archaeology of the Israelite Settlement.* Jerusalem: Israel Exploration Society, 1988.

Fishbane, Michael. *Biblical Interpretation in Ancient Israel.* Oxford: Oxford University Press, 1985.

————. *Biblical Myth and Rabbinic Mythmaking.* New York: Oxford University Press, 2003.

Foster, Benjamin. *Before the Muses.* 2 vols. Bethesda: Maryland University Press, 1993.

Fowden, Garth. *The Egyptian Hermes: A Historical Approach to the Late Pagan Mind.* Cambridge: Cambridge University Press, 1986.

————. *Empire to Commonwealth: Consequences of Monotheism in Late Antiquity.* Princeton, N.J.: Princeton University Press, 1993.

Frankfurter, David. *Elijah in Upper Egypt: The Apocalypse of Elijah and Early Egyptian Christianity.* Minneapolis, Minn.: Fortress Press, 1993.

Frei, Peter, and Klaus Koch. *Reichsidee und Reichsorganisation im Perserreich.* Freiburg: Universitätsverlag, 1984.

Freud, Sigmund. *Moses and Monotheism.* Translated by Katherine Jones. New York: Vintage Books, 1939.

Gager, John G. *Moses in Greco-Roman Paganism.* Nashville, Tenn.: Abingdon, 1972.

Galtung, Johan. *Strukturelle Gewalt.* Reinbek: Rowohlt, 1975.

Gardiner, Alan H. *Late-Egyptian Stories.* Brussels: Editions de la Fondation Egyptologique Reine Elizabeth, 1932.

Gehrke, Hans-Joachim, ed. *Rechtskodifizierung und soziale Normen im interkulturellen Vergleich.* Tübingen: Gunter Narr, 1994.

Geller, Stephen A. "The God of the Covenant." In Porter, *One God or Many?* 273–319.

————. "The Rape of Dinah: Sexuality and Transcendence." In his *Sacred Enigmas: Literary Religion in the Hebrew Bible,* 142–56. London: Routledge, 1996.

Georgoudi, Stella. "À propos du sacrifice humain en Grèce ancienne." *Archiv für Religionsgeschichte* 1, no. 1 (1999): 61–82.

Gladigow, Burkhard. "Polytheismus und Monotheismus: Zur historischen Dynamik einer europäischen Alternative." In *Polytheismus und Monotheismus in den Religionen des Vorderen Orients*, ed. Manfred Krebernik and Jürgen van Oorschot, 3–20. Munster: Ugarit-Verlag, 2002.

Godelier, Maurice. "Mythos und Geschichte: Überlegungen über die Grundlagen des wilden Denkens." In *Seminar: Die Entstehung von Klassengesellschaften*, ed. Klaus Eder, 309–29. Frankfurt: Suhrkamp, 1973.

Goedicke, Hans. "A Neglected Wisdom Text." *Journal of Egyptian Archeology* 48 (1962): 25–35.

———. *The Quarrel of Apophis and Seqenenre*. San Antonio, Tex.: Van Sicklen, 1986.

Goelet, Ogden, and Baruch A. Levine. "Making Peace in Heaven and on Earth: Religious and Legal Aspects of the Treaty between Ramesses II and Hattušili III." In *Boundaries of the Ancient Near Eastern World: A Tribute to Cyrus H. Gordon*, ed. Meir Lubetski, Claire Gottlieb, and Sharon Keller, 252–99. Sheffield, Eng.: Sheffield Academic Press, 1998.

Goldwasser, Orly. "King Apophis of Avaris and the Emergence of Monotheism." In *Timelines: Studies in Honour of Manfred Bietak*, 3 vols., ed. Ernst Czerny et al., 2:129–33. Leiden: Peeters, 2006.

Goodenough, E. R. "Die politische Philosophie des hellenistischen Königtums." In *Ideologie und Herrschaft in der Antike*, ed. Hans Kloft, 27–89. Darmstadt: Wissenschaftliche Buchgesellschaft, 1979.

Götze, Albrecht. *Hattusilis: Der Bericht über seine Thronbesteigung nebst den Paralleltexten*. Darmstadt: Wissenschaftliche Buchgesellschaft, 1967.

———. "Die Pestgebete des Mursilis." In *Kleinasiatische Forschungen*, ed. Ferdinand Sommer and Hans Ehelolf, pt. 1, 16–251. Weimar: H. Böhlaus, 1930.

———, ed. *Die Annalen des Mursilis*. Leipzig, 1933. Reprint, Darmstadt, Wissenschaftliche Buchgesellschaft, 1967.

Grevemeyer, Jan-Heeren. "Im Windschatten des Widerstands." In *Traditionale Gesellschaften und europäischer Kolonialismus*, ed. Jan-Heeren Grevemeyer, 16–46. Frankfurt: Suhrkamp, 1981.

Griffiths, John Gwyn. *The Divine Verdict: A Study of Divine Judgment in the Ancient Religions*. Leiden: Brill, 1991.

———, ed. and trans. *Plutarch's De Iside et Osiride*. Cardiff: University of Wales Press, 1970.

Grimm, Alfred. "Altägyptische Tempelliteratur: Zur Gliederung und Funktion der Bücherkataloge von Edfu und et-Tod." *Studien zur Altägyptischen Kultur*, Suppl. 3 (1988): 162–69.

Gruen, Erich. *Heritage and Hellenism: The Reinvention of Jewish Tradition*. Berkeley: University of California Press, 1998.

Güterbock, Hans G. "The Deeds of Suppiluliuma as Told by His Son Mursili II." *Journal of Cuneiform Studies* 10 (1956): 41–130.

Habermas, Jürgen. *Theorie des kommunikativen Handelns.* 2 vols. Frankfurt: Suhr-kamp, 1981.

Halbertal, Moshe. *People of the Book: Canon, Meaning, and Authority.* Cambridge, Mass.: Harvard University Press, 1997.

——, and Avishai Margalit. *Idolatry.* Cambridge, Mass.: Harvard University Press, 1992.

Halbwachs, Maurice. *La Mémoire collective.* Paris: Presses Universitaires de France, 1950. Translated by Francis J. Ditter and Vida Qazdi Ditter as *The Collective Memory* (New York: Harper and Row, 1980).

——. *On Collective Memory.* Edited and translated by Lewis A. Coser. Chicago: University of Chicago Press, 1992.

Halpern, Baruch. *The Emergence of Israel in Canaan.* Chico, Cal.: Scholars Press, 1983.

Handel, Michael I. *Weak States in the International System.* London: Frank Cass, 1981.

Hanson, K. C. "The Mesha Stele." Available at http://www.kchanson.com/ANCDOCS/westsem/mesha.html (last accessed December 10, 2007).

Hegel, Friedrich. *Vorlesungen über die Philosophie der Geschichte.* Edited by Theodor Litt. Stuttgart: Reclam, 1961.

Helck, Wolfgang, and Eberhard Otto, eds. *Lexikon der Ägyptologie.* 7 vols. Wies-baden: Harrassowitz, 1972–1992.

Hendel, Ronald. *Remembering Abraham: Culture, Memory, and History in the Hebrew Bible.* Oxford: Oxford University Press, 2005.

Hengel, Martin. *Judentum und Hellenismus.* 3rd ed. Tübingen: Mohr, 1988.

Hillers, Delbert R. *Treaty-Curses and the Old Testament Prophets.* Rome: Pontifical Biblical Institute, 1964.

Hoffner, Harry A. "Histories and Historians of the Near East: The Hittites." *Orientalia* 49 (1980): 283–332.

——. "Propaganda and Political Justification in Hittite Historiography." In *Unity and Diversity: Essays in the History, Literature, and Religion of the Ancient Near East,* ed. Hans Goedicke and J. J. M. Roberts, 49–64. Baltimore, Md.: Johns Hopkins University Press, 1975.

Holy Bible: English Standard Version. Wheaton, Ill.: Crossway Bibles, 2001.

Homer, *Iliad.* Translated by Samuel Butler. New York, 1898. Web edition published by ebooks@Adelaide. http://etext.library.adelaide.edu.au/h/homer/h8i/ (last accessed December 10, 2007).

Hopfner, Theodor, ed. *Fontes historiae religionis aegypticaoe.* Bonn: Marcus & Weber, 1923.

Hornung, Eric. *Akhenaten: The Religion of Light.* Ithaca, N.Y.: Cornell University Press, 2000.

——. *Conceptions of God in Ancient Egypt.* Ithaca, N.Y.: Cornell University Press, 1982.

———. "Das Denken des Einen im alten Ägypten." In Krebernik and van Oorschot, *Polytheismus und Monotheismus*, 21–32.

———. *Geschichte als Fest: Zwei Vorträge zum Geschichtsbild der frühen Menschheit.* Darmstadt: Wissenschaftliche Buchgesellschaft, 1966.

———. "Zum altägyptischen Geschichtsbewusstsein." In *Archäologie und Geschichtsbewusstsein*, ed. Hermann Müller-Karpe, 13–30. Munich: C. H. Beck, 1982.

———, ed. *Der ägyptische Mythos von der Himmelskuh: Eine Ätiologie des Unvollkommen.* Freiburg: Universitätsverlag, 1982.

Hout, Theo P. J. van den. "Khattushili III of Khattusha." In *Civilizations of the Ancient Near East,* ed. Jack M. Sasson et al., 1107–20. New York: Scribner, 1995.

Hughes, Dennis D. *Human Sacrifice in Ancient Greece.* London: Routledge, 1991.

Hülkeskamp, Karl-Joachim. "Written Law in Archaic Greece." *Proceedings of the Cambridge Philogical Society* 38 (1992): 87–117.

Hume, David. "Comparison of these Religions, with Regard to Persecution and Toleration." In *Writings on Religion,* ed. Antony Flew, 145–48. LaSalle, Ill.: Open Court, 1992.

Iamblichus. *De mysteriis Aegyptiorum.* Translated by Edouard Des Places as *Les Mystères d'Egypte* (Paris: Les Belles Lettres, 1993).

Josephus, Flavius. *Contra Apionem.* In *Flavii Iosephi Opera,* vol. 5. Edited by Benedikt Niese. Berlin: Weidmann, 1892.

Keel, Othmar. *Kanaan—Israel—Christentum: Plädoyer für eine "vertikale" Ökumene.* Münster: Institutum Judaicum Delitzschianum, 2002.

———. "Monotheismus—ein göttlicher Makel? Über eine allzu bequeme Anklage." *Neue Zürcher Zeitung,* October 30–31, 2004, 68.

———. *Remembering Abraham: Culture, Memory, and History in the Hebrew Bible.* Oxford: Oxford University Press, 2005.

———. "Warum im Jerusalemer Tempel kein anthropomorphes Kultbild gestanden haben dürfte." In *Homo Pictor,* ed. Gottfried Boehm, 244–82. Munich: Saur, 2001.

———, and Christoph Uehlinger. *Gods, Goddesses, and Images of Gods in Ancient Israel.* Minneapolis, Minn.: Fortress Press, 1998.

Kessler, Rainer. *Die Ägyptenbilder der Hebräischen Bibel: Ein Beitrag zur neueren Monotheismusdebatte.* Stuttgart: Katholisches Bibelwerk, 2002.

Kippenberg, Hans G. "Die jüdischen Überlieferungen als patrioi nomoi." In *Die Restauration der Götter: Antike Religion und Neo-Paganismus,* ed. Richard Faber and Renate Schlesier, 45–60. Würzburg: Königshausen & Neumann, 1986.

———. *Die vorderasiatischen Erlösungsreligionen in ihrem Zusammenhang mit der antiken Stadtherrschaft.* Frankfurt: Suhrkamp, 1991.

Kirsch, Jonathan. *God against the Gods: The History of the War between Monotheism and Polytheism.* New York: Viking Compass, 2004.

Kitchen, Kenneth A. *Ramesside Inscriptions*. 8 vols. Oxford: Blackwell, 1966–1990.

Korostovtsev, Mikhail. "La Stèle de Ramses IV (avec deux planches)." *Bulletin de l'Institut français d'archéologie orientale* 54 (1947): 155ff.

Kratz, Reinhard Gregor. *Reste hebräischen Heidentums am Beispiel der Psalmen*. Göttingen: Vandenhoeck & Ruprecht, 2004.

———. *Translatio imperii: Untersuchungen zu den aramäischen Daniel-Erzählungen und ihrem theologie-geschichtlichen Umfeld*. Neukirchen-Vluyn: Neukirchener Verlag, 1991.

Krause, Martin, and Pahor Labib, trans. *Gnostische und hermetische Schriften aus Codex II und Codex VI*. Glückstadt, Ger.: Augustin, 1971.

Krauss, Rolf. *Das Ende der Amarnazeit*. Hildesheim, Ger.: Gerstenberg, 1978.

Krebernik, Manfred. "Vielzahl und Einheit im altmesopotamischen Pantheon." In Krebernik and van Oorschot, *Polytheismus und Monotheismus*, 33–51.

———, and Jürgen van Oorschot, eds. *Polytheismus und Monotheismus in den Religionen des Vorderen Orients*. Munster: Ugarit-Verlag, 2002.

Kristeva, Julia. *Les Pouvoirs de l'horreur: essai sur l'abjection*. Paris: Seuil, 1980. Translated by L. S. Roudiez as *Powers of Horror: An Essay on Abjection* (New York: Columbia University Press, 1982).

Kurth, Dieter. "Götter determinieren Götter." *Studien zur altägyptischen Kultur* 5 (1977): 175–81.

Lang, Bernhard. *Der Einzige Gott: Die Geburt des biblischen Monotheismus*. Munich: C. H. Beck, 1981.

———. "Vom Propheten zum Schriftgelehrten: Charismatische Autorität im Frühjudentum." In *Theologen und Theologien in verschiedenen Kulturkreisen*, ed. Heinrich von Stietencron, 89–114. Düsseldorf: Patmos, 1986.

———. "The 'Writings': A Hellenistic Literary Canon in the Hebrew Bible." In *Canonization and Decanonization*, ed. A. van der Kooij and K. van der Toorn, 41–66. Leiden: Brill, 1998.

Leclerc, Gérard. *Anthropologie und Kolonialismus*. Translated by Hanns Zischler. Munich: Hanser, 1973.

Leiman, Shnayer Z. *The Canonization of Hebrew Scripture: The Talmudic and Midrashic Evidence*. Hamden: Connecticut Academy of Arts and Sciences, 1976.

Leroi-Gourhan, André. *Le Geste et la parole*. Vol. 2, *La Mémoire et les rhythmes*. Paris: Albin Michel, 1965.

Lethen, Helmut. *Verhaltenslehren der Kälte: Lebensversuche zwischen den Kriegen*. Frankfurt: Suhrkamp, 1994.

Levenson, Jon D. "Is There a Counterpart in the Hebrew Bible to New Testament Antisemitism?" *Journal of Ecumenical Studies* 22, no. 2 (1985): 242–60.

Levinson, Bernard M. "'But you shall surely kill him': The Text-Critical and Neo-Assyrian Evidence for MT Deuteronomy 13:10." In *Bundesdokument und Gesetz: Studien zum Deuteronomium*, ed. Georg Braulik, 37–63. Freiburg: Herder, 1995.

Lewis, C. S. *The Allegory of Love.* Oxford: Oxford University Press, 1958.

Liebeschuetz, Wolf . "Significance of the Speech of Praetextatus." In Athanassiadi and Frede, *Pagan Monotheism,* 185–205.

Litke, Richard L. *Reconstruction of the Assyro-Babylonian God-lists, AN: dA-nu-um and AN: Anu sá ameli.* New Haven, Conn.: Yale Babylonian Collection, 1998.

Livingstone, Alasdair. *Court Poetry and Literary Miscellanea.* Helsinki: Helsinki University Press, 1989.

Lloyd, A. B. "The Inscription of Udjahorresnet, a Collaborator's Testament." *Journal of Egyptian Archaeology* 68 (1982): 166–80.

Lohfink, Norbert. "Der Begriff des Gottesreichs vom Alten Testament her gesehen." In *Unterwegs zur Kirche: Alttestamentliche Konzeptionen,* ed. Josef Schreiner, 33–86. Freiburg: Herder, 1987.

———. "Der gewalttätige Gott des Alten Testaments und die Suche nach einer gewaltfreien Gesellschaft." In *Der eine Gott der beiden Testamente,* ed. Ingo Baldermann, 106–36. Neukirchen-Vluyn: Neukirchener Verlag, 1987.

———. "Der Glaube und die nächste Generation: Das Gottesvolk der Bibel als Lerngemeinschaft." In his *Das Jüdische am Christentum,* 144–66. Freiburg: Herder, 1987.

Loprieno, Antonio. *La Pensée et l'écriture.* Paris: Cybèle, 2002.

Loretz, Oswald. "Die Einzigkeit eines Gottes im Polytheismus von Ugarit: Zur Levante als Ursprungsort des biblischen Monotheismus." In Krebernik and van Oorschot, *Polytheismus und Monotheismus,* 71–89.

———. *Des Gottes Einzigkeit: Ein altorientalisches Argumentationsmodell zum "Schma Jisrael."* Darmstadt: Wissenschaftliche Buchgesellschaft, 1997.

Luckenbill, Daniel David. *Ancient Records of Assyria and Babylonia: Histories and Mysteries.* 2 vols. 1926–27. Reprint, Winona Lake, Ind.: Eisenbrauns, 1989.

Luhmann, Niklas. "Rechtszwang und politische Gewalt." In his *Ausdifferenzierung des Rechts: Beiträge zur Rechtssoziologie und Rechtstheorie,* 154–72. Frankfurt am Main: Suhrkamp, 1999.

Mahé, Jean-Pierre. *Hermès en Haute-Égypte.* Vol. 2, *Le Fragment du Discours Parfait et les définitions hermétiques arméniennes* (NH VI, 8.8a). Quebec: Presses de l'Université Laval, 1982.

Malamat, Abraham. "The Kingdom of Judah between Egypt and Babylon: A Small State within a Great Power Confrontation." *Studia Theologica* 44 (1990): 65–77.

Martin, Dale B. *Inventing Superstition: From Hippocrates to the Christians.* Cambridge, Mass.: Harvard University Press, 2004.

McCarthy, Dennis J. *Treaty and Covenant.* Rome: Pontifical Biblical Institute, 1978.

Mendelssohn, Moses. *Jerusalem oder religiöse Macht und Judentum.* 1783. Reprint, Hamburg: Felix Meiner Verlag, 2005. Translated and edited by Alfred Jospe as *Jerusalem, or, On Religious Power and Judaism* (New York: Schocken, 1969).

Merkelbach, Reinhold. *Isis-Regina, Zeus Sarapis: Die griechisch-ägyptische Religion nach den Quellen dargestellt.* Stuttgart: Teubner, 1995.

———, and Maria Totti-Gemünd, eds. *Abrasax: Ausgewählte Papyri religiösen und magischen Inhalts.* 5 vols. Opladen, Ger.: Westdeutscher Verlag, 1990.

Mettinger, Tryggve N. D. *No Graven Image? Israelite Aniconism in Its Near Eastern Context.* Stockholm: Almquist, 1995.

Metzler, Dieter. "A. H. Anquetil-Duperron (1731–1805) und das Konzept der Achsenzeit." *Achaemenid History* 7 (1991): 123–33.

Meyer, Eduard. *Aegyptische Chronologie.* Leipzig: Abhandlungen der Preussischen Akademie der Wissenschaften, 1904.

———. *Ägyptische Dokumente aus der Perserzeit.* Berlin: Akademie Verlag, 1915.

Miller, Patrick D. *The Religion of Ancient Israel.* London: SPCK, 2000.

Mitchell, Stephen. "The Cult of Theos Hypsistos between Pagans, Jews, and Christians." In Athanassiadi and Frede, *Pagan Monotheism in Late Antiquity,* 81–148.

Momigliano, Arnaldo. "The Disadvantages of Monotheism for a Universal State." In his *On Pagans, Jews, and Christians,* 142–58. Middletown, Conn.: Wesleyan University Press, 1987.

Montserrat, Dominic. *Akhenaten: History, Fantasy, and Ancient Egypt.* London: Routledge, 2000.

Moor, Johannes Cornelis de. *The Rise of Yahwism: The Roots of Israelite Monotheism.* Rev. ed. Leiden: Peeters, 1997.

Niditch, Susan. *War in the Hebrew Bible: A Study on the Ethics of Violence.* New York: Oxford University Press, 1993.

Nietzsche, Friedrich. *On the Genealogy of Morality.* Edited by Keith Ansell-Pearson. Translated by Carol Diethe. Cambridge: Cambridge University Press, 1994.

———. *On the Genealogy of Morals.* Translated by Walter Kaufmann and R. J. Hollingdale. 1967. Reprinted in *Basic Writings of Nietzsche* (New York: Modern Library, 1989).

Nock, Arthur Darby, ed. *Corpus Hermeticum II.* Translated by André-Jean Festugière. Paris: Collection Budé, 1960.

———. "Oracles théologiques" (1928). In *Essays on Religion and the Ancient World,* 2 vols., ed. Zeph Stewart, 1:160–68. Cambridge, Mass.: Harvard University Press, 2005.

Otto, Eckart. *Das Deuteronomium.* Berlin: W. de Gruyter, 1999.

———. "Political Theology in Judah and Assyria: The Beginning of the Hebrew Bible as Literature." *Svensk Exegetisk Årsbok* (Special issue: Festschrift T.N.D. Mettinger) 65 (2001): 59–76.

Parker, Richard Anthony, Jean Leclant, and Jean Claude Goyon. *The Edifice of Taharqa.* Hanover, N.H.: University of New England Press, 1979.

Parpola, Simo. "Monotheism in Ancient Assyria." In Porter, *One God or Many?* 165–209.

Peterson, Erik. *Heîs Theós: Epigraphische, formgeschichtliche und religionsgeschichtliche Untersuchungen.* Göttingen: Vandenhoeck & Ruprecht, 1926.

———. *Monotheismus als politisches Problem.* 1935. Reprinted in his *Theologische Traktate* (Munich: Kösel, 1951).

Porter, Barbara Nevling, ed. *One God or Many? Concepts of Divinity in the Ancient World.* [Chebeague, ME]: Casco Bay Assyriological Institute, 2000.

Posener, Georges. "La Piété personelle avant l'age amarnien." *Revue d'Égyptologie* 27 (1975): 195–210.

———. "Sur le monothéisme dans l'ancienne Égypte." In *Mélanges bibliques et orientaux en l'honneur de M. Henri Cazelles,* ed. André Caquot and M. Delcor, 347–51. Kevelear, Ger.: Butzon and Bercker, 1985.

Quack, Joachim Friedrich. *Studien zur Lehre für Merikare.* Wiesbaden: Harrassowitz, 1992.

Preuss, Horst Dietrich. *Verspottung fremder Religionen im Alten Testament.* Stuttgart: Kohlhammer, 1971.

Rackham, H. *Pliny: Natural History I. Praefatio. Libri I, II,* LCL. Cambridge, Mass.: Harvard University; London: William Heinemann, 1938.

Redford, Donald B. "The Hyksos Invasion in History and Tradition." *Orientalia* 39 (1970): 1–51.

———. *Pharaonic King-Lists, Annals, and Day-Books.* Mississauga, Ont., Can.: Benben, 1986.

Reeves, Nicholas. *Akhenaten: Egypt's False Prophet.* London: Thames & Hudson, 2001.

Reliefs and Inscriptions at Karnak I. Chicago: University of Chicago Press, 1936–86.

Reymond, E. A. E. *From the Contents of the Libraries of the Suchos Temples in the Fayyum.* Pt. 2, *From Ancient Egyptian Hermetic Writings.* Vienna: Österreichische Akademie der Wissenschaften, 1977.

Römer, Thomas. "Le Sacrifice humain en Juda et Israël." *Archiv für Religionsgeschichte* 1, no. 1 (1999): 17–26.

Ross, David. "The Stela of Mesha." Available at http://pages.sbcglobal.net/zimriel/Mesha/index.html (last accessed December 10, 2007).

Sanders, E. P. *Jewish and Christian Self-Definition.* 3 vols. Philadelphia: Fortress Press, 1980–82.

Sanders, James A. *Canon and Community.* Philadelphia: Fortress Press, 1984.

———. *From Sacred Story to Sacred Text.* Philadelphia: Fortress Press, 1987.

———. *Torah and Canon.* Philadelphia: Fortress Press, 1972.

Sandman, Maj. *Texts from the Time of Akhenaten.* Brussels: Fondation Reine Élizabeth, 1938.

Santner, Eric. *On the Psychotheology of Everday Life: Reflections on Freud and Rosenzweig.* Chicago: University of Chicago Press, 2001.

Sauneron, Serge. *Le Papyrus Magique Illustré de Brooklyn.* New York: Brooklyn Museum, 1970.

Schaeder, Hans Heinrich. *Ezra der Schreiber.* Tübingen: Mohr, 1930.

Schäfer, Peter. "Die heilige Gewalt." *Frankfurter Allgemeine Zeitung,* May 18, 2005.

———. *Judeophobia: Attitudes toward the Jews in the Ancient World.* Cambridge, Mass.: Harvard University Press, 1997.

———. "Das jüdische Monopol: Jan Assmann und der Monotheismus." *Süddeutsche Zeitung,* August 11, 2004.

———. *Der Triumph der reinen Geistigkeit: Sigmund Freuds Der Mann Moses und die monotheistische Religion.* Berlin: Philo, 2003.

Schenkel, W. "Eine neue Weisheitslehre?" *Journal of Egyptian Archeology* 50 (1964): 6–12.

Schindler, Alfred, ed. *Monotheismus als politisches Problem: Erik Peterson und die Kritik der politischen Theologie.* Gütersloh: Gütersloher Verlagshaus, 1978.

Schluchter, Wolfgang. *Religion und Lebensführung.* 2 vols. Frankfurt: Suhrkamp, 1988.

Schmidt, Francis, ed. *The Inconceivable Polytheism: Studies in Religious Historiography.* New York: Harwood Academic, 1987.

Schmitt, Carl. *The Concept of the Political.* Translated by George Schwab. Chicago: University of Chicago Press, 1996.

Schott, Siegfried, ed. *Urkunden mythologischen Inhalts.* 2 vols. Leipzig: J. C. Hinrichs, 1929–39.

Schwager, Raymund. *Brauchen wir einen Sündenbock? Gewalt und Erlösung in den Schriften des Alten Testaments.* Vienna: Kulturverlag, 1994.

Schwartz, Benjamin I. "The Age of Transcendence." In *Wisdom, Revelation, and Doubt.* Special issue. *Daedalus* 104, no. 2 (Spring 1975): 1–7.

Schwartz, Regina M. *The Curse of Cain: The Violent Legacy of Monotheism.* Chicago: University of Chicago Press, 1997.

Seibert, Peter. *Die Charakteristik: Untersuchungen zu einer ägyptischen Sprechsitte und ihren Ausprägungen in Folklore und Literatur.* Wiesbaden: Harrassowitz, 1967.

Seneca. *Ad Lucilium Epistulae morales.* Edited by Manfred Rosenbach. Darmstadt: Wissenschaftliche Buchgesellschaft, 1995.

Sethe, Kurt. *Amun und die acht Urgötter von Hermopolis: Eine Untersuchung über Ursprung und Wesen des ägyptischen Götterkönigs.* Berlin: W. de Gruyter, 1929.

———. *Thebanische Tempelinschriften aus griechisch-römischer Zeit.* Edited by Otto Firchow. Berlin: Akademie-Verlag, 1957.

Singer, Itamar. "'The Thousand Gods of Hatti': The Limits of an Expanding Pantheon." In *Concepts of the Other in Near Eastern Religions,* ed. Ilai Alon, Ithamar Gruenwald, and Itamar Singer, 81–102. Leiden: Brill, 1994.

Smelik, K. A. D., and E. A. Hemelrijk. "Who Knows Not What Monsters Demented Egypt Worships? Opinions on Egyptian Animal Worship in Antiquity as Part of the Ancient Conceptions of Egypt." *Aufstieg und Niedergang der Römischen Welt* 2.17.4 (1984): 1852–2000, 2337–57 (indices).

Smith, Mark S. *The Early History of God: Yahweh and the Other Deities in Ancient Israel.* 2nd ed. Grand Rapids, Mich.: Eerdmans, 2002.

———. *The God in Translation: Cross-Cultural Recognition of Deities in the Biblical World.* Forthcoming.

———. "Louvre E3229: A Demotic Magical Text." *Enchoria* 7 (1977): 115–49.

———. *The Memoirs of God: History, Memory, and the Experience of the Divine in Ancient Israel.* Minneapolis: Fortress Press, 2004.

———. *The Origins of Biblical Monotheism: Israel's Polytheistic Background and the Ugaritic Texts.* Oxford: Oxford University Press, 2001.

Smith, Morton. *Palestinian Parties and Politics That Shaped the Old Testament.* New York: Columbia University Press, 1971.

Speelers, Louis. "Un papyrus funéraire de Basse Époque aux Musées Royaux du Cinquantenaire de Bruxelles." *Recueil des Travaux* 39 (1921): 25–43.

Spence, Donald P. *Narrative Truth and Historical Truth: Meaning and Interpretation in Psychoanalysis.* New York: Norton, 1982.

Spiegelberg, Wilhelm. *Die sogenannte Demotische Chronik.* Leipzig: Hinrichs, 1914.

Stark, Rodney. *One True God: Historical Consequences of Monotheism.* Princeton, N.J.: Princeton University Press, 2001.

Steck, Odil Hannes. *Der Abschluß der Prophetie im Alten Testament: Ein Versuch zur Vorgeschichte des Kanons.* Neukirchen-Vluyn: Neukirchener Verlag, 1991.

Stegemann, Hartmut. *Die Essener, Qumran, Johannes der Täufer und Jesus.* 3rd ed. Freiburg: Herder, 1994.

Stern, Menachem, ed. *Greek and Latin Authors on Jews and Judaism.* 3 vols. Jerusalem: Magnes, 1974–84.

Stern, Philip D. *The Biblical Herem: A Window on Israel's Religious Experience.* Atlanta, Ga.: Scholars Press, 1991.

Steymans, Hans Ulrich. *Deuteronomium 28 und die adê zur Thronfolgeregelung Asarhaddons: Segen und Fluch im Alten Orient und in Israel.* Freiburg: Universitätsverlag, 1995.

Stock, Brian. "Textual Communities." In his *The Implications of Literacy: Written Language and Models of Interpretation in the Eleventh and Twelfth Centuries,* 88–240. Princeton, N.J.: Princeton University Press, 1983.

Stolz, Fritz. *Weltbilder der Religionen.* Zurich: Pano, 2001.

Störk, Lothar. "Die Flucht der Götter." *Göttinger Miszellen* 155 (1996): 105–8.

Streck, Maximilian, ed. *Assurbanipal und die letzten assyrischen könige bis zum untergange Ninivehs.* 3 vols. Leipzig: J. C. Hinrichs, 1916.

Stricker, B. H. *Asenarii* I. *Oudheidkundige Mededelingen uit het Rijksmuseum van Oudheden te Leiden* 46 (1965): 52–75.

———. *Asenarii* II. *OMRO* 48 (1967): 23–43.

———. *Asenarii* III. *OMRO* 52 (1971): 22–53.

———. *Asenarii* IV. *OMRO* 56 (1975): 65–74.

Sundermeier, Theo. "Religion, Religionen." In *Lexikon missionstheologischer Grundbegriffe,* ed. Karl Müller and Theo Sundermeier, 411–23. Berlin: Dietrich Reimer, 1987.

———. *Was ist Religion? Religionswissenschaft im theologischen Kontext.* Gütersloh: Gütersloher Verlagshaus, 1999.

Tadmor, Hayim. "Autobiographical Apology in the Royal Assyrian Literature." In *History, Historiography, and Interpretation: Studies in Biblical and Cuneiform*

Literatures, ed. Hayim Tadmor and Moshe Weinfeld, 36–57. Jerusalem: Magnes, 1986.

Tait, W. J. *Papyri from Tebtunis in Egyptian and in Greek.* London: Egypt Exploration Society, 1977.

Tasinato, Maria. *Sulla curiosità: Apuleio e Agostino.* Parma: Pratiche, 1994. Translated by Jean Paul Manganaro as *La Curiosité: Apulée et Augustin* (Lagrasse, France: Verdier, 1999).

Traunecker, Claude. *Les Dieux de l'Égypte.* Paris: Seuil, 1992.

Uehlinger, Christoph. "The 'Canaanites' and Other 'Pre-Israelite' Peoples in Story and History." *Freiburger Zeitschrift für Philosophie und Theologie* 46 (1999): 546–78, and 47 (2000): 173–98.

———. "Du culte des images à son interdit." *Le Monde de la bible* 110 (April 1998): 52–63.

van den Brook, R. "The Sarapis Oracle in Macrobius, *Sat.* I, 20, 16–17." In *Hommages à Maarten J. Vermaseren,* ed. Margreet B. de Boer and T. A. Edridge, 123–41. Leiden: Brill, 1978.

Vandier, Jacques. *Le Papyrus Jumilhac.* Paris: Centre National de la Recherche Scientifique, 1960.

van Seters, John. *In Search of History: Historiography in the Ancient World and the Origins of Biblical History.* New Haven, Conn.: Yale University Press, 1983.

Versnel, H. S. "Thrice One: Three Greek Experiments in Oneness." In Porter, *One God or Many?* 79–163.

Voegelin, Eric. *Der Gottesmord: Zur Genese und Gestalt der modernen politischen Gnosis* [The Murder of God]. Munich: W. Fink, 1999.

———. *Order and History.* 4 vols. Baton Rouge: University of Louisiana Press, 1956–74.

———. *Die politischen Religionen.* Vienna, 1938. Reprint, Munich: Peter Opitz, 1993.

———. *Das Volk Gottes: Sektenbewegungen und der Geist der Moderne* [The People of God]. Edited by Peter-Joachim Opitz. Translated by Heike Kaltschmidt from an unpublished English text. Munich: W. Fink, 1994.

Volten, Aksel Peter Fritz. *Zwei altägyptische politische Schriften.* Copenhagen: Einar Munksgaard, 1945.

Waddell, W. G., trans. *Manetho.* Cambridge, Mass.: Harvard University Press, 1940.

Weber, Max. *Gesammelte Aufsätze zur Religionssoziologie.* 3 vols. Tübingen: Mohr, 1920.

Weinfeld, Moshe. "The Ban on the Canaanites in the Biblical Codes and Its Historical Development." In *History and Traditions in Early Israel,* ed. André Lemaire and Benedikt Otzen, 142–160. Leiden: Brill, 1993.

———. "The Common Heritage of Covenantal Traditions in the Ancient World." In Canfora, Liverani, and Zaccagnini, *I Trattati nel Mondo Antico,* 175–91.

———. *Deuteronomy and the Deuteronomic School.* Oxford: Clarendon Press, 1972.

———. *Deuteronomy 1–11* New York: Doubleday, 1991.

White, H. G. E., ed. and trans. *Ausonius*. 2 vols. Cambridge, Mass.: Harvard University Press, 1985.

Whitehead, James D., and Evelyn E. Whitehead. "cong yishi dao liangzhi." *Fudan Journal* (Fudan University, Shanghai) 3 (2001): 143–49.

Widengren, Geo. *Religionsphänomenologie*. Berlin: W. de Gruyter, 1969.

Wilcke, Claus. "Die sumerische Königsliste und erzählte Vergangenheit." In *Vergangenheit in mündlicher Überlieferung*, ed. Jurgen von Ungern-Sternberg and Hansjörg Reinau, 113–40. Stuttgart: Teubner, 1988.

Wilson, John A. "The Theban Tomb (No. 409) of Si-Mut, Called Kiki." *Journal of Near Eastern Studies* 29 (1970): 187–92.

Wimbush, Vincent L. "Ascetic Impulse in Ancient Christianity." *Theology Today* 50, no. 3 (October 1993): 417–28.

Yerushalmi, Yosef Hayim. *Freud's Moses: Judaism Terminable and Interminable*. New Haven, Conn.: Yale University Press, 1991.

———. "Réflexions sur l'oubli." In his *Usages de l'oubli*, 7–21. Paris: Seuil, 1988.

Younger, K. Lawson, Jr. *Ancient Conquest Accounts: A Study in Ancient Near Eastern and Biblical History Writing*. Sheffield, Eng.: JSOT Press, 1990.

Zandee, Jan. *Der Amunshymnus des Papyrus Leiden I 344, Verso*. 3 vols. Leiden: Rijksmuseum van Oudheden, 1992.

———. *De Hymnen aan Amon van Papyrus Leiden I 350*. Leiden: Brill, 1948.

INDEX

185

INDEX LOCORUM

Page numbers in the current text appear in italics.

GEORGE L. MOSSE SERIES
IN MODERN EUROPEAN CULTURAL AND
INTELLECTUAL HISTORY

Series Editors

Stanley G. Payne, David J. Sorkin, and John S. Tortorice

Of God and Gods: Egypt, Israel, and the Rise of Monotheism
Jan Assmann

Collected Memories: Holocaust History and Postwar Testimony
Christopher R. Browning

Cataclysms: A History of the Twentieth Century from Europe's Edge
Dan Diner; Translated by Joel Golb

*Carl Schmitt and the Jews: The "Jewish Question," the Holocaust, and
German Legal Theory*
Raphael Gross; Translated by Joel Golb

Confronting History: A Memoir
George L. Mosse

Nazi Culture: Intellectual, Cultural, and Social Life in the Third Reich
George L. Mosse

What History Tells: George L. Mosse and the Culture of Modern Europe
Stanley G. Payne, David J. Sorkin, and John S. Tortorice

The Jews in Mussolini's Italy: From Equality to Persecution
Michele Sarfatti; Translated by John and Anne C. Tedeschi

*Jews and Other Germans: Civil Society, Religious Diversity, and
Urban Politics in Breslau, 1860–1925*
Till van Rahden; Translated by Marcus Brainard